Physical Medicine and Rehabilitation

STATE OF THE ART REVIEWS

Foot and Ankle Rehabilitation

Guest Editors:

Dennis D. J. Kim, MD
Associate Clinical Professor
Department of Rehabilitation Medicine
Montefiore Medical Center/
Albert Einstein College of Medicine
Bronx, New York

Stanley F. Wainapel, MD, MPH
Clinical Director
Department of Rehabilitation Medicine
Montefiore Medical Center
Bronx, New York
Professor of Clinical Rehabilitation Medicine
Albert Einstein College of Medicine
Bronx, New York

Volume 15/Number 3
HANLEY & BELFUS, INC.

October 2001
Philadelphia

Publisher: HANLEY & BELFUS, INC.
210 South 13th Street
Philadelphia, PA 19107
(215) 546-7293
(215) 790-9330 (Fax)
Web site: http://www.hanleyandbelfus.com

PHYSICAL MEDICINE AND REHABILITATION: State of the Art Reviews is included in *BioSciences Information Service, Current Contents, ISI/BIOMED,* and *Cumulative Index to Nursing & Allied Health Literature.*

PHYSICAL MEDICINE AND REHABILITATION: State of the Art Reviews   ISSN 0888-7357
Volume 15, Number 3   ISBN 1-56053-344-7

PHYSICAL MEDICINE AND REHABILITATION: State of the Art Reviews is published triannually (three times per year) by Hanley & Belfus, Inc., 210 South 13th Street, Philadelphia, Pennsylvania 19107.

POSTMASTER: Send address changes to PHYSICAL MEDICINE AND REHABILITATION: State of the Art Reviews, Hanley & Belfus, Inc., 210 South 13th Street, Philadelphia, PA 19107.

The 2001 individual subscription price is $89.00 per year U.S., $99.00 outside U.S. (add $45.00 for air mail). The institution subscription price is $114.00 per year U.S., $124.00 outside U.S. (add $45.00 for air mail). Single issue copies are $39.00 (outside U.S., add $15.00 for single copy air mail).

Physical Medicine and Rehabilitation: State of the Art Reviews
Vol. 15, No. 3, October 2001

FOOT AND ANKLE REHABILITATION
Dennis D. J. Kim, MD, and Stanley F. Wainapel, MD, MPH, Editors

CONTENTS

This chapter reviews the topographic anatomy of the foot with emphasis on the local-ization of the easily palpable superficial structures and articulations. Familiarity with the normal placement of these structures facilitates a better appreciation of their action and interaction during the activity of walking, and permits the examiner to assess potential deviations. The chapter next reviews the underlying architecture of the major joints within the foot and their potential freedom of movement. These joint complexes are examined individually and in relationship to associated structures. The chapter proceeds to integrate this information into a study of the sequential stages in the gait cycle with emphasis on stance phase. The sequence of coordinated muscular activity as well as the influence of overlying body structures, including the effects of momentum, is reviewed with cognizance of the foot's major design objectives: provision of an adaptive but stable base of support during ambulation.

Proper history taking and physical examination of the foot have not been priorities in the residency-training curriculum in physical medicine and rehabilitation. Most diag-noses of foot pain can be made without the use of expensive investigative tools such as CT or MRI. This chapter's purpose is to guide practicing physiatrists through select aspects of the history taking and physical examination that lead to logic-based diagnoses and successful conservative management of the foot in an office setting.

Imaging of the foot and ankle is a fascinating but intricate area. The complexity of the anatomy and the spectrum of diseases affecting the foot and ankle increase the demands upon the medical imager. This chapter is not exhaustive in scope. The au-thors have attempted to provide a foundation for the physiatrist when confronted with imaging and diagnostic dilemmas in clinical practice.

Heel pain is one of the most commonly encountered complaints of the lower ex-tremity in physiatric practice. Clear distinction between the confusing complex of symptoms is controversial and often difficult. This chapter emphasizes the differen-tial diagnosis as well as treatment options and their appropriate application based on biomechanical principles.

Rehabilitation professionals often treat patients with complaints related to the foot. Patients with known neuromuscular disease usually present with typical foot findings. This chapter provides a short overview of the foot conditions related to neuromuscular disorders in the adult patient, according to the location of the lesion. Patients with acquired disorders such as stroke and spinal cord injury, as well as those with hereditary disorders such as Charcot-Marie-Tooth disease, are discussed.

The biomechanical, anatomic, and pathologic consequences of Achilles and other tendons of the foot are more common than often recognized. In this chapter, functional anatomy and the role of these tendons in biomechanics of the foot are considered, as a lower extremity response to functional pronation/supination in weight bearing and locomotion. The purpose of this chapter is to provide a basis for the comprehension of biomechanical causal factors in effect during weight bearing that create an environment conducive to the development of tendon pathologies. The majority of patients with Achilles tendon, posterior tibial, or peroneal tendon dysfunction can effectively be treated with conservative treatment. In managing these tendon pathologies, identification of the outlined biomechanical factors and their proximal related kinematics is crucial. The use of biomechanical orthoses, therapeutic exercises, and non-surgical and surgical principles of management are outlined. Rehabilitative interventions that address these biomechanical factors can provide effective and long-lasting results.

In the specialty of physical medicine and rehabilitation, physiatrists frequently see patients with complications secondary to diabetes mellitus. Prevention of amputation in diabetics has not been an area our specialty has emphasized. Physiatrists must learn how to care for the feet of diabetics, thereby preventing further complications of this undertreated area.

The ideal goal of partial foot amputation is to remove as little tissue as possible with a clear understanding of the potential functional outcome for the patient. Wound healing is best achieved the more proximal the amputation is performed, while prosthetic management and rehabilitation are better the more distal the amputation level. Chronic arterial occlusion must be seen as an illness associated with diabetes, tobacco use, and reduced activity. Partial foot amputations should be considered a treatment option when full skin thickness coverage can be provided. Ideally, full body weight should be tolerated by the residual limb, which will have sensate skin that can provide protective feedback. Syme's amputation can provide an excellent weight bearing surface that permits short distance ambulation without the use of prosthesis. In older people, one should refrain from the "salami approach" to limb amputation, which can cause secondary consequences and sometimes even threaten the life of the patient. This chapter reviews the surgical techniques, postoperative management, acute pain control, and phantom limb and pain.

1999 ISSUES

Practice Management
Julie K. Silver, MD, Editor

Clinical Electrophysiology
Steve R. Geiringer, MD, Editor

Low Back Pain
Dennis M. Lox, MD, Editor

2000 ISSUES

Manual Medicine
Mark A. Tomski, MD, Editor

Pediatric Rehabilitation
Michael A. Alexander, MD, and Gabriella E. Molnar, MD, Editors

Orthotic Devices
John B. Redford, MD, Editor

2001 ISSUES

Osteoarthritis
Todd P. Stitik, MD, Editor

Traumatic Brain Injury
James McDeavitt, MD, Editor

Foot and Ankle Rehabilitation
Dennis D. J. Kim, MD, and Stanley F. Wainapel, MD, MPH, Editors

2002 ISSUES

Functional Disorders
Nathan Zasler, MD, and Michael Martelli, PhD, Editors

Gait Analysis
Alberto Esquenazi, MD, Editor

Hip and Knee Rehabilitation
Victoria A. Brander, MD, Editor

Subscriptions for full year and single issues available from the publisher—
Hanley & Belfus, Inc., 210 South 13th Street, Philadelphia, PA 19107.
Telephone (215) 546-7293; (800) 962-1892. Fax (215) 790-9330.

CONTRIBUTORS

Dudley K. Angell, MD
Assistant Professor, Department of Rehabilitation Medicine, Columbia Presbyterian Medical Center, New York, New York

Lila Bartkowski-Abbate, MA, PT
Physical Therapist, Department of Rehabilitation Medicine, Albert Einstein College of Medicine; Weiler Hospital, Bronx, New York

Wen Chao, MD
Clinical Instructor, Orthopaedic Surgery, University of Pennsylvania, Philadelphia, Pennsylvania; Active Medical Staff at Pennsylvania Hospital and Lankenau Hospital, Philadelphia and Wynnewood, Pennsylvania

John A. DiPreta, MD
Clinical Assistant Professor of Surgery, Division of Orthopaedics, Albany Medical College; Staff, Albany Medical Center Hospital, St. Peter's Hospital, Albany Memorial Hospital, Albany, New York

Alberto Esquenazi, MD
Director, MossRehab Regional Amputee Center and Gait & Motion Analysis Laboratory; Associate Professor, Department of Rehabilitation, Jefferson College of Medicine, Philadelphia, Pennsylvania

Sireen M. Gopal, MD
Assistant Professor, Department of Rehabilitation, Albert Einstein College of Medicine; Montefiore Medical Center, Bronx, New York

Sikha Guha, MD
Assistant Professor, Rehabilitation Medicine, Montefiore Medical Center, Albert Einstein College of Medicine; Department of Rehabilitation, Montefiore Medical Center, New York

Nogah Haramati, MD
Associate Professor of Radiology and Orthopaedic Surgery; Director, Musculoskeletal Radiology, Albert Einstein College of Medicine and Montefiore Medical Center, Bronx, New York

Phala A. Helm, MD
Professor, Department of Physical Medicine and Rehabilitation, University of Texas Southwestern Medical Center, Dallas, Texas

Dennis D. J. Kim, MD
Associate Clinical Professor, Department of Rehabilitation Medicine, Montefiore Medical Center/Albert Einstein College of Medicine, Bronx, New York

Yoon-Tae Kim, MD
Assistant Professor, Department of Rehabilitation Medicine, Uijungbu St. Mary's Hospital, Catholic University Medical Center, Uijungbu City, Kyunggi-Do, Korea (South)

Young-Jin Ko, MD
Associate Professor, Department of Rehabilitation Medicine, Kangnam St. Mary's Hospital, The Catholic University of Korea, Seoul, Korea (South)

Stephen R. Lebduska, MD
Lead Physiatrist, Syracuse Veterans Affairs Medical Center; Clinical Assistant Professor, Department of Physical Medicine and Rehabilitation, State University of New York Upstate Medical University, Syracuse, New York

Kenneth J. Mroczek, MD
New York University Medical Center, New York, New York

Mooyeon Oh-Park, MD
Assistant Professor, Rehabilitation Medicine, Montefiore Medical Center, Albert Einstein College of Medicine, Bronx, New York

Geetha Pandian, MD
Associate Professor, Department of Physical Medicine and Rehabilitation, University of Texas Southwestern Medical Center, Dallas, Texas

Barry Rodstein, MD, MPH
Assistant Professor, Rehabilitation Medicine, Albert Einstein College of Medicine; Beth Israel Medical Center, New York, New York

Lew C. Schon, MD
Department of Orthopaedics, Union Memorial Hospital, Baltimore, Maryland

Nancy E. Strauss, MD
Assistant Professor of Clinical Rehabilitation Medicine, Department of Rehabilitation Medicine, Columbia University College of Physicians and Surgeons; Director of Residency Training in Physical Medicine and Rehabilitation, New York Presbyterian Hospital, New York, New York

C. Christopher Stroud, MD
Department of Orthopaedics, Union Memorial Hospital, Baltimore, Maryland

Hilary R. Umans, MD
Associate Professor, Radiology and Orthopedic Surgery, Albert Einstein College of Medicine; Montefiore Medical Center, Bronx, New York

Keith L. Wapner, MD
Clinical Professor, Orthopaedic Surgery, University of Pennsylvania, Philadelphia, Pennsylvania; Active Medical Staff at Pennsylvania Hospital, Hahnemann University Hospital, and Lankenau Hospital, Philadelphia and Wynnewood, Pennsylvania

Cornelia Wenokor, MD
Assistant Professor, Department of Radiology, UMDNJ-NJ Medical School, Newark, New Jersey

PREFACE

Rehabilitation medicine, to coin a term I once heard at a conference at Sloan Kettering Institution in New York, is "upright" medicine. The ultimate goal of our field is to improve our patients' ability to stand, walk, and perform the daily physical tasks that are critical to the quality of their lives. One need not have extensive experience in the field to understand that diagnosing and treating foot disorders are pivotal to this goal. By the same token, how can the physiatrist perform good "upright" medicine without understanding the intricacies of the human foot?

Within the last decade, the practice of medicine has evolved from a hospital-based field to one that is geared toward providing cost-effective outpatient services. In physiatry, this trend is sometimes furthered by reluctance from managed care to approve expensive surgical procedures unless conservative options have failed. This results in an increased demand for rehabilitation services and knowledge that can be met by incorporating a practical hands-on approach.

Rehabilitation medicine has the greatest potential to successfully provide comprehensive, conservative foot care to a large mobile population of patients searching for practical options. The ability to utilize a holistic approach and to incorporate medical and non-medical means to improve their function is an invaluable service.

As physiatrists, we have the necessary understanding of the complicated network of muscles, connective tissue, nerves, and vasculature to properly diagnose and treat foot disorders. We also strive to study conditions as they influence the practical realities of the patient's life. That is, as physiatrists treating foot disorders, we are as concerned about our patients' footwear, socks, insoles, and aesthetics as we are with the pathology that underlies their disease. In addition, we have the ability to provide biomechanically sound, disease-specific physical therapy that is not limited to monotonous protocols. In spite of this great potential, from my experience in completing this publication I've learned that physiatrists do not have an extensive history of studying the human foot. It was difficult to find many authors within our specialty who could confidently discuss the subject matter presented in this volume. Over the years, my peers at Albert Einstein and I have studied the foot and its complicated influence on the quality of life of our patients to devise practical ways to manage their complaints. It is with great honor that I present our experience and knowledge on this subject matter in this issue of *Physical Medicine and Rehabilitation: State of the Art Reviews*.

I would like to thank the contributors to this edition; my daughters Ryul, June, and Azalea (my private editors); and my wife, who lost endless hours of sleep by allowing me to keep the light on all night.

Dennis D. J. Kim, MD
Guest Editor

PUBLISHED ISSUES 1989–1998
(available from the publisher)

PREFACE

With its remarkable combination of suppleness and tactile sensitivity, the human hand has been celebrated in science, art, and literature for its unique contribution to the evolution, communication, and creativity of our species. The foot has attracted far less attention or recognition, including a relative paucity of medical literature dealing with its rehabilitation. Yet the scientific name for man, *Homo erectus*, attests to the crucial importance of the foot to human development and civilization. It can be conceptualized as the final common pathway of stance and locomotion. Anatomically and physiologically, the foot is as complex as the hand, and it is subject to weight bearing stresses that produce a wide range of disabling consequences. Vascular, neuromuscular, rheumatologic, and orthopedic diseases produce distinctive clinical presentations in the foot.

This volume presents an overview of the anatomy, physiology, radiology, and pathophysiology of the foot with particular attention to practical rehabilitation strategies for the clinician. It is not intended to be a comprehensive text on all relevant areas. Special diagnostic and therapeutic issues in children, principles of physical therapy for the foot, and rehabilitation management of fractures (to cite but three) have not been covered. Nevertheless, we believe that physiatrists will be able to approach and manage a wide range of foot problems after reading these chapters. The foot is literally and figuratively the foundation of upright posture, and it is our hope that this volume will serve as a foundation of knowledge for the health professional who encounters these challenging patients.

Stanley F. Wainapel, MD, MPH
Guest Editor

PHYSICAL MEDICINE AND REHABILITATION: STATE OF THE ART REVIEWS (PM&R: STARS)

Instructions for Authors

PM&R: STARs, published three times a year, features special topic-related issues with peer-reviewed articles by experts in particular fields. Although manuscripts are usually requested from specific authors based on the theme of each issue, others are welcome to query the publisher regarding their desire to write specific review articles or to guest edit an entire issue. Articles are peer-reviewed by the guest editor(s), experts in the particular field covered by the article, and by outside reviewers as appropriate. Manuscripts are closely edited as necessary.

Peer Review
After your manuscript has been peer-reviewed, it may be returned to you for revision prior to publication. We ask your cooperation in accomplishing revisions, if any, expeditiously.

The Text
Two copies of the manuscript and a diskette along with the original illustrations should be sent to the guest editor. Unless otherwise indicated by the guest editor, the manuscript should be no longer than 20–25 double-spaced, typewritten pages, including references. Tables and figures are not included in the page count because they should be used wherever appropriate to enhance the text. The author's name and degrees, school and/or hospital appointments, mailing address, telephone number, fax number, and e-mail address should appear on the opening page.

Tables and Illustrations
Please consider the visual impact of your article. Tables and figures may be used to break up long blocks of text, and can be both informative and aesthetically pleasing.

Tables. Information given in tables may be commented on but should not be repeated in the text. Each table should be numbered, given a brief descriptive title, typed on a separate sheet, and attached to the manuscript. Placement in the text should be indicated.

Illustrations. Illustrations may be used generously. Best results are obtained from original artwork and photographs in the form of crisp computer art (laser printer) or glossy prints (pref. 5″ × 7″). Avoid the use of fuzzy halftones or blurred photocopies of charts or graphs. Line art should not contain gray scale or shading. Illustrations cannot be printed in color. Color prints, transparencies, or slides may be submitted for printing in black and white, but they often do not reproduce well. One copy of each illustration, identified by marking *lightly* in pencil the figure number and author's name on the back, is sufficient. Art created in Photoshop or Illustrator may be submitted on disk along with a reproducible hard copy. Do *not* mount illustrations or mark them with pens or markers. Please prepare legends on a separate sheet attached to the manuscript. Indicate in the text where figures should be placed. *Illustrations are not returnable.*

Abstracts
You must supply an abstract of your paper of not more than 200 words. The abstract should briefly describe the matter or issue being addressed in the paper, how the research or study was conducted (if applicable), the results, and the author's conclusions.

References
References should be listed **alphabetically** rather than in order of occurrence, numbered for citation, and typed double-spaced. Each reference should contain, in the order and format indicated, the author's last name and initials; the title of the article; the name of the periodical; and the volume, inclusive page numbers, and year. If a book is cited, give chapter author's name, chapter title, editor's name, title of book, edition, place of publication, publisher, and year. The latest edition of any textbook should be cited. For works with five or more authors, use the first three authors' names followed by *et al.* The *Index Medicus* abbreviations for journals and periodicals should be used.

Borrowed Material
It is the *author's* responsibility to obtain letters of permission for borrowed material from the publisher and/or the author of the original material. Copies of the letters granting permission should be forwarded to **Hanley & Belfus, Inc.**, when they are received. Complete reference to original place of publication should be given to a borrowed figure or as a footnote to a borrowed table. Permission forms are available from the editor or publisher to expedite this process.

Proof
The first-named author of each article will receive page proof, unless otherwise specified, to be read carefully and returned to the publisher with only essential corrections. Please proofread your article carefully; because you are most familiar with the content of your article, you are in the best position to identify substantive errors.

Complimentary Copy
Each contributor will receive a complimentary copy of the completed volume.

STEPHEN R. LEBDUSKA, MD

TOPOGRAPHIC AND FUNCTIONAL ANATOMY AND BIOMECHANICS OF THE FOOT

From the Department of Physical
  Medicine and Rehabilitation
State University of New York
  Upstate Medical University
Syracuse, New York

Reprint requests to:
Stephen R. Lebduska, MD
Lead Physiatrist, Syracuse VAMC
Clinical Assistant Professor, Dept.
  of PM&R
SUNY Upstate Medical University
750 East Adams Street
Syracuse, NY 13210

The physiatric approach to assessment and management of clinical problems relies upon a heightened understanding of the relationship between structural components and their overall function. In this chapter, I attempt to familiarize the reader with the normal surface anatomy of the foot and the underlying bone and soft tissue architecture. I also review the biomechanics of the foot, at rest and in motion, as it transitions from weight bearing to free suspension and back again.

Cognizance of the design objectives pertaining to the foot from a teleologic perspective helps us better understand the evolution of the human foot into its current structure. As the terminal device of the weight bearing lower extremities which are almost exclusively responsible for human locomotion, the foot must accomplish several design objectives. These include provision of a stable base of support while in contact with the ground. During ambulation, the foot must be capable of instantaneous adaptability to uneven terrain as well as shock attenuation. Additionally, the foot should function to optimize the use of muscle energy in terms of efficiency and control. With these features in mind, we can examine the foot and study the static and dynamic relationship of its components.

SURFACE STRUCTURE

Through visual inspection and palpation, we can generally identify a number of important structural components including all of the bones of the foot as well as their major articulations, tendinous insertions of the major extrinsic muscles

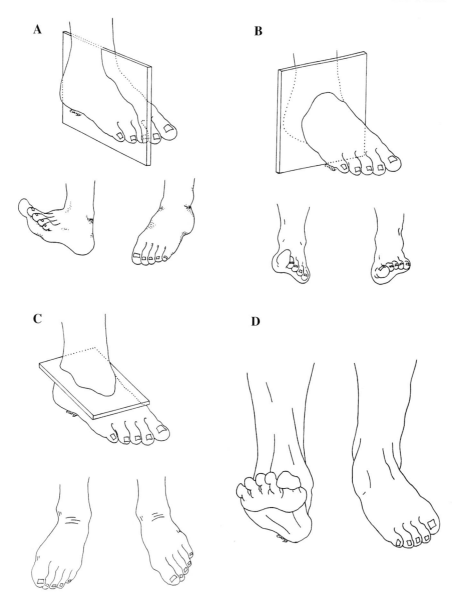

FIGURE 1.   *A,* Foot dorsiflexion and plantarflexion. *B,* Foot inversion and eversion. *C,* Foot adduction and abduction. *D,* Foot supination and pronation.

acting on the foot, superficial ligaments and neurovascular elements. In an effort to eliminate ambiguity, some descriptive terms relating to position and movement must be clarified. All positions will be in reference to the sagittal, frontal and transverse planes as illustrated (Fig. 1). The discussion will begin by describing joints in a neutral standing position with the feet on a flat horizontal surface. The potential movement of the foot or part of the foot in terms of these planes can then be described.

We must, however, keep in mind that owing to the obliquity and complexity of these articulations, no movements occur truly in congruence with any of these planes.

Dorsiflexion is basically a sagittal plane movement of the foot which reduces the angle between the long axis of the foot and that of the tibia (see Fig. 1A). Plantarflexion reverses this process.

Inversion describes an essentially frontal plane movement which elevates the medial aspect of the foot relative to the lateral aspect (see Fig. 1B). Eversion reverses this process. Adduction of the foot is primarily a transverse plane movement in which the forefoot rotates medially about a vertical axis (see Fig. 1C). Abduction occurs as the foot rotates laterally about this same axis.

When we actively attempt to invert the foot, this movement typically occurs in combination with some adduction of the forefoot. This combined movement is frequently termed *supination* (see Fig. 1D). Conversely, active eversion normally occurs in combination with abduction. This combined movement is termed *pronation*. The terms varus and valgus are also scattered throughout the literature. These terms refer to position rather than movement. A *varus* foot is in a position of inversion (or supination), and a *valgus* foot is everted (or pronated).

In general, the foot should be observed and examined in both a weight bearing and non-weight bearing condition. This is easily accomplished with the patient standing upright in a posture of optimal comfort, and with the patient sitting, with the knees flexed and the feet suspended. This discussion will look at the medial, lateral, superior and plantar aspects of the foot and list structures found accordingly.

Medial View

Inspection of the medial aspect of the foot and ankle reveals the universally evident *medial malleolus*, which is the most distal medial prominence of the tibia (Fig. 2). We can utilize this as a starting point for systematic palpation of other easily identifiable structures.

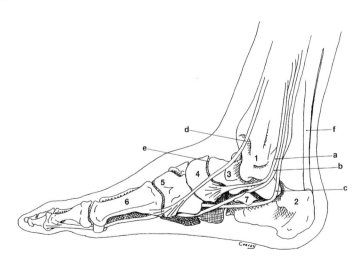

FIGURE 2. Palpable structures on the medial aspect of the foot. 1: medial malleolus; 2: calcaneus; 3: talus; 4: navicular; 5: medial cuneiform; 6: 1st metatarsal; 7: sustentaculum tali; a: tibialis posterior tendon; b: flexor hallucis longus tendon; c: flexor digitorum longus tendon; d: tibialis anterior tendon; e: talonavicular joint; f: Achilles tendon.

Extending from the distal margin of the medial malleolus, a broad fan shaped retinaculum spreads out to insert along the peripheral margin of the heel. This medial or flexor retinaculum is easily appreciated as an elastic structure especially if we evert the calcaneus as we palpate inferior to the malleolus. Deep to the flexor retinaculum and posterior to the medial malleolus, several important structures "wrap around" the malleolus in close proximity as they course anteriorly to more distal insertions in the foot. These structures include the *tibialis posterior tendon*, the *flexor hallucis longus tendon*, the *posterior tibial artery and vein*, the *tibial nerve*, and the *flexor digitorum longus tendon*. This region is known as the *tarsal tunnel*, and although it is difficult to identify individual structures by palpation, they are organized from anterior to posterior as listed above.

Deep to these structures lies the deltoid ligament, which is actually composed of four separate ligaments that attach the medial distal tibia to the talus, calcaneus and the navicular. If we palpate with moderate pressure approximately 1 cm distal to the inferior end of the medial malleolus, we can locate a rounded bony protuberance. This is the *sustentaculum tali*, which is a medial shelf like extension of the calacaneus that supports the talus as its name implies. A small portion of the talus may be palpable just above this with deep pressure. We can appreciate movement in the subtalar joint, which is the articulation between the talus and calcaneus, if we passively invert and evert the calcaneus while maintaining pressure with our thumb just proximal to the sustentaculum tali.

Moving more distally (towards the great toe), we encounter the *navicular tuberosity*. This is an easily palpable prominence of the bone which is the "keystone" of the medial longitudinal arch. We can take time to appreciate the tendons of two important extrinsic foot muscles from this point. If we ask the subject to actively plantarflex the foot against a little resistance from the examining hand, we can palpate the insertion of the *tibialis posterior tendon* on the inferior surface of the navicular tuberosity, where it arrives after descending obliquely from behind the medial malleolus. If we move superior to the tuberosity and ask the subject to actively dorsiflex the foot, we can easily palpate the prominent *anterior tibialis tendon* as it courses anteriorly and inferiorly. We can then trace this tendon to its insertion on the lateral proximal aspect of the first metatarsal. Just proximal to this insertion, we can palpate the first tarso-metatarsal joint as a shallow groove. We can also appreciate the *talonavicular joint* by grossly grasping the forefoot while maintaining our thumb in the space between the navicular tubercle and the medial malleolus, and gently abducting and adducting the foot. This vertically oriented joint will widen with forefoot abduction and close with adduction as the navicular glides posteriorly. Just inferior to this palpable articulation, we can appreciate a band or cord-like ligament coursing from the anterior aspect of the sustentaculum tali to the posterior aspect of the navicular tuberosity. This is the *plantar calcaneonavicular* or *spring ligament*, and it attaches to the navicular in an area adjacent to the insertion of the tibialis posterior tendon which descends obliquely from behind the medial malleolus.

Lateral View

Just as we started our survey of the medial aspect of the foot, we begin our inspection of the lateral aspect of the foot at the lateral malleolus (Fig. 3). This slightly more pointed prominence represents the distal end of the fibula and is typically easily visible. We may also notice a concavity lying just anterior to the lateral malleolus. Palpation will confirm a significant depression known as the *tarsal sinus* (sinus tarsi in some literature). Here we can palpate the origin of the *extensor digitorum brevis* muscle if we ask the subject to actively extend the digits. When we apply sufficient

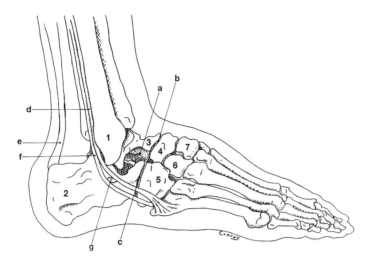

FIGURE 3. Palpable structures on the lateral aspect of the foot. 1: lateral malleolus; 2: calcaneus; 3: talar neck; 4: navicular; 5: cuboid; 6: lateral cuneiform; 7: intermediate cuneiform; a: tarsal sinus; b: talonavicular joint; c: calcaneocuboid joint; d: peroneus brevis tendon; e: Achilles tendon; f: peroneus longus tendon; g: peroneal tubercle.

pressure to "touch the floor" of the tarsal sinus, we are palpating the dorsolateral aspect of the calcaneus. As we move slowly toward the distal edge of this bony (calcaneal) floor, we can usually appreciate a fairly sharp edge. Just distal to this edge, the *calcaneocuboid joint* runs in a predominantly vertical (frontal plane) orientation. If we maintain a finger at this juncture while passively inverting the foot, we can appreciate the cuboid sliding medially and increasing the bony step-off. When we press against the medial margin of the tarsal sinus, we are palpating the neck of the talus. As we move distally, we slide onto the talar head, which becomes even more prominent if the foot is inverted.

When we palpate just posterior to the lateral malleolus, we can identify tendons of the peroneal muscles as they extend inferiorly and anteriorly. As the tendons of these two muscles pass below the distal tip of the lateral malleolus, they are separated by another bony prominence, the *peroneal tubercle* or *trochlea*. This lateral projection of the calcaneus can easily be located by palpating approximately 1 cm inferior and just anterior (distal) to the tip of the lateral malleolus. The *peroneus brevis tendon* courses above the trochlea, and the *peroneus longus tendon* runs below it. If we ask the subject to evert the foot against resistance, we can identify the peroneus brevis tendon as it inserts on the tuberosity of the fifth metatarsal. We can also palpate the peroneus longus tendon until it dives to the plantar aspect of the foot to insert on the first cuneiform and first metatarsal.

The lateral ankle ligaments are somewhat difficult to identify by palpation, but we should be aware of their orientation and restraining actions. These three ligaments all originate on the lateral malleolus and consist of the anterior talofibular ligament, posterior talofibular ligament, and calcaneofibular ligament.

Superior View

As we observe the dorsal aspect of the foot from an anterior vantage point, we can evaluate the general alignment of the foot in relationship to the crural bones and the ankle mortice. We can utilize the contours of both malleoli to estimate the central axis of the foot. Although we have already located aspects of the talus from medial and lateral palpation, location from the supero-anterior approach is extremely useful in orienting this bone in relation to the remainder of the foot.

As the subject gently dorsiflexes the foot, the tendons of the *tibialis anterior*, *extensor digitorum longus*, and the *extensor hallucis longus* are generally visible to their points of insertion. The tibialis anterior inserts on the medial aspect of the medial cuneiform and first metatarsal. The extensor hallucis longus inserts on the distal phalanx of the great toe.

We can generally observe the contour and positioning of the metatarsals and their relationship to the toes. The length of the toes and their relationship to one another are also noted from this vantage point. The resting position of the metatarsophalangeal joints and the interphalangeal joints is easily observed as well.

Plantar View

Inspection of the plantar aspect can be accomplished with the patient supine or seated. We can observe the distribution of calluses to indicate areas of significant weight bearing. The *calcaneal tuberosity* is easily palpable posteriorly, as are the metatarsal heads anteriorly. Two *sesamoids* are usually palpable at the level of the first metatarsal head, contained within the tendon of the *flexor hallucis brevis*. The plantar aponeurosis covers most of the remainder of the plantar aspect of the foot.

JOINT STRUCTURE

We now discuss the functional architecture of the major joint complexes of the ankle and foot. The most proximal joint in our survey is the ankle joint proper, or the

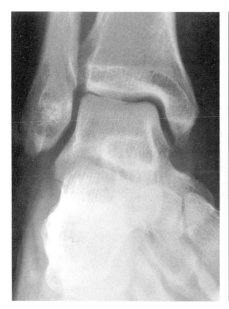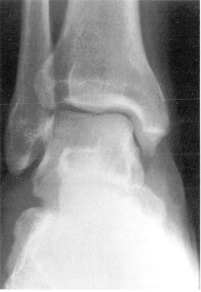

FIGURE 4.   Two plain x-rays of the ankle joint. A-P view on the right, and "mortise view" with 20 degrees internal rotation on the left.

talocrural joint. The talus, with its biconvex superior weight bearing surface, the trochlea, articulates almost exclusively with the distal expansion of the tibia, which has a conforming contour. The trochlear surface is slightly broader anteriorly and contains a shallow central longitudinally oriented furrow. Medially, the tibia extends distally alongside the talus as the medial malleolus. The fibula, which is tightly bound to the tibia through most of its length by the interosseus membrane with additional ligamentous reinforcements distally, extends further down the lateral aspect of the talus as the lateral malleolus. It is also situated significantly posterior to the medial malleolus. The medial and lateral collateral ligaments of the ankle extend from the malleoli to the talus and calcaneus, serving to maintain the trochlear and tibial articulating surfaces in close approximation between the malleoli. As a consequence, mediolateral movement is extremely limited at this joint. We therefore observe dorsiflexion and plantarflexion as the predominant movements occurring at this joint.

Owing to the configuration of the talar surface, the axis of rotation in this joint is not in the transverse plane and elevates by approximately 8 degrees above horizontal on the medial side. Additionally, as a result of the posterior placement of the fibula in relation to the medial malleolus, the axis of rotation is also oriented 20 to 30 degrees posterior to the frontal plane on the lateral side.[13] We can confirm this oblique axis by noting that x-rays taken to best visualize the "ankle mortise" require internal rotation of the leg by about 20 degrees (Fig. 4). Inman related the orientation and structure of the talar trochlea to that of a cone with its central axis running nearly through the distal tips of the malleoli[12] (Fig. 5).

Consequently, although the ankle permits motion principally in the sagittal plane, some degree of abduction will be associated with dorsiflexion, and conversely, some adduction will accompany plantarflexion. It is extremely important to recognize that this very configuration, which associates obligatory abduction during active dorsiflexion while the foot is off the ground (open chain movement), analogously results in internal rotation of the overlying tibia during the passive dorsiflexion which occurs in early stance phase. At this stage, the foot is fixed horizontally on the ground and the tibia is rotating over it.

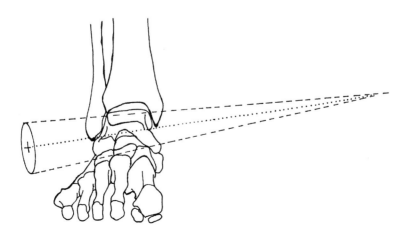

FIGURE 5. Axis of rotation and structure of the talar trochlea. (Redrawn from Morris J: Clin Orthop 122:13, 1977.)

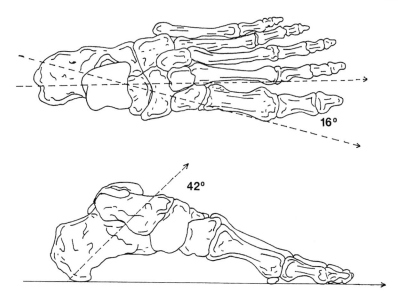

FIGURE 6.   Axis of the subtalar joint.

The *subtalar joint* or *talocalcaneal joint* lies distal to the tibiotalar joint. This joint consists of three separate areas (facets) of articulation between the superior surface of the calcaneus and the inferior articulating surface of the talus. The broadest of these is the posterior facet, which articulates with the posterior body of the talus. The middle facet consists of an articulation between the sustentaculum tali and the medial talus. The anterior facet is smaller in surface area and articulates with the inferior surface of the talar head.[20] Five ligaments in addition to a thin surrounding capsule serve to stabilize this joint.[8] A very strong, two part *interosseus talocalcaneal ligament* limits the amount of inversion and eversion occurring at the subtalar joint with more significant limitation of eversion.[1,14] The posterior portion of this ligament originates on the superior surface of the calcaneus, beginning just anterior to the posterior facet, and runs superiorly in the tarsal sinus to insert on the inferior surface of the talus. The anterior portion of this ligament, also known as the *cervical ligament*, originates just laterally from the floor of the tarsal sinus and runs superiorly to insert on the neck of the talus. Additionally, the lateral talocalcaneal ligament assists in limiting inversion, assisted by the extensor retinaculum. The medial talocalcaneal ligament runs from the posterior process of the talus to the sustentaculum tali and assists in limiting eversion. There is a fourth (posterior talocalcaneal), which is of lesser significance.

The multiple points of articulation between these two bones result in an overall joint axis which runs from plantar and posterolateral to dorsal and anteromedial. This oblique axis is variable but typically demonstrates approximately 42 degrees of inclination in the sagittal plane and deviates medially from this plane by 16 to 23 degrees[18] (Fig. 6). This joint has been described by Inman and Mann as acting as a mitered hinge, rotating about a single axis with motion determined by talar rotation in the transverse plane[16] (recall that tibial rotation results in obligatory talar rotation). The inclination of the subtalar axis depends upon the architecture of the foot. Positional variations of this axis influence the degree to which rotation of the vertically

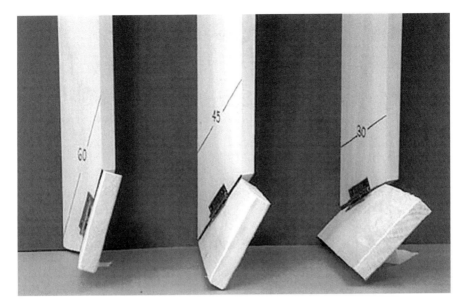

FIGURE 7. Effect of subtalar axis of inclination on relative foot pronation with tibial rotation. Thirty, forty-five, and sixty degree models.

oriented tibia translates into inversion or eversion of the horizontally oriented foot. We can see from the models in Figure 7 that with an axis angle of 45 degrees, rotation occurs in a 1 to 1 ratio in the vertical and horizontal segments. A more vertically oriented axis results in proportionately less horizontal segment rotation for each degree of vertical segment rotation. The converse is true for an axis angle of less than 45 degrees. Several authors have investigated the broad variation in the functional axis of the subtalar joint with angles of between 20 and 68 degrees observed.[5,7,25] During stance phase in the gait cycle, there is an average of 19 degrees of tibial rotation,[15] which will translate into a greater or lesser degree of subtalar rotation.

Moving distally to the subtalar joint, we encounter the *midtarsal* or *transverse tarsal joint*. This joint is actually composed of the articulations of two hindfoot bones, namely the talus and calcaneus, with two midfoot bones, the navicular and cuboid. A gliding motion occurs between the talus and navicular as well as between the calcaneus and cuboid during pronation and supination of the hindfoot. Once again, extremely strong ligamentous restraints are provided to limit pronation and supination at the midtarsal joint. The short and long plantar ligaments as well as the plantar calcaneonavicular ligament and the bifurcate ligament supply these restraints.[26]

The complex contour of the surface between these four bones, combined with the fact that movement of the talus and calcaneus occurs in a sequential fashion, results in motion at the midtarsal joint which cannot be described about a single axis. The net consequence of movement at the midtarsal joint has been described as though it occurs about two separate axes. One of these runs roughly longitudinally through the foot, and the other runs obliquely[18] (Fig. 8). These two axes have no anatomic relationship to the joint lines, but represent net movement occurring simultaneously within these two complex articulations.[22] The (descriptive) longitudinal axis runs slightly medially from the midline of the foot and moves dorsally from the horizontal plane. We can

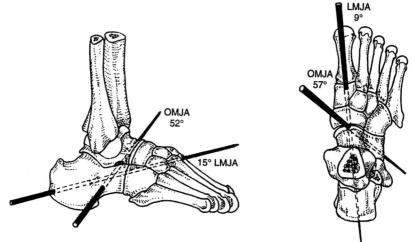

FIGURE 8.   Functional (non anatomic) axes of the midtarsal joint. (From Michaud TC: Foot Orthoses and Other Forms of Conservative Foot Care. Baltimore, Williams & Wilkins, 1993, with permission.)

logically speculate that this axis describes permissible movement which is largely inversion and eversion. This will then potentially allow the forefoot to remain horizontal (on the ground) during hindfoot pronation and supination. The second or oblique axis runs more steeply medially and dorsally from posterior to anterior. Visualizing rotation about this axis, we can appreciate the association of abduction with dorsiflexion of the forefoot, and adduction in combination with plantarflexion. Just as we saw in the subtalar joint, there is a significant range in the observed inclination of these axes based on anatomic variation.[18] This will in turn effect the proportional amount of abduction or adduction associated with dorsiflexion or plantarflexion.

Although we can best explain the cumulative motion of the midtarsal joint as occurring about two "non anatomic" axes, the two individual articulations do have distinct axes of rotation. More importantly, the two discrete axes of movement occurring at the talonavicular joint and the calcaneocuboid joint actually change in relationship to each other depending upon the position of the subtalar joint. Additionally, the relationship of these two axes determines the overall flexibility of the midtarsal joint. Elftman observed that with a pronated subtalar joint, the talonavicular and calcaneocuboid joint axes assume a more parallel position (Fig. 9). This parallel configuration permits greater flexibility or overall increase in range of motion at the midtarsal joint as a whole. With subtalar supination, these two axes diverge, resulting in a loss of overall flexibility.[4]

Distal to the navicular lie three cuneiform bones on the medial aspect of the forefoot. The medial, intermediate and lateral cuneiforms articulate with the first, second and third metatarsals, respectively. Lateral to the navicular, the cuboid extends further longitudinally and articulates primarily with the fifth metatarsal.

We easily appreciate the larger caliber of the bones comprising the first ray, namely the first (or medial) cuneiform and the first metatarsal. These bones are held tightly together by dorsal and plantar ligaments. This ray is in turn also firmly united to the navicular by dorsal and plantar ligaments.[26] Approximately one third of the overall weight shared by the forefoot in standing is carried by the first ray. This fraction

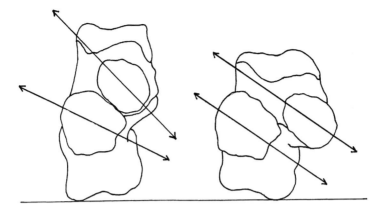

FIGURE 9. Talonavicular and calcaneocuboid joint axes in supination (*left*) and pronation (*right*).

increases in the later stages of stance phase during walking. Motion in the first ray occurs about an oblique axis which runs from a proximal medial superior point through a distal lateral and inferior point.[22] This is in contrast to the oblique axes of the subtalar and midtarsal joints which run in a medial direction distally. Therefore, first ray dorsiflexion is coupled with inversion and plantarflexion results in eversion. The second through fifth rays consist of the second metatarsal articulating with the intermediate cuneiform, the third metatarsal articulating with the lateral cuneiform, and the fourth and fifth metatarsals acting alone. Motion in the second through fourth rays is primarily in the sagittal plane with dorsiflexion and plantarflexion occurring.[24] The fifth ray axis is more oblique, resulting in pronation and eversion associated with dorsiflexion; and supination and inversion associated with plantarflexion.

DYNAMIC ANALYSIS

After reviewing the bony and ligamentous architecture of the major ankle and foot joints, we have an appreciation of the potential range of motion permitted at each articulation, as well as the fixed structural restraints to movement. We also recognize the potentiating (or limiting) effect which the position of one joint may exert on the range of motion of other foot joints. This discussion will now look at the dynamic influences on foot movement and positioning during walking. The effects and timing of muscular activity as well as momentum and ground reaction forces will be reviewed. The focus will be on the stance phase of the gait cycle. It is assumed that most readers are familiar with normal human gait patterns. For those who require a review, various text sources are available.[12,23] The subdivision of the gait cycle and nomenclature for specific phases varies in the literature. This discussion will use the scheme outlined in Jacqueline Perry's book *Gait Analysis*.[23] Also listed will be some of the familiar equivalent or analogous terminology. The five divisions of stance phase that will be analyzed include *initial contact, loading response, mid stance, terminal stance,* and *pre swing* (Fig. 10).

Stance Phase

1. **Initial Contact** (Heel Strike)

At the instant of heel contact, the vector of ground reaction is directed behind the axis of the ankle joint. The magnitude of this ground reaction force may be

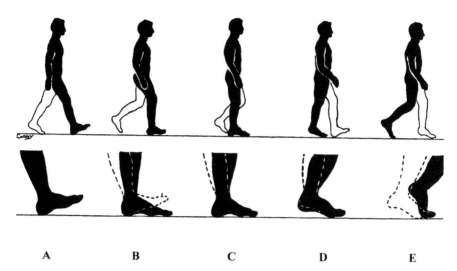

A   **B**   **C**   **D**   **E**

FIGURE 10.   Divisions of stance phase. *A*, Initial contact. *B*, Loading response. *C*, Mid stance. *D*, Terminal stance. *E*, Pre swing.

significantly greater than actual body weight. The ankle (talocrural joint) acts as a pivot, resulting in rapid plantarflexion of the forefoot. Almost simultaneously, the pretibial muscle groups begin an eccentric contraction to resist this motion. The net result is some attenuation of the extreme initial ground reaction force. There is also some conservation of momentum as the eccentrically contracting pretibial muscles help to pull the more proximal tibia over the plantarflexing foot.

The calcaneus typically contacts the ground in a slightly inverted position. This is due to the inversion of the longitudinal axis of the midtarsal joint, which occurs in terminal swing phase as a result of the primarily medially pulling ankle dorsiflexors, which ensures ground clearance and prepares the foot for initial contact. This slightly inverted calcaneal position results in the majority of ground reaction force being applied to the lateral calcaneal condyle. This generates an everting (pronatory) force on the calcaneus and subtalar joint. Eccentric contractions of the anterior tibialis muscle as well as the extensor hallucis longus, which insert over the medial aspect of the foot, result in supination of the longitudinal axis of the midtarsal joint.

Pronation of the subtalar joint (i.e., pronation of the calcaneus) assists in internal rotation of the leg. (Recall our mitered hinge model.) Once the forefoot contacts the ground, friction prevents adduction, and tibial internal rotation is "absorbed" by subtalar pronation (Fig. 11). This subtalar pronation also serves to unlock the midtarsal joint, facilitating adaptation to terrain.

2. **Loading Response** (Foot Flat)

Weight rapidly transfers to the foot in early stance phase, with some 60% of the total body weight accepted within the first 2% of the gait cycle (i.e., in the first 20 milliseconds!). The initial ground reaction vector is behind the ankle, and the initial impact vector is essentially vertical. In order to preserve forward momentum, the early muscular action of the pretibial group plays a major role. First, by slowing the rapid plantarflexion of the foot after heel contact, these muscles serve to prolong the action of the heel as a "rocker," causing the body weight to roll over this single point of contact with the floor. Additionally, eccentric contraction of the pretibial group

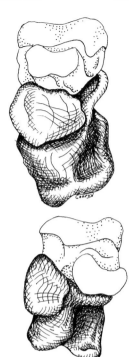

FIGURE 11. Upper illustration shows inverted position of calcaneus at initial contact. Lower illustration shows pronated subtalar joint position.

simultaneously tends to pull the more proximal tibia forward over the ankle joint. It is important to realize that the (eccentrically) controlled plantarflexion of the ankle after initial heel contact actually smoothes and diminishes the overall effect of the ankle rocker on tibial advancement. If the foot were maintained at a fixed angle with the tibia (say 90 degrees), a much more abrupt and rapid tibial advancement would need to occur in order to achieve positioning of the foot flat on the floor.

Once the forefoot has contacted the floor, the relative direction of ankle movement reverses. The foot can plantarflex no further (assuming a hard surface), and the forward moving body causes proximal tibial advancement which results in passive dorsiflexion of the ankle and more complete loading of this limb.

3. Mid Stance

With both the heel and forefoot on the ground, the axis of rotation now occurs about the ankle joint. The support limb therefore transitions from a heel rocker to an ankle rocker.[23] As the body continues to move forward over the observed foot, the vertical load vector also progresses forward to pass through and then anterior to the axis of the ankle joint. This generally occurs as the contralateral foot is leaving the ground, defining a period of single support. Through this progression, forefoot loading continues to increase. The relative position of the ankle transitions from approximately 8 degrees of plantarflexion to 5 degrees of dorsiflexion during this phase.

Just as the pretibial muscles slowed ankle plantarflexion early in stance phase, the calf muscles must now restrain the passive dorsiflexion which is occurring as the body moves forward. Once again, we observe muscles contracting eccentrically to control limb movement. The soleus muscle is initially active early in midstance and is later joined by the gastrocnemius.[28] The soleus provides a majority of the decelerating force as a result of its larger size and its direct attachment to both the calcaneus and the tibia. Recall that the gastrocs, which originate on the femur, will act to flex the knee as well as plantarflex the ankle until late in midstance when the body's center of mass has moved anterior to the ankle.

Through the duration of the midstance phase in the support limb, the contralateral swing phase limb has advanced from well behind to in front of the support limb. The contralateral pelvis is advancing as well, resulting in external rotation of the entire support limb. With the foot fixed on the ground, external rotation of the tibia now results in reversal of the "mitered hinge" action, and supination of the subtalar joint occurs. This supination is assisted by the muscular activity of the posterior tibialis, flexor digitorum longus, flexor hallucis longus, and the gastrocs-soleus. Subtalar supination subsequently moves the axes of the two midtarsal joint complexes (talonavicular and calcaneocuboid) out of parallel, resulting in increased rigidity of the midtarsal joint.

4. Terminal Stance (Heel Off)

By the end of midstance, the forefoot has been transformed (by joint motion) into a more rigid structure in preparation for its role as a weight bearing extension of the distal limb. The body has progressed forward to a position where the center of gravity is well in front of the ankle joint. The terminal stance period begins with heel rise off the floor.

In order to reduce the overall drop in the body's center of mass (for energy conservation), passive ankle dorsiflexion must be minimized. This is accomplished by strong eccentric contraction of the soleus and gastrocnemius muscles which permit only an additional 5 degrees of dorsiflexion during this period.[6] This muscular locking of the ankle joint, in combination with a relatively rigid midfoot, results in anterior translation of the "rocker" to the metatarsal heads[23] (Fig. 12). The body proceeds forward and the heel continues to rise as a result of the relatively fixed ankle with the tibia rolling over the metatarsal heads in contact with the floor.[21] We have now reached a point at which all the supported body weight is borne by the forefoot in the final stages of single support. Owing to its multiple articulations, the foot must rely on the combined contributions of several coordinated mechanisms to transform into an adequately rigid support. First, the rapidly advancing swing limb

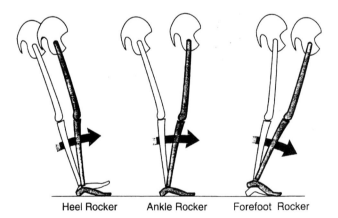

Heel Rocker	Ankle Rocker	Forefoot Rocker

FIGURE 12.   Transition from *heel rocker* to *ankle rocker* to *forefoot rocker* during stance phase. (From Perry J: Gait Analysis Normal and Pathological Function. Thorofare NJ, Slack, 1992, with permission.)

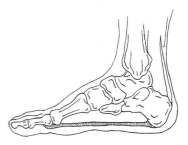

FIGURE 13.   "Windlass effect" of plantar fascia.

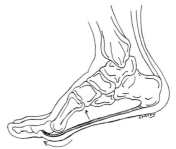

causes additional external rotation in the supporting limb. With the heel off the ground, this external rotation results in rapid further subtalar joint supination. This in turn results in continued locking of the midtarsal joints. Second, the plantar fascia, which extends from the calcaneus to the base of the proximal phalanges, acts to support the foot. During terminal stance, as the body weight rolls over the metatarsal heads, the toes are passively dorsiflexed. This results in a tightening of the plantar fascia known as the windlass effect[9] (Fig. 13). Due to the fact that the fascia is drawn around a metatarsal head of significantly greater radius on the medial side of the foot (the first metatarsal head), there is a greater windlass effect on the medial side of the foot. The higher medial arch is therefore better supported, and subtalar supination is assisted as well.[19] Third, a number of extrinsic and intrinsic foot muscles act to stabilize the first ray. The peroneus longus contracts to plantarflex the first ray and stabilize it against the proximal tarsal bones. The peroneus brevis compresses the cuboid into the calcaneus, helping to stabilize the lateral column. The flexor hallucis longus and the flexor digitorum longus aid in supinating the oblique axis of the midtarsal joint. The abductor hallucis assists in plantarflexing the first ray.[29]

The body falls forward during the end of terminal stance resulting in a significant force of forward progression and preservation of momentum. Studies suggest that the eccentrically contracting soleus and gastrocs support heel rise adequately, but *do not* generate a propulsory plantar flexion. In fact, the net effect of activity in these muscles is to restrain forward momentum.[27] This phase ends with the contralateral swing phase foot contacting the floor. Just prior to this event, owing to rapidly diminishing weight on the support leg, the ankle begins to plantarflex.

5. **Pre Swing** (Toe Off)

The pre swing portion of the stance phase represents an interval at which the load on the now trailing limb is rapidly diminishing to zero. The leading contralateral support limb has accepted the majority of the body's weight. As a result, the continued (although diminished) contraction of the gastrocnemius and soleus results

TABLE 1. Muscle Activity During the Subdivisions of Stance Phase

Muscle	Initial Contact	Loading Response	Midstance	Terminal Stance	Pre Swing
Anterior tibialis	↑↑↑↑	↑↑↑↑			↑↑↑
Extensor hallucis longus	↑↑↑	↑↑↑			↑↑↑
Extensor digitorum longus	↑↑↑	↑↑↑			↑↑↑
Soleus		↑	↑↑↑	↑↑↑↑	
Gastrocnemius		↑	↑↑↑	↑↑↑↑	
Posterior tibialis		↑↑	↑	↑↑↑	
Peroneus longus		↑	↑↑	↑↑↑	
Peroneus brevis			↑	↑↑↑	
Flexor digitorum longus		↑	↑↑	↑↑↑	↑
Flexor hallucis longus			↑	↑↑↑	↑
Extensor digitorum brevis			↑↑↑	↑↑↑	↑↑↑
Flexor hallucis brevis			↑↑↑	↑↑↑	↑↑↑
Abductor digiti quinti			↑↑↑	↑↑↑	↑↑↑
Abductor hallucis				↑↑↑	↑↑↑
Flexor digitorum brevis				↑↑↑	↑↑↑
Interossei				↑↑↑	↑↑↑

in a more rapid heel rise in the now off-loaded foot which continues to roll over the metatarsal heads. Continued tibial advancement combined with gastrocsoleus contraction (recall that the gastrocs also cross the knee joint) results in generation of a flexion torque at the knee. The knee joint subsequently commences the requisite flexion needed for ground clearance during swing phase. Just as the pretibial muscle groups contracted to slow rapid plantarflexion after initial contact, they begin to contract at the very end of stance phase to decelerate the rate of further plantarflexion. At this time, they are also preparing for the continued (concentric) contraction necessary to return the foot to an ankle neutral position for ground clearance during swing phase. A summary of the muscular activity occurring during the subdivisions of stance phase is detailed in Table 1.

Swing Phase

Swing phase describes a period of nonsupport in which the trailing limb, having just left the ground, must advance more rapidly than the forward moving trunk and assume a position ready to accept weight at the instant of contact. Movements at all lower extremity joints during this phase are of course in open chain.

The work of several investigators suggest that the swing phase limb generates much of the momentum to power forward motion.[2,3,17] Concentric contraction of the iliopsoas, combined with momentum generated by the rotating pelvis, generates a rapid hip flexion which must be damped by eccentric contraction of the hamstrings at the end of swing phase in preparation for initial contact. Sufficient knee flexion for ground clearance is achieved by a combination of biceps femoris contraction and the momentum generated by the rapidly flexing hip. This momentum continues to carry the distal lower extremity forward ahead of the torso and into nearly full knee extension. Eccentric hamstring contraction is also required here at the end of swing phase to prevent knee hyperextension and prepare the limb for weight acceptance.

The ankle, which begins swing phase in slight plantarflexion, is actively dorsiflexed by the pretibial muscles initially. Once adequate foot clearance is achieved at midswing, these muscles relax until just before heel contact when they once again become active.

The foot must also transition into a position prepared for ground contact by the end of swing phase. The subtalar joint initially pronates as a result of extensor digitorum longus activity early in swing phase. Later in swing, with combined activation of the much stronger anterior tibialis, the joint re-supinates in preparation for initial contact. The (functional) longitudinal axis of the midtarsal joint, which is pronated at the end of pre swing, also undergoes supination from the action of the anterior tibialis. The oblique axis, which is in a position of supination at the end of pre swing, is pronated by the early action of the extensor digitorum longus. At this point, the foot is positioned to repeat the gait cycle again.

We have reviewed the observable and palpable anatomy of the normal foot and ankle, as well as the underlying relationships of the bony and soft tissue components. The elegant adaptability and efficiency of this joint complex depend on inherent structural constraints in combination with precisely coordinated muscular activity. Recall that the entire sequence of events described above occurs in the course of about 1 second, repetitively and without concentration as we walk from place to place.

REFERENCES

1. Cahill DR: The anatomy and function of the contents of the human tarsal sinus and canal. Anat Rec 153:1, 1965.
2. Dananberg HC: Functional hallux limitus and its relationship to gait efficiency. J Am Podiatr Med Assoc 76: 6–18, 1986.
3. Dannanberg HC: Gait styles as an etiology to chronic postural pian, Part II. J Am Podiatr Med Assoc 83: 615–624, 1993.
4. Elftman H: The transverse tarsal joint and its control. Clin Orthop 16: 41, 1960.
5. Englesberg JR, Andrews JG: Kinematic analysis of the talocalcaneal/talocrural joint during running support. Med Sci Sports Exer 3: 275–284, 1987.
6. Gilbert JA, Maxwell GM, McElhaney JH, Clippinger FW: A system to measure the force and movements at the knee and hip during level walking. J Orthop Res 2: 281–288, 1984.
7. Green DR, Whitney AK, Walter P: Subtalar joint motions. J Am Podiatr Med Assoc 56: 149, 1966.
8. Hamilton WG: Surgical anatomy of the foot and ankle. CIBA Clinical Symposia 37 Number 3, 1985.
9. Hicks JH: The mechanics of the foot II. The plantar aponeurosis and the arch. J Anat 88:25–30, 1954.
10. Herman R, Wirta R, Perry J: Human Solutions for Locomotion. New York, Plenum Press, 1976.
11. Inman VT: UC-BL dual axis ankle-control system and UC-BL shoe insert: biomechanical considerations. Bull Prosth Res BPR10-11 : 130, 1969.
12. Inman VT, Ralston HJ, Todd F: Human Walking. Baltimore, Williams & Wilkins, 1981.
13. Isman RE, Inman VT: Anthropometric studies of the human foot and ankle. Biomechanics Laboratory, University of California, San Francisco and Berkeley. Technical Report 58, San Francisco, The Laboratory, 1968.
14. Kapanji IA: The Physiology of Joints: Lower Limb, Vol 2. Edinburgh, Churchill Livingstone, 1970.
15. Levens AS, Inman VT, Blosser JA: Transverse rotation of the segments of the lower extremity in locomotion. J Bone Joint Surg (Am) 30A: 859–874, 1948.
16. Mann RA, Inman VT: Phasic activity of intrinsic muscles of the foot. J Bone Joint Surg (Am) 46:469, 1964.
17. Mann RA, Moran GT, Dougherty SE: Muscle activity during running, jogging, and sprinting. Am J Sports Med 14, 1986.
18. Manter JT: Movements of the subtalar and transverse tarsal joints. Anat Rec 80:397–409, 1941.
19. Michaud TC: Ideal motion during the gait cycle. In: Foot Orthoses and Other Forms of Conservative Foot Care. Baltimore, Williams & Wilkins, 1993, pp 27–55.
20. Morris JL: Biomechanics of the foot and ankle. Clin Orthop 122:10–17, 1977.
21. Murray MP, Drought AB, Kory RC: Walking pattern of normal man. J Bone Joint Surg 46A (2):335–360, 1964.

22. Oatis CA: Biomechanics of the foot and ankle under static conditions. Phys Ther 68:1815–1821, 1982.
23. Perry J: Gait Analysis Normal and Pathological Function. Thorofare, NJ, Slack, 1992.
24. Root ML, Orien W, Weed JH: Clinical biomechanics, 10–17 In: Normal and Abnormal Function of the Foot. Los Angeles, 1977.
25. Root ML, Weed JH, Sgarlato TE: Axis of motion of the subtalar joint. J Am Podiatr Assoc 56:149, 1966.
26. Serrafian SK: Anatomy of the Foot and Ankle: Descriptive, Topographic, Functional, 2nd ed. Philadelphia, JB Lippincott, 1993.
27. Simon SR, Mann RA, Hagy JL, Larsen LJ: Role of the poserior calf muscles in normal gait. J Bone Joint Surg 60A:465–472, 1978.
28. Sutherland D: An elctromyographic study of the plantar flexors of the ankle in normal walking on the level. J Bone Joint Surg 48A:66–71, 1966.
29. Wernick J, Volpe RG: Lower extremity function and normal mechanics. In Valmassy RL (ed): Clinical Biomechanics of the Lower Extremities. St. Louis, Mosby, 1996, pp 1–57.

YOUNG-JIN KO, MD
YOON-TAE KIM, MD
DENNIS D. J. KIM, MD

PROBLEM-ORIENTED HISTORY TAKING AND PHYSICAL EXAMINATION OF PATIENTS WITH FOOT PAIN

From the Department of
  Rehabilitation Medicine
Kangnam St. Mary's Hospital
College of Medicine
The Catholic University of Korea
Seoul, Korea (South)

Reprint requests to:
Young-Jin Ko, MD
Associate Professor, Department
  of Rehabilitation Medicine
Kangnam St. Mary's Hospital
College of Medicine
The Catholic University of Korea
505 Banpo-Dong, Seocho-Ku
Seoul, 137-040, Korea (South)

Since the art of rehabilitation aims to restore the mobility, fitness, and independence of patients, skills in making accurate diagnoses and instituting the proper management of foot pain can be an important asset to all practicing physiatrists. However, proper history taking and physical examination of the foot have not been priorities in the residency-training curriculum in physical medicine and rehabilitation. Rehabilitation training programs and a plethora of references focus mainly on AFOs, footwear, or foot orthoses rather than on the diagnostic and therapeutic approach to foot pain and foot disorders. Most diagnoses of foot pain can be made without the use of expensive investigative tools such as the CT or MRI. This chapter is not intended to describe all of the physical examination techniques. Rather, its purpose is to guide practicing physiatrists through select aspects of the history taking and the physical examination that lead to logic-based diagnoses and successful conservative management of the foot in an office setting.

PREPARING THE VISIT

During the process of arranging an office appointment, the office receptionists should request that the patient bring any footwear or foot orthoses (FOs) which were made specifically for a therapeutic purpose or were worn most frequently by the patient. This will provide the examiner with an opportunity to assess the success or failure of previous treatments with a more analytic eye.[14] In this case, the maxim "you can tell a lot about a person from his shoes" holds true.

In addition, prior to interviewing the patient about foot pain, it is helpful for the examiner to first obtain general information about the patient's medical history (e.g., diabetes mellitus, vascular disease, previous operations), occupation, body weight, duration of the foot pain, and treatment history of foot disorders. Such pertinent information can be obtained in the waiting room of the doctor's office by having the patient fill out a one-page questionnaire or a simple checklist.

HISTORY TAKING

Because of the realities of medical practice today, the most important goal in eliciting a history is to capture the essence of foot-related complaints within a limited amount of office time. It is therefore an asset for a practicing physiatrist to be adept at recognizing **the typical patterns in the history and symptom presentation** that are associated with several common foot disorders.[13]

Because **foot pain** is the most common foot-related presentation that physiatrists manage in their offices, it will be the focus of this chapter, although other complaints such as numbness, weakness, stiffness, swelling, instability, disfiguration, calluses, ulceration, and blister formation are also frequent. The physiatrist should ask begin first with locating the foot pain, then proceed to identifying the mode of onset, the nature of pain, and aggravating factors.

Location of the Pain

Localizing the pain and identifying the relationship to the topographic anatomy are the most important steps in the assessment of foot pain. The examiner should be able to induce the patient to pinpoint the location of pain. It may require several repetitions of questioning before a satisfactory answer can be extracted from the patient. Once the location of the patient's subjective pain is identified, the relationship to local tenderness is sought since **most of local foot pain originates from the foot**.

Poorly localized bilateral foot pain is seen in patients who wear tight shoes. The foot pain of interdigital neuralgia is commonly associated with tight footwear. The foot pain in interdigital neuralgia is usually located around the **lateral forefoot**, although the patient may complain of pain in the entire foot including the dorsal aspect as well as the proximal foot.

Posterior heel pain may be a result of superficial calcaneal bursitis (pump bumps), retrocalcaneal bursitis, FHL tendinitis, os trigonum syndrome, insertional Achilles tendinitis, seronegative spondylotic arthropathy, peroneal tendinitis, and sural nerve injuries or entrapment. Haglund deformity and posterior calcaneal exostoses should be under a differential diagnosis. The posterosuperior portion of the calcaneus becomes more prominent in the patients with the HF varus, cavus foot and rigidly plantar flexed first ray, and may lead a patient being more prone to develop retrocalcaneal bursitis.[22]

Plantar heel pain is discussed in detail in the chapter Hindfoot Pain and Plantar Fasciitis.

Medial heel pain may be related to the lesions of the saphenous nerve, medial calcaneal nerve (calcaneal branch neurodynia,[2] inferior calcaneal nerve,[3] or medial plantar nerve (jogger's foot) lesions. The examiner, in particular, should not miss the medial HF pain with tendinitis of the **posterior tibialis muscle**.

For complaints of *lateral midfoot (MF) and HF pain*, the examiner may look for tendinitis of the peroneus longus and peroneus brevis, calcaneo-cuboid arthropathy, pericuboid synovitis and arthritis, recurrent cuboido–4th metatarsal subluxation, sinus tarsi syndrome, calcaneofibular (subfibular) impingement of various causes, or osteochondritis of the lateral ankle. Pain with **peroneus longus tendinitis** may be felt at the forefoot where the insertion site is rather than behind the lateral malleolus or under the cuboid. Pain due to repetitive stress to the peroneus longus muscle may even be felt at the main muscle belly at the proximal fibula.

Lateralization of foot pain implies lateral side foot pain while the pathologies are at the medial side of the foot. Lateralized foot pain can be seen in hallux rigidus, in the painful medial strands of the plantar fascia in plantar fasciitis, or can be the result of excessive pronation secondary to posterior tibial tendon insufficiency

For the complaints of medial FF pain, bunions, sesamoiditis, hallux rigidus, hallux limitus, or gouty arthritis should be considered. Pain in gouty arthritis frequently involves the first MTP, but patients can have complaints about any part of the foot including the heel.

Other Foot-Related Complaints

Complaints of *stiffness and heaviness* provide little help in arriving at a specific etiologic diagnosis. A diabetic patient may have a stiff foot, but the patient usually does not complain. In elderly patients, taking medications such as calcium channel blockers or NSAIDs can cause swelling and heaviness of the feet. The feeling of *cold feet* without measurable low temperature of the feet suggests peripheral polyneuropathy.

A *feeling of insecurity and weakness* should be differentiated from true muscle weakness or fatigue. This should be confirmed by an appropriate physical examination. A *feeling of a foot that gives* in a patient with an inversion injury may represent ankle mortis or STJ pathologies with a ligament injuries.

The patient may blame his/her foot pain for *loss of balance or ataxia*. However, loss of balance during standing and gait is rarely caused by foot disorders. Therefore, hidden neurologic conditions such as diabetic neuropathy, vitamin B_{12} deficiency, CIDP, cervical spondylotic myelopathy, parkinsonism, undiscovered stroke, or normal pressure hydrocephalus should be excluded in the elderly population. *Tight Achilles tendon* may aggravate the postural abnormalities that occur in the elderly.

Recurrent *blister formation* is related to a too-tight shoe, a too-loose shoe, or insufficient protective socks in athletes. Severe foot pain, preceded by blisters or vice versa, may be seen in patients with herpes zoster.

Mode of Onset, Progression, and Activity Related Pain

PATTERN OF ONSET

Most foot pain is presented with a "progressively worsening" pattern. It is well known that this gradual onset of pain suggests repetitive stress as the mechanism behind the symptom. Underlying pathology to consider includes plantar fasciitis, posterior tibial tendinitis, and stress fractures.

Though this is the general rule, a clear distinction should be made in the history between the onset of the pathology and the onset of the pain that brought the patient to the physiatrist. Many patients with pathology that have a gradual progression describe their foot pain as being of sudden onset. This may be true because many patients tend to interpret the first appearance of a bothersome symptom as the moment the pathology began. For example, a patient with degenerative tendinitis or arthritis may not be symptomatic until at some point a minor trauma triggers the pain. The wary physiatrist will consider this phenomenon when making a diagnosis.

Take another instance of misinterpretation: A patient who has been bedridden in the hospital for an extended period of time may experience an acute onset of pain in the plantar aspect of the foot or calf as a result of the stretching of the muscle or plantar fascia when he or she resumes weight bearing and walking. Without a proper history and physical examination, a practitioner may misinterpret this acute onset of pain as being as vascular in origin while the true source of the pain is mechanical. Under the suspicion of **acute vascular origin** of the pain simply by reason of its mode of onset, the clinician may unnecessarily prescribe exhaustive investigative studies, although the patient's symptom may be relieved simply by a heel-lift.

SPECIAL WORK OR ACTIVITY RELATED

In addition, patients with minor biomechanical problems in their feet may not experience problems until they push their feet to the physical limit that can be tolerated. For example, a patient who has mild hindfoot (HF) varus or cavus foot may not experience foot pain until he/she has engaged in long distance running.

Also, some sports activities are prone to cause certain foot injuries to develop more frequently. For example, posterior heel pain by posterior impingement with os trigonum, anterior ankle pain due to osteophytes, and interdigital neuritis are more common in ballet dancers.[9,19] Retrocalcaneal bursitis and insertional tendinitis with Haglund deformity would be most commonly found in dancers and mountain climbers because their ankles and feet are used in the activities requiring hyper-dorsiflexion.

Activities promoting endurance tend to cause tenosynovitis, shin splints, compartment syndromes, fasciitis, and stress fractures. Those activities that put a premium on maneuverability produce strains and avulsion fractures.[4]

Heel pad atrophy with pain is common in an overweight person whose job demands long hours of standing.

It is therefore important to obtain a history of special work and activities in order to widen the differential in particular patients.

Associated Symptoms

Foot pain may be a part of systemic disorders. For example, in rheumatoid arthritis, the joints of the forefoot (FF) are mostly involved and a significant HF joint arthritis is uncommon, although it can cause considerable pain and disability when it occurs.[10]

Heel pain may be a local representation of the more generalized diseases such as ankylosing spondylitis, psoriatic arthritis, or Reiter's syndrome. Such entities should be considered when a history of foot pain is presented with other constitutional symptoms.

In addition, history regarding the proximal joints and upper extremity involvement should be inquired for possible generalized arthropathies, myelopathies, or neuropathies. Severe burning foot pain and ataxia, with or without upper motor neuron signs, may be an associated presentation in an HIV-infected patient. In diabetic patients, recurrent foot pain and swelling after walking or exercise may be a sign of the neurogenic osteoarthropathy (Charcot foot).

Radiating Pain and Concurrent Pain

Describing **a low back pain radiating to the foot** is not an uncommon characterization by the patient as well as by the referring physician when the patient is referred for an electrodiagnostic study for foot pain. Many patients who have LBP and foot pain simultaneously may misinterpret this **concurrent pain** as radiating pain. Many of the foot-originated concurrent pain may be due to interdigital neuritis, plantar fasciitis, and metatarsalgia, and they are easily identifiable by proper history taking and physical examination. These patients often wear tight-fitting shoes. Viewing their footwear and proper physical examination may be helpful to make a diagnosis and developing ways to relieve the foot pain. Misdiagnosing concurrent pain as a radiating pain will veer the physiatrist toward the wrong path in making a diagnosis and in treating the patient.

Nature of Foot Pain

Burning pain usually represents a neural origin such as neuralgia, entrapment, nerve irritation, erythromeralgia, or RSD rather than a musculoskeletal etiology. Pain in erythromeralgia is usually described as the pain of a burn, pain of mustard, or pain of intense sunburn.[6] When a patient who has been treated for plantar fasciitis complains of burning, tingling, or "pins and needle sensation" in the foot, the practitioner should be alert for coexisting focal nerve entrapment syndromes.

Patients with lymphangitis or superficial thrombophlebitis may also complain of a burning pain. The locations are, however, usually at the ankle and leg rather than in the foot, and other signs such as red streak of lymphangitis or lymphadenopathy would be noticed.

Tingling or pins and needles sensation usually suggests a neural origin. It may, however, be reflective of an inflammatory process close to the neural tissue such as tenosynovitis around the interdigital nerve branches.

Throbbing or pulsating pains suggest vascular origin or an inflamed/infected tissue with congestion. Often the patients obtain relief from throbbing pain by elevating the limb. *Disproportionately severe aching pain* relative to the degree of injury or pain during passive stretching of the involved muscle is characteristic of compartment syndrome.

In a patient who complains of severe excruciating foot pain with minor stimulation, the clinician should search for other clinical clues for RSD or gouty arthritis.

Relieving or Aggravating Factors

RELATIONSHIP WITH FOOTWEAR

Many foot conditions become symptomatic only when the patients wear their shoes. A patient with *interdigital neuritis* rarely feels pain when barefoot. Often he or she prefers to wear loose sandals over formal shoes. Upon more careful questioning, the examiner may discover that the patient changes to loose slippers or goes barefoot as soon as she/he arrives at home. An elderly patient may use an open sandal in the winter months to avoid FF pain caused by the constrictive design of ordinary women's shoes. *Faulty shoes and foot orthoses (FOs)* cause foot pain rather frequently. Lateral foot pain with peroneal muscle overuse may suggest inversion stress caused by faulty shoes (worn-out laterally) or faulty FOs due to over-enthusiastic medial posting without balancing laterally. In this instance, the patient would reveal that her/his lateral foot pain occurs only when she/he uses that particular shoe or insole.

Patients with cavus foot feel comfortable with *Western style cowboy boots* because the construction of the cowboy boot is suitable for the cavus with FF equinus of the patient's foot.

Again, having patients bring in their footwear to the encounter and distinguishing what shoes are the most comfortable or the most uncomfortable would make the diagnosis rather obvious in these instances.

Relationship with Previous Surgical Procedures

A surgical history may provide clues as to the source of patient's foot pain. The saphenous nerve can be damaged or entrapped under the scar after a surgery at the knee, harvesting the saphenous vein, arthroscopic procedures at the knee or ankle, or fracture of the ankle.[7] Superficial peroneal nerve as well as the sural nerve injury could be the result of arthroscopic surgery of the ankle.[11] Severe pain on the plantar medial aspect of the first MTP may result from the medial plantar hallucal nerve injury after medial sesamoidectomy.[1]

Relationship with Medications

It is often helpful to ask patients how their foot pain is related to the intake of their medications. The clinician should suspect erythromeralgia whenever patients mention substantial and prolonged relief of burning pain in the foot as a result of using acetylsalicylic acid.[21] Meanwhile, the vasodilating medications such as bromocriptine, nifedipine, and verapamil may aggravate the erythromeralgia.[16]

It is also well known that the acute gouty arthritis may respond dramatically to the administration of cochicine. If a patient complains of foot swelling and heaviness, obtain a history of non-steroidal anti-inflammatory medication and calcium channel blocker intake. Side effects of these common medications may be the source of the discomfort.

Ischemic Pains

Ischemic claudication of the calf or foot is activity related and promptly relieved when the patient stops walking. A history of pain while standing is not likely due to ischemic claudication. Claudication is most often "symptomatically unilateral" in spite of its bilateral vascular involvement since the patient rarely goes beyond his or her pain tolerance in the symptomatic limb. Patients with **ischemic rest pain** prefer to sit at the edge of the bed and dangle their feet to obtain relief of their foot discomfort. Significant pedal edema rather than the foot pain itself may be a clue of the ischemic rest pain in this instance.

Position of the Weight Bearing Foot

Pain changing with the position of weight bearing provides clues to the diagnosis. Worsening hindfoot pain by standing on either the inner or outer border of the foot suggests **STJ origin of the pain**. By this maneuver, the mobility of the subtalar, talonavicular, and calcaneocuboid joints and eversion and inversion powers are also evaluated.[23] If the patient shows significant relief of pain by reversing the **aggravating weight bearing foot posture** with medial or lateral wedges, this information should be adopted into the management plan (i.e., footwear or FOs for STJ control).

Although both the pain due to impingement of **os trigonum** and **peroneal tendinitis** is located posterolaterally behind the lateral malleolus, peroneal tendinitis is aggravated by resisted eversion, while the pain secondary to os trigonum impingement is triggered by forced plantar flexion of the ankle in activities such as kicking a football.

Time Relationship with Pain

In certain instances, a history of temporal relationship to pain is helpful.

Seasonal Pain.   Burning foot pain in *erythromeralgia* is related to the elevated skin temperature. The patient's pain may be greater during the summer months and when the patient has a fever, but would be less in the wintertime.[16,21]

Night Pain.   Foot pain during the night while the patient is in the bed could be indicative of neuralgic pain or ischemic rest pain. An ischemic rest pain may not be symptomatic until the patient has had a few hours of sleep in the bed. In contrast to other musculoskeletal origins of foot pain, a neuralgic pain tends to be relieved significantly by standing or walking.

RELATIONSHIP WITH THE GAIT CYCLE

Classic foot pain in plantar fasciitis is most severe during the initial period of weight bearing in the morning, eases out after several minutes of walking, and then returns after prolonged walking. The timing of the pain is mostly between *the midstance and push-off* period of gait cycle. The heel pain due to the bursitis under the calcaneal spur occurs at the initial *heel contact period* rather than at the late stance period of the gait cycle.

Foot pain aggravated by *climbing stairs or pivoting* may suggest peroneus longus tendon pathology because this muscle plays a major role in first ray plantarflexion, which is essential in these dynamic situations.

PHYSICAL EXAMINATION

Equipment for Examination

A hand goniometer, reflex hammer, magnifying glasses, and tuning fork are usually sufficient to perform a routine office physical examination of the foot. More sophisticated devices such as a high chair, pedoscope, biothesiometer, Semmes-Weinstein monofilaments, Harris mattress, and thermometer (infrared or laser) are used in certain conditions.

Marking the painful spot on the foot with **lipstick** is an excellent technique in locating and defining the relationship of the tender point in the patient's foot with the footwear or FOs (lipstick technique). Compression or percussion with a **sharpened rubber-tip of a pencil** is extremely useful in localizing a neuroma or nerve entrapment site by reproducing the patient's symptoms.

Once the history is taken, the patient should remove his/her shoes and socks and disrobe.

Examination with Patient Standing and Walking

During the standing evaluation, valgus or varus deformity of hindfoot and changes in proximal chain responses to pronation or supination of the foot can be observed.

Patellar squinting at knee level suggests that the pronated foot may be secondary to a compensatory effort of the patient in relation to femoral anteversion (horizontal plane compensation). The indiscriminate use of FOs in an effort correcting foot pronation would not be successful in this circumstance.

Slight pronation of the hindfoot on standing is a normal finding. On the other hand, excessive STJ pronation and resultant FF abduction allow the observer to see two or more toes when looking from behind (*too many toes sign*). This sign represents FF abduction or an externally rotated limb and should not be considered specific for any single pathologic condition, although it has been described frequently in tibialis posterior insufficiency.

TABLE 1. Pronation-Supination Responses

	Pronation Response	Supination Response
Calcaneal (frontal)	Eversion	Inversion
Fore/midfoot (sagittal)	Dorsiflexion	Plantar flexion
Forefoot (transverse)	Abduction	Adduction
Ankle	Dorsiflexion	Plantar flexion
Tibia	Internal rotation	External rotation
Knee	Flexion, valgus	Extension, varus
Femur	Internal rotation	External rotation
Hip	Flexion	Extension
Leg length	Shortened	Lengthened
Effect during gait	Absorbs impact, adapting the uneven terrain	Provides solid leverage for push-off

Hyperpronation can be caused by many different reasons including idiopathic, compensation for triceps surae tightness, insufficiency of the posterior tibial tendon, ruptured anterior tibialis tendon, Charcot neuroarthropathy foot, and tarsal coalition (congenital and acquired).

In examining the adequacy of the posterior tibialis muscle and tendon, the patient is asked to stand on one or both forefeet. Visible fullness of the medial HF between the medial malleolus and navicular bone should alert the examiner for tibialis posterior tendinitis. A *single or double heel raise test* and first metatarsal raise test[12] are designed for posterior tibialis tendon insufficiency.

Pronated or supinated foot deformity causes a so-called pronation or supination response (Table 1) in the proximal kinetic chain up to the spinal segments. Looking for the signs of hyperpronation-related pathologies in the proximal chain is an important role of the physiatrist in patient care (Table 2).

A small amount of *limb length discrepancies* (LLD) can be assessed easily by adding 3–6 mm heel lifts inside or outside of the shoes. For larger discrepancies, various thickness of plates that can be placed underneath the shorter side and horizontal levels of both shoulders and iliac crests can be assessed.

TABLE 2. Flexible Flatfoot Associated Pathology of the Proximal Chain

Peroneus longus spasm

Tibialis posterior overuse (posterior shin splints)

Patellofemoral syndrome

Medial collateral knee ligament strain

Iliotibial band syndrome at the knee or hip level

Patellar tendinitis

Popliteus muscle syndrome

Hip adductor tendinitis

Greater trochanteric bursitis

Lumbosacral muscle spasms

Piriformis syndrome

Sacroiliac joint stress syndrome

Modified from Yale JF: Clin Podiatr Med Surg 6(3):555–560, 1989.

It should be kept in mind that a small amount of *flexion (contracture) of the hip* may result in rather significant leg length shortening. Therefore, thorough examination of the ROM of the hips, knees, and ankles should be performed in every patient with LLD.

Foot pronation normally causes functional shortening of the leg length by about 3–6 mm, while supination results in functional lengthening. The total shortening of the limb in pronation, however, can be much greater because the pronation response includes knee valgus, knee flexion, and hip flexion at the same time.

In a patient with LLD, the patient may walk with supinated foot on the shorter side and pronated foot on the longer side (*windswept gait*). A poorly thought-out correction of the pronated foot would be harmful to the patient in this instance.

In the walking evaluation, the examiner basically looks for symmetry and fluency of gait. Walking evaluation without footwear may yield more information regarding the biomechanical abnormalities of foot than with the shoe on, unless the examiner is looking for the effect of footwear on the patient's symptom.

Observing the *relationship between the medial mallelolus, navicular bone, and first MTP* provides valuable information regarding the HF, MF, and FF behavior during gait.

The direction in which the patella faces will provide information regarding the rotational relationship between the femur and tibia.

Externally rotated limb places less demand on the foot during pronation to re-supination in the gait cycle because of the shortened lever arm for push-off. This gait pattern may be observed in tibialis posterior insufficiency, hallux limitus, hallux valgus, sesamoiditis, plantar fasciitis, fractures of the FF or MF midfoot, etc. Since the externally rotated limb does not require full dorsiflexion of the ankle to clear the ground, this gait pattern may also be seen in the patient with a functionally longer limb.

Valgus knee with pronated foot is a common condition presenting together. It is often difficult to differentiate whether the pronated foot caused valgus knee or valgus knee promoted pronated foot. An important point to remember, however, is that without properly addressing the valgus deformity or valgus force of the knee, any correction or accommodation with footwear and FOs would not be effective.

Examination with Patient Sitting: The Foot Is a Palpable Organ

In contrast to other musculoskeletal organs, almost all the basic anatomic structures of the foot are accessible to the examiner's palpating hands.[24] Most foot examinations can be performed in a sitting or supine position except in several special examinations that require a prone position. A high chair is commercially available to facilitate a foot evaluation in a sitting position.

When the patient sits on the examination table with legs dangling over the side, a normal foot is in equinus, mild varus, and slight supination and has an adequately formed longitudinal arch. Both feet are compared, while the patient is asked to perform inversion/eversion of both HF and adduction/abduction of the both FF.

As in all types of physical exam, a systematic approach is always best. Because they are the most reliable references even in patients with excessive edema or inflammation, begin first with palpation of *bony reference points*. Palpation may reveal invaluable clues such as tenderness, bogginess, fluctuations, gaps, subluxation, and local heat, and may also trigger the characteristic neuroma pains.

Starting from the medial side of the foot, palpate the medial malleolus, sustentaculum tali, navicular bone, talar head, medial cuneiform, and first MTPJ. Then laterally,

TABLE 3.   Points of Maximum Tenderness According to Foot and Ankle Disorders

Disorders	Tender Point
Morton's neuritis	3rd (2nd) interdigital
Hallux rigidus	Dorsal aspect of 1st MTPJ
Hallux valgus/bunion	Medial aspect of 1st MTPJ
Sesamoiditis	Medial plantar at 1st MTPJ, shifts with DF of G. toe
Metatarsalgia	Plantar aspects of all MTPJs
Plantar fasciitis	Calcaneal insertion of the plantar fascia Along the medial and middle strands of fasciae
Entrap. of 1st branch LPN (Baxter's n., inf. calc. n.)	Medial plantar aspect of hind foot
Bursitis under the heel spur	Plantar aspect of medial anterior quadrant of heel
Pericuboidal synovitis/arthritis	4th metatarsocuboid and calcaneocuboid joints
Sinus tarsi syndrome	Sinus tarsi, occasionally retrocalcaneal region
Retrocalcaneal bursitis	Between calcaneus and Achilles tendon
Precalcaneal bursitis	Posterior to Achilles tendon at heel
Achilles tendinitis	6–7 cm above the insertion of Achilles tendon
Tibialis posterior tendinitis	Between medial malleolus and navicular
Peroneus longus tendinitis	Between lateral malleolus and cuboid, across plantar aspect toward 1st metatarsal base
Peroneus br. injury/tendinitis	Lateral dorsal aspect of 5th metatarsal styloid
PB tendon rupture	Styloid process of 5th metatarsal

palpate the lateral malleolus, peroneal trochlea (tuberosity), calcaneo-cuboid articulations, sinus tarsi, cuboid, and cuboido–4th metatarsal, base of 5th metatarsal, and the fifth MTPJ (Table 3).

The examiner may then palpate the posterior calcaneal tubercle, and anteriorly the individual metatarsal heads up through their shafts to their proximal articulations. Particular attention should be paid to the 2nd MTPJ because a wide variety of pathology involves this joint.

Unlike the bony references, the palpation of tendons is a more difficult endeavor. Even in normal patients, it is difficult to delineate all small tendons. Therefore, the goal of this part of the exam is to roughly assess the major tendons first. The major tendons to palpate include the gastrocsoleus (Achilles tendon), anterior tibialis, and extensor digitorum longus.

Then if smaller, specific tendons need to be examined, the patient should be asked to contract against the examiner's resistance to make hidden tendons more prominent and more accessible to palpation. Such tendons include those of the extensor hallucis longus, posterior tibialis (between the medial malleolus and navicular bone), flexor hallucis longus, peroneus longus, peroneus brevis, and peroneal tertius muscles. The examiner should remember that the peroneus longus tendon winds under the cuboid, crosses the midfoot, and inserts in the base of the first metatarsal and medial cuneiform plantarly.

Palpating ligaments is an even more troublesome experience. Like those tendons that required maneuvers for palpation, ligaments also require active manipulation of the foot by the examiner. For example, the calcaneal-fibular ligament becomes more accessible to palpation when the subtalar joint is inverted. Likewise, the plantar fascia can also be made palpable by the dorsiflexion of the MTPJ.

Though it is not possible to palpate other ligaments, it is important for the examiner to be able to pinpoint the location of ligaments that can be part of the pathology underlying the patient's pain. Ligaments to be familiar with include the anterior-inferior tibiofibular ligament at the ankle mortis, anterior talofibular ligament, deltoid ligament, and spring ligament.[18]

In our experience, most practitioners are already familiar with examining the major muscle bellies that may be involved in foot pain. These will not be discussed in this chapter. However, it is worthwhile to mention that most practitioners fail to palpate the posterior tibialis muscle—a muscle that is frequently involved in pain associated with excessive pronation; and the peroneus longus muscle—a muscle that is excessively abused in pathology rooted in supinated conditions.

As mentioned earlier, it is to the benefit of the practitioner to recognize patterns of pain in the history and physical exam to reach the proper diagnosis. The following are some conditions with certain unique characteristics that may be helpful in defining the precise pathology and guiding the proper treatment.

Sesamoiditis or sesamoid injury presents as a pain in the medial plantar aspect of the 1st MTPJ. One of the characteristic features of this typically point specific sesamoid pain is its tendency to shift anteriorly with passive dorsiflexion of the 1st MTP. This shifting logically occurs because the sesamoids are contained in and move with the tendons of FHB.

Hallux rigidus is suspected if there is a limitation of extension of the 1st MTPJ associated with pain at the dorsal surface. As mentioned earlier, the patient ironically may also have pain and tenderness along the lateral foot. Owing to pain and limitations in the extension of the 1st MTPJ, the patient is unable to toe-break in the usual manner and tends to toe-break laterally (lateralization). On examination of the patient's footwear, the shoe crease may be directed along this lateral toe-break line.

Achilles tendon tightness can be assessed by measuring the angle formed by the longitudinal axis of the fibula and 5th metatarsal while the knee is in full extension and the STJ is in neutral. Tightness in the soleus and gastrocnemius are assessed separately. Normally there should be 20 degrees of ankle dorsiflexion. At least 10 degrees of ankle dorsiflexion is required for normal gait pattern. The condition where no dorsiflexion occurs in the ankle is termed ***equinus deformity***, while dorsiflexion less than 10 degrees is termed ***equinus state***. Achilles tendon tightness is the most common cause of these conditions in the adult.

Forefoot equinus usually occurs with cavus foot (i.e., Charcot-Marie-Tooth) and practitioners often fail to recognize the biomechanical significance of the FF-equinus. A patient with FF-equinus will use compensation mechanisms in the sagittal plane to achieve heel contact on the ground during weight bearing. As a result, the patients "use up" all the tibio-talar (ankle) DF as well as the available maximum length of the Achilles tendon. In other words, there may not be any true Achilles tendon tightening or true equinus deformity at the ankle. An inexperienced practitioner may falsely assume that a FF equinus is an ankle equinus.

It is for this reason that Achilles tendon lengthening exercise will not improve the FF equinus or the patient's pain at the anterior ankle caused by abutting between the tibia and anterior talus. In addition, the patient may complain of pain at the posterior knee as a result of over-stretching the posterior capsules and muscles of the knee. The best solution would be surgical correction of the FF-equinus deformity or accommodating the FF-equinus with heel lifts. Unnecessary Achilles stretching exercises should be avoided in this instance.

Examination with Patient Prone

The range of internal and external rotation of the hips in the prone position should be evaluated for rotational abnormalities whenever the patient complains of pain in the knee as well as in the foot. This is a good habit to assume because rotational problems in the proximal joints maybe be manifested as pain and/or deformity in the foot. During the examination, be wary of patients with excessive internal rotation with limited external rotation of hips. These patients may have foot pain due to torsional abnormalities such as femoral anteversion. In these cases, correction of foot pain is futile without addressing the abnormalities in the more proximal joints.

In the prone position, heel pad atrophy, fat herniation, plantar fascia, Haglund deformity, retrocalcaneal bursitis, peroneal tendinitis, and Achilles tendinitis can be evaluated.

Defining the subtalar joint (STJ) neutral is a crucial to the examination process. This is typically performed in a prone position—although it could be done in any other position.

In *heel pad atrophy*, the patient complains of diffuse pain in the entire heel that is not confined to the medial calcaneal tubercle. There is no specific guideline regarding the definition and degree of fat pad atrophy. However, a good rule of thumb is that when the examiner is able to palpate the calcaneal bone through the fat pad, the fat pad would be considered atrophic. A *bursa under the heel spur* may be palpable at the anterior medial quadrant of heel as a fluctuating soft mass. Differentiating between the retrocalcaneal bursitis, FHL tendinitis, and os trigonum syndrome can be difficult because these three conditions occur at the same anatomic area and may also coexist.

In summary, with good knowledge of the local anatomy and related biomechanics, proper physical exam techniques, and a detailed history, the practitioner can establish a list of the most likely pathologic conditions (see Table 3).

Neurologic Examination of Foot

A neurologic exam of the foot is both difficult to perform and difficult to interpret for multiple reasons. Anatomically, the distribution of sensory and motor nerve branches is not as well defined as in the hand. In addition, for some unknown reason, the patient's subjective expression of pain in the foot is extremely variable. Often patients have difficulty differentiating cutaneous pain versus the pain from the deep anatomic structures, and have a tendency to widen the extent of and location of abnormal sensations. In addition, the differentiation of normal versus abnormal neurologic exams becomes more difficult as patients age. For example, elderly adults generally lose some level of vibratory acuity over time. Therefore, this deficit should not be considered pathologic in such patients unless other findings coexist.

Motor power is also difficult to appraise, especially in the elderly patients. In a healthy adult, it is hard to assess the isolated power of intrinsic foot muscles because of the overlay/synergy of these with extrinsic muscles. Assessment of these intrinsic muscles therefore relies on the actual palpation of the muscles. Owing to physiologic muscle atrophy in the elderly, even this basic level of assessment may become particularly difficult.

In addition, the triceps surae reflexes may not be obtainable in the normal elderly. The posterior tibialis muscle reflex is difficult to perform and is frequently unobtainable even in a healthy individual. The Babinski sign is useful for the upper motor neuron disorders, but it also represents the existence of normal peroneal (peripheral nerve) nerve function at the time when the patient presents with a foot drop.

Nevertheless, routine sensory examinations should include pinprick, light touch, temperature, position, and vibration sensations. Other diagnostic considerations to be included in the neurologic assessment are systemic neurologic disorders or diseases that involve more proximal segments. The detailed examination is described in the chapter Foot Conditions Related to Neuromuscular Disorders in Adults.

It is worthwhile to mention here that locating *a painful neuroma* is one of the skills that a practitioner should acquire. An unsuspected neuroma after trauma or other various operative procedures can create a diagnostic dilemma if it is not considered in the differential. If there is a strong clinical suspicion, the examiner may utilize the sharpened tip of an ordinary pencil eraser to locate the neuroma and trigger the pain in the patient.

Other Tests and Assessment Methods

DEFINING SUBTALAR JOINT NEUTRAL

Defining STJ neutral is a mandatory skill for a physiatrist. It is necessary in assessing the biomechanical status of a patient's foot, in designing the foot orthosis, and in evaluating the shoes or FO modifications.[1]

To define the subtalar joint neutral position, the patient is placed in a prone position and places the medial malleolus of the opposite leg in the popliteal fossa of the examining leg (figure-4 position). This is done to place the long axis of the examining foot to vertical orientation. The examiner grasps the 4th–5th metatarsal heads gently between the ipsilateral thumb and index fingers. The thumb of the opposite hand is placed on the medial aspect of the talonavicular joint and the index

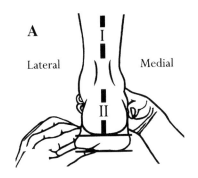
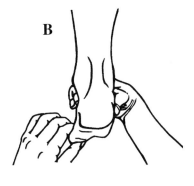
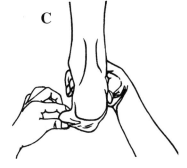

FIGURE 1. Determination of subtalar joint neutral. *A*, Subtalar joint neutral. I: line connecting mid-calf to mid-calcaneus; II: mid-calcaneal bisecting line. *B*, Forefoot varus. *C*, Forefoot valgus.

finger on the lateral side of the talus. The examiner repeatedly supinates and pronates the forefoot gently with the ipsilateral hand until the talonavicular joint is congruent (head of talus resting in the cup of the navicular) and the laxity of the Achilles tendon disappears at the same time. This position of the subtalar joint is defined as a subtalar neutral.

Once the subtalar neutral position has been defined, hindfoot valgus and varus deformity can be assessed with the angle formed by the line connecting mid-calf to ankle and the midcalcaneal bisect line (central sagittal axis). Also with this position, measuring the angle connecting calcaneus bisecting line and line of the metatarsal heads can assess FF valgus and varus deformities (Fig. 1).

If the pronated position of the FF is easily obtained and maintained with minimum force, the secondary changes of the MF and FF capsulo-ligamentous structures are still flexible. On the contrary, if the pronated FF position is difficult to obtain, the secondary varus changes in the FF and MF are severe and inflexible (i.e., longstanding posterior tibial tendon insufficiency).[17]

STJ AXIS PALPATION (KIRBY'S METHOD)

A method for STJ axis determination in reference to the transverse plane has been developed and is performed in a supine position. The STJA in relation to the plantar surface of the foot may be determined by finding the point on the plantar aspect of the foot at which no STJA rotation occurs with manual thumb pressure. For the right foot, the examiner uses the left hand to sense subtalar joint motion by gently holding the lateral two MTPs and uses the right hand to produce subtalar joint motion by pressing on the plantar foot (Fig. 2).

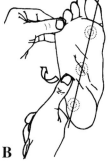

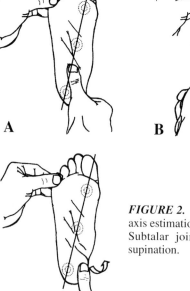

FIGURE 2.   Kirby's method of subtalar joint axis estimation. *A*, No subtalar joint rotation. *B*, Subtalar joint pronation. *C*, Subtalar joint supination.

If thumb pressure is medial to the STJA, STJ supination will occur. If thumb pressure is lateral to the STJA, STJ pronation will occur. If thumb pressure is directly on the STJA, no STJ motion will occur. The points of non-rotation are plotted on the foot to indicate the STJA location on the plantar aspect of foot.[15]

The plotted line is usually pointed toward the great toe or first interdigital space in a normal person. This method can be applied to children easily but is difficult in the adult, especially if the HF and MF rigid deformity has occurred already. A flexible pronated foot with an excessively medially deviated STJA axis may require UCBL or modified AFO to achieve direct control of STJ pronation, instead of an ordinary shoe insert.[15]

COLMAN'S LATERAL BLOCK TEST

This test is designed to assess the flexibility of the compensatory HF varus deformity in the presence of fixed FF valgus deformity (i.e., Charcot-Marie-Tooth disease). A long wooden block of varying thickness is placed under the lateral heel to the metatarsal, allowing the first metatarsal to drop to the floor. If the compensatory HF deformity is flexible, it will correct with the lateral block in place. If the HF deformity were fixed, the HF varus alignment would not be changed. For further information, readers should refer to the chapter Foot Conditions Related to Neuromuscular Disorders in Adults.

SQUEEZING AND PINCHING

Since the anatomy of the foot easily allows squeezing, pinching, and probing, in certain circumstances, these methods can be utilized for their considerable diagnostic yield.

Pinching of the 3rd or 2nd interdigital space between the examiner's thumb and index finger in the patient with pain in the forefoot is used to localize the interdigital neuritis.

Forefoot squeeze test is performed by wrapping the hand around the dorsum of the metatarsals and squeezing the heads together. In this maneuver, both tenosynovitis, bursitis, as well as interdigital neuritis can result in pain. Clicking felt by the patient as well as by the examiner during the squeeze test (Mulder's click) has been considered in the past to be a specific sign of an interdigital neuroma, though it is now regarded as less specific than originally thought.

Calcaneal squeeze test for calcaneus is useful for evaluation of heel pain. In this squeeze, the examiner's thenar eminences of both hands are used to squeeze the lateral aspects of the calcaneus. Because no major neurovascular or tendinous structures are passing through this area, deep heel pain on this particular maneuver represents calcaneal pathology such as stress fracture, rather than heel pad, heel spur, or Achilles tendon–related pathologies.

Squeezing of the proximal tibia and fibula results in separating the distal tibiofibular syndesmosis. The patient with severe inversion ankle sprain with lingering anterior ankle pain may represent the anterior-inferior tibiofibular ligament injury. Since the examiner does not make any direct contact with other anterior ankle structures, ankle pain elicited in this maneuver would most likely to be syndesmosis origin.

Foot Examination in Patients with Peripheral Vascular Insufficiency and Diabetes Mellitus

In the *pallor on elevation test*, both of the patient's legs and feet are elevated above the heart level. The color is milked from the soles of the feet by gentle pressure.

After approximately 30 seconds, the amount of color that reappears is noted. If the patient has significant arterial disease, there will be persistent pallor on elevation.[26]

Venous filling time is a time-honored assessment method available in the office. After pallor on elevation has been noted, the patient sits up quickly, and the length of time that it takes the first vein to fill on the dorsum of the foot is recorded. This venous filling time is normally within 10–15 seconds in a normal person. In a patient with significant arterial disease, there will be a delay in venous filling time up to 30–60 seconds. The amount of rubor in the feet after 2–3 minutes should be noted.[26]

Rubor (redness) in dependency is indicative of clinically significant tissue ischemia. The rubor should be considered a warning sign to the surgeon. An amputated stump through this level may not heal without additional procedures such as arterial bypass surgery. A similar rule may be applied to the physician treating foot ulcers. The longer it takes (> 2–3 minutes) for rubor in dependency to appear, the more severe is the degree of arterial insufficiency.

During *supine evaluation*, the proximal popliteal, femoral, and external iliac artery pulses are accessible. A *manually palpable pulse* in the foot may be more meaningful than the detection of the pulsating sound by a handheld Doppler probe, unless the pulse-volume recordings are performed at the same time. Pulse palpation assesses volume changes better than the Doppler does.

For an objective examination of sensation in diabetic patients, vibration perception threshold (VPT) is performed by using a *biothesiometer*. It has been found that subjects with values greater than VPT of 25 V (predictive value) have a seven times higher risk of developing foot ulcer when compared with subjects with VPT less than 15 V.[20] In the diabetic population, *Semmes-Weinstein monofilaments (5.07)* are used to screen for protective sensation. This method is simple and inexpensive with high reliability and validity.[5]

The *elevation test* is a valuable method providing differential diagnosis when a diabetic patient presents with erythema of the foot. Erythema of the foot due to *hyperemia* (i.e., Charcot neuropathic osteoarthropathy) would fade by elevating the foot above the heart level for a few minutes, whereas erythema due to *cellulitis* would not fade on elevation. This simple test is reliable and provides direction of the treatment plan.

The *probing test* is a simple clinical test which can be utilized for clinical assessment of a foot ulcer in the diabetic patients and provides a practical guide in the assessment of osteomyelitis.[8] Gently squeezing the various compartments of the foot after probing may yield unexpected communicating sinuses deep inside the foot although the wound seems to be only superficial.

Foot Pain Related to FOs and AFOs

Evaluation of the most comfortable and uncomfortable footwear, wear pattern, and foot orthoses can provide remarkable diagnostic clues as well as management guides. These problems and clues are discussed in detail in the chapter Physiatric Management of Sports-Related Foot and Ankle Injury.

Medial foot pain in AFO users are frequently caused by excessive pressure at the top of the arch or at the medial-inferior aspect of the talar head. A patient who has spasticity of the plantar flexor or a tight heel cord would use a pronation response to gain dorsiflexion. This repeated pronation on each gait cycle forces the talar head to deviate medially and the medial longitudinal arch to be flattened. Without reducing spasticity of the plantar flexors, Achilles tendon stretching, or accommodative heel lifting under the patient's heel, the patient's pain will persist in spite of repeated relief provided by an orthotist at these painful locations.

Local pain at the forefoot, at the edge of the AFO, can be caused by similar circumstances described above. The physiatrist should be aware of the FF equinus deformity in designing an AFO for a patient with Charcot-Marie-Tooth disease. Cursory designed AFOs for ankle equinus will be troublesome owing to the pain at the distal edge of the AFO. Accommodation with heel elevation would be an appropriate orthotic approach.

CONCLUSION

When a patient complains of foot pain, there is always a reason. The clinical clues needed to find the underlying cause are usually waiting there for the clinician to discover. The proper diagnosis can be reached by taking a problem-oriented history and physical examination. Regardless of the extensive literature that correlates such pains to a number of ornate causes involving multiple systems, one must remember that *most foot pains originate from the foot*. A well-informed examiner should start first with a sound knowledge of the anatomy and biomechanics of the foot, search for the relevant clues in the history and physical, and then narrow the differential. This, however, does not eliminate the need for the examiner to study the ankle, knee, and the rest of the proximal kinetic chain. A tight Achilles tendon should be identified and treated appropriately, since shortened gastrocsoleus muscletendon is an important culprit for almost every foot pain regardless of the etiology.

REFERENCES

1. Alexander IJ: The Foot. Examination and Diagnosis, 2nd ed. New York, Churchill-Livingstone, 1997.
2. Bateman JE: The adult heel. In Jahss MH (ed): Disorders of Foot. Philadelphia, WB Saunders, 1982, pp 764–775.
3. Baxter DE, Peiffer GB: Treatment of chronic heel pain by surgical release of the first branch of the lateral plantar nerve. Clin Orthop 279:235, 1999.
4. Coker TP, Arnold JA: Sports injuries to the foot and ankle: In Jahss MH (ed): Disorders of foot. Philadelphia, WB Saunders, 1982 pp 1573–1606.
5. Coleman WC: Footwear for injury prevention: Correction with risk category. In Bowker JH, Pfeifer MA (eds): The Diabetic Foot, 6th ed. St. Louis, Mosby, 2001, pp 422–438.
6. Fairbarian JF: Clinical manifestations of peripheral vascular disease. In Jurgens JL, Spittell JA, Fairbarian JF (eds): Peripheral Vascular Disease. Philadelphia WB Saumders, 1980, pp 3–49.
7. Frey C: Foot and ankle arthroscopy and endoscopy. In Myerson MS (ed): Foot and Ankle Disorders. Philadelphia, WB Saunders, 2000, pp 1477–1511.
8. Grayson ML, Balogh K, Levin E, Karchmer AW: Probing to bone in infected pedal ulcers. A clinical sign of underlying osteomyelitis in diabetic patients. JAMA 273:721–723, 1995.
9. Hamilton WG: Stenosing tenosynovitis of the flexor hallucis longus tendon and posterior impingement upon the os trigonum in ballet dancers. Foot Ankle 3:74–80, 1982.
10. Hansen ST: The ankle and foot. In Kelly WN (ed): Rhematology, 5th ed. Philadelphia, WB Saunders, 1997, pp 1759–1772.
11. Heinen GT, Ferkel RD: Arthroscopy of the ankle and subtalar joints. Foot Ankle 4(4):833–864, 1999.
12. Hinterman B, Gachter A: The first metatarsal rise sign. A sensitive sign of tibialis posterior tendon dysfunction. Foot and Ankle Int 17:236–241, 1996.
13. Hoppenfeld S: Physical examination of the foot by complaint. In Jahss MH (ed): Disorders of the Foot. Philadelphia, WB Saunders, 1982, pp 103–115.
14. Hughes JR: Footwear assessment. In Merriman LM, Tollafield DR (eds): Assessment of the Lower Limb. Edinburgh, Churchill Livingstone, 1995.
15. Kirby KA, Green DR: Evaluation and nonoperative management of pes valgus. In DeValentine SJ (ed): Foot and Ankle Disorders in Children. New York, Churchill Livingstone, 1992, pp 295–327.
16. Olin JW, Arrabi W: Vascular diseases related to extremes in environmental temperature. In Young JR, Olin JW, Bartholomew JR (eds): Peripheral Vascular Diseases. St. Louis, Mosby, 1996, pp 614–617.

17. Richardson EG: Tarsal coalition. In Myerson MS (ed): Foot and Ankle Disorders. Philadelphia, WB Saunders, 2000, pp 729–748.

18. Sarrafian SK: Anatomy of the Foot and Ankle. Descriptive, Topographic, Functional. Philadelphia, JB Lippincott, 1983.

19. Schon LC: Nerve entrapment, neuropathy, and nerve dysfunction in athletes. Orth Clin North Am 25(1):4759, 1994.

20. Song J, Spadone SJ: Sensory examination. Comparison of instruments. Clin Podiatr Med Surg 16:29–48, 1999.

21. Spittell, JA: Vascular syndromes related to environmental temperature. In Jurgens JL, Spittell JA, Fairbairn JF (eds): Peripheral Vascular Diseases. Philadelphia, WB Saunders, 1980, pp 601–604.

22. Stephens MM: Haglund's deformity and retrocalcaneal bursitis. Ortho Clin North Am 25(1):41–45, 1994.

23. Sullivan JA: Pes planus. In Myerson MS (ed): Foot and Ankle Disorders. Philadelphia, WB Saunders, 2000, pp 645–727.

24. Winkel D, Matthijs O, Phelps V: Examination of the ankle and foot. In Winkel D (ed): Diagnosis and Treatment of the Lower Extremity. Gaithersburg, MD, Aspen, 1997, pp 375–401.

25. Yale JF: The conservative treatment of adult flexible flatfoot. Clin Podiatr Med Surg.6(3):555–560, 1989.

26. Young JR: Physical examination. In Young JR (ed): Periphreal Vascular Diseases, 2nd ed. St. Louis, Mosby, 1996, pp 18–32.

CORNELIA WENOKOR, MD
HILARY R. UMANS, MD
NOGAH HARAMATI, MD

IMAGING OF THE FOOT AND ANKLE

From UMDNJ-NJ Medical School
Newark, New Jersey (CW)
    and
Albert Einstein College of Medicine
and Montefiore Medical Center
Bronx, New York (HU, NH)

Reprint requests to:
Department of Radiology
UMDNJ-NJ Medical School
Room C-320
150 Bergen Street
Newark, NJ 07103

STANDARD PROJECTIONS

A standard ankle series consists of an antero-posterior (AP), lateral, and oblique or mortise views. For the AP view, the patient is positioned supine, and the beam is centered at the tibiotalar joint with the ankle in slight dorsiflexion and the foot mildly pronated. On a normal AP view, there is at least 5 mm of overlap of the distal fibula with the tibia at a level 1 cm above the tibial plafond. The mortise view is obtained at 15–20° of internal rotation with the beam centered at the ankle joint. This view facilitates evaluation of the talofibular joint. Special views may permit additional evaluation of bony structures or joints. The **external oblique view** of the ankle, taken with 45° external rotation, allows better assessment of the medial malleolus.

The standard AP projection of foot demonstrates forefoot anatomy, particularly phalanges and metatarsophalangeal joints, and permits measurement of the following:

Metatarsus primus varus angle (< 25°)
Intermetatarsal angle (< 10°)
Hallux valgus angle (< 20°)
Interphalangeal angle (< 15°)
Talocalcaneal angle (35° ± 20°)

An angled (15°) AP projection improves detail of midfoot anatomy, particularly illustrating normal alignment of the lateral border of the 1st tarsometatarsal joint and medial border of the 2nd tarsometatarsal joint.

The lateral projection of the foot (see Fig. 1) permits measurement of the talocalcaneal angle (50° ±- 20°) and Boehler's angle (20–40°).

The medial oblique view complements both the AP and lateral views in evaluating forefoot and hindfoot. One of its primary roles is evaluating the midfoot, including the third through fifth tarsometatarsal joints. This view demonstrates normal medial border alignment of the 3rd and 4th tarsometatarsal joints. It also allows evaluation of the talonavicular and calcaneocuboid relationship.

The lateral oblique view offers additional information about the tarsal and Chopart's joint. The detail of the talonavicular joint can be evaluated.

SPECIAL PROJECTIONS

Special views may permit additional evaluation of bony structures or joints. The Harris-Beath view is an axial view of the calcaneus and is obtained with 45° caudal angulation of the central beam. This view allows evaluation of subtalar joint and is used for fracture evaluation of the calcaneus and evaluation of tarsal coalition. Computed tomography (CT) and magnetic resonance imaging (MRI), however, afford a more sensitive evaluation of the subtalar joint and hindfoot anatomy in the axial and coronal planes.

Broden's view is a medial oblique view of the ankle and hindfoot with approximately 20° cephalad beam angulation. It also permits evaluation of the subtalar joint, the sinus tarsi, and the middle talocalcaneal facet. The lateral oblique view provides similar information but does not demonstrate the sinus tarsi.

Sesamoid views are taken with the beam tangential to the sesamoid bones and 40° beam angulation toward the heel. Both lateral and axial views may be obtained. These are useful if fracture, osteonecrosis, or inflammation of the sesamoid bones is suspected.

STRESS VIEWS

Stress views can be used for differentiation of ligament injuries from sprains at the ankle joint in the absence of fractures. This might be painful in an acutely injured patient and injection of local anesthetic can facilitate the examination. AP projections are obtained with both varus and valgus stress applied as the foot is held in neutral and plantar flexion. Comparison views of the unaffected side are necessary to distinguish ligamentous injury from laxity. A side-to-side discrepancy of 5° is suggestive of injury, and 10° is diagnostic of ligament tear. Lateral stress views are performed with a double exposure technique. The first exposure is performed with the heel supported in neutral position; the second exposure follows with stress applied to the anterior tibia. Tibial shift relative to the talus of > 2.5 mm is diagnostic of instability.

WEIGHT BEARING VIEWS

Weight bearing views apply reproducible stress to the foot and allow functional evaluation of bony relationships. AP and lateral projections are routine. For infants or patients unable to stand, the AP view can be achieved with the patient supine, knees flexed, and the feet pressed against the film cassette. The tibia must be aligned with the hindfoot with the central ray angled 15° toward the heel to eliminate overlap of the lower leg with the heel. For the lateral projection, the patient leans forward to dorsiflex the ankle, or plantar pressure may be applied to achieve maximal dorsiflexion.

COMPUTED TOMOGRAPHY

CT uses a narrowly collimated x-ray beam that rotates around the patient permitting acquisition of multiple contiguous slices. Newer (spiral or helical) scanners obtain a volumetric data set permitting high-resolution two dimensional or three dimensional multiplanar reconstructions. Images may be printed in soft tissue and bone windows. For fine bone detail, bone algorithm should be employed. Typically 3-mm-thick slices are obtained, but for reconstructions, best results are achieved using contiguous 1.0–1.5-mm-thick slices. The ankle and foot are ideally imaged in both the direct axial and coronal plane. Axial images are obtained with the patient supine and soles of the feet perpendicular to the CT table; great toes should be close together and knees held straight. Direct coronal images can be acquired with the knee in flexion and the sole of the foot seated on the table. If necessary, foot wedges or gantry tilt can optimize positioning. Alternatively, good results are possible using thin section axial imaging with reformations in the coronal plane.

Indications for CT include fracture and post-traumatic deformities, arthritides, congenital deformities including tarsal coalition, tumors, and infection; intravenous contrast is primarily reserved for detection of soft tissue abscesses and sinus tracts. Implanted surgical hardware, shrapnel, or metallic foreign bodies may cause significant image degradation because of beam hardening (streak) artifact. Plaster or fiberglass casts usually do not cause significant artifact, but may prevent proper patient positioning.

MAGNETIC RESONANCE IMAGING

Following plain films, MRI is now the modality of choice for the imaging evaluation of ankle and foot disorders. In many conditions, MR complements CT. MR images are generated using a stationary magnetic field in conjunction with radiofrequency pulses but no ionizing radiation. Images are acquired in at least two orthogonal planes. Axial, coronal, and sagittal planes are routinely obtained. Pulse sequences and imaging planes are tailored to the specific clinical question. MR provides superior soft tissue contrast, making it ideal for evaluation of ligaments, tendons, and soft tissue masses. It is also optimal for bone marrow evaluation and assessment of articular cartilage integrity. Intravenous gadolinium is typically reserved for the imaging of osteomyelitis, abscess and sinus tracts, and evaluation of inflammatory arthritis and occasionally for tumors.

MR ARTHROGRAPHY

MR arthrography uses intra-articular injection of either saline or a dilute gadolinium solution to enhance detection of ligament injury, cartilage damage, loose bodies, or osteochondritis dissecans. Injection is performed using sterile technique and local anesthetic control, guided by fluoroscopy, palpation, or ultrasound. A 22-gauge, $1\frac{1}{2}$-inch needle is placed anteromedial to the dorsalis pedis artery, the tip tilted slightly inferiorly to avoid the anterior lip of the tibia. Once the needle tip lies intra-articular, 6–8 ml of fluid are injected. MR following arthrography is performed using fat suppressed T1-weighted spin echo sequences, gradient recalled echo sequences (which may be acquired volumetrically), or T2-weighted sequences.

TARSAL COALITION

Tarsal coalition implies tarsal fusion that can be fibrous (syndesmosis), cartilaginous (synchondrosis), or osseous (synostosis). Coalitions are generally congenital, but can be acquired, following trauma, surgery, infection, or inflammation. Patients typically become symptomatic in adolescence, presenting with vague pain and limitation of the subtalar joint, a rigid flat foot deformity, or intermittent peroneal spasm. Ordinary flatfoot deformities are flexible and generally not painful.

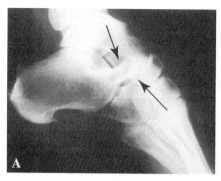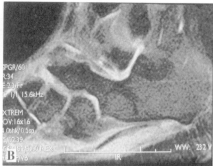

FIGURE 1. *A*, Calcaneonavicular coalition. A lateral radiograph shows an osseous bridge connecting the calcaneus with the navicular bone (arrows). *B*, A FSEIR sagittal MR image shows the osseous calcaneonavicular coalition.

Tarsal coalition occurs most commonly between the calcaneus and navicular or at the middle talocalcaneal facet. Secondary radiographic signs include talar beaking (more common in talocalcaneal coalition); the"anteater sign" of calcaneonavicular coalition refers to the elongated and squared anterior calcaneal process (Fig. 1). Calcaneonavicular coalition is often demonstrated on medial oblique radiographs of the foot, while talocalcaneal coalition is optimally evaluated using CT or MR, which are of equal diagnostic value (Fig. 2). Both forms may be bilateral; therefore, both feet are usually imaged. Talonavicular and calcaneocuboid fusions constitute less than 10% of tarsal coalition cases and often occur in conjunction with other more common forms of tarsal coalition.[15]

HALLUX VALGUS

Hallux valgus deformity, which may result from constricting footwear and deficient tendon slings, is present when there is lateral deviation of the great toe and medial deviation of the first metatarsal head (Fig. 3). This deformity is often accompanied and aggravated by metatarsus primus varus (widening of the angle between the base of the first and second metatarsal base > 25°). Although hallux valgus does not affect alignment at the second ray, increased stress of weight bearing shifts to the second metatarsophalangeal (MTP) joint and may result in secondary metatarsal stress fracture and/or secondary plantar plate rupture with ensuing hammer toe or crossover toe deformities.

Both the adductor (lateral) and abductor (medial) hallucis tendons insert on the base of the proximal phalanx and send fibers to the sesamoid complex. The flexor hallucis longus and brevis tendons insert, respectively, on the plantar aspect of the distal and proximal phalanges of the great toe and anchor the hallucal sesamoids. The extensor hallucis longus tendon inserts on the dorsal base of the distal phalanx. A hallux valgus deformity develops if the balance between these tendons is disturbed. The abductor hallucis, adductor hallucis, and the sesamoid complex all shift laterally.

If footwear change and orthotic use fails, the surgical approach will vary depending on the severity of the hallux valgus and metatarsus primus varus deformities. Surgical correction includes repair of the medial soft tissue structures, resection of the bony bunion, and osteotomy of the first metatarsal and/or the proximal phalanx.

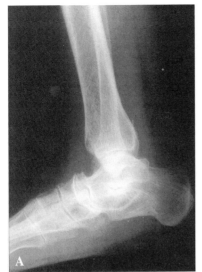

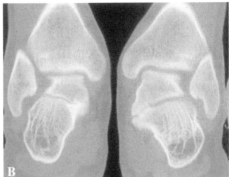

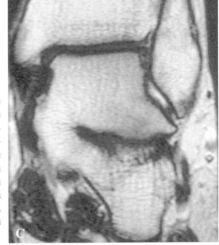

FIGURE 2. *A*, Talocalcaneal coalition. The lateral radiograph does not demonstrate the posterior subtalar joint and middle talocalcaneal facet. A C-shaped curvilinear radiodense line (the "C"-sign) courses beneath the posterior subtalar joint. *B*, Coronal CT scan shows bilateral talocalcaneal coalition with an osseous bridge on the right and a cartilaginous or fibrous bridge on the left. *C*, Sagittal SE T1-weighted MR shows an osseous talocalcaneal coalition.

OSTEOARTHRITIS

Osteoarthritis, the most common form of degenerative joint disease (DJD), is associated with advancing age, obesity and either overt or repetitive microtrauma to a joint. Radiographic changes include asymmetric articular narrowing, subchondral sclerosis, subchondral pseudocysts, and marginal osteophytes. Preservation of bone mineral density, osteophytosis, and absence of erosions help distinguish degenerative from inflammatory arthritis. Cartilage destruction tends to predominate at weight bearing areas. With increased intra-articular pressure, subchondral pseudocysts, often delineated by sclerotic margins, form as a result of entrance of synovial fluid through articular cartilage fissures and defects or microfractures of the subchondral cortex. Atraumatic osteoarthritis rarely affects the ankle. In the foot, the first MTP and the first TMT joints are most commonly affected.

HALLUX RIGIDUS

Hallux rigidus is osteoarthritis at the first MTP joint (Fig. 4). It is usually idiopathic, but can result from chronic or acute trauma, traumatic compression of the cartilaginous surfaces (turf toe), or can be postinfectious or postinflammatory. Typical changes include joint space narrowing, subchondral sclerosis, osteophytosis, and subchondral cystic changes.[11] The osteophytes typically form at the lateral and

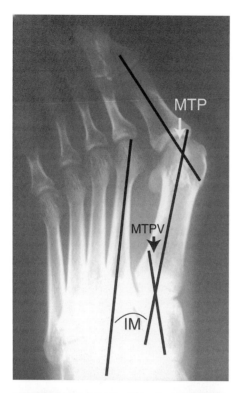

FIGURE 3. Hallux valgus. Standard AP radiograph shows lateral deviation of the great toe with mild medial deviation of the first metatarsal head. The metatarsophalangeal (MTP) angle measures 49°. The metatarsus primus varus (MTPV) angle measures 26°. The intermetatarsal (IM) angle measures 9°. Note the laterally shifted sesamoids.

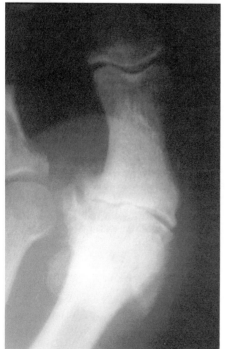

FIGURE 4. Hallux rigidus. AP radiograph of the first toe demonstrates joint space narrowing and lateral osteophyte formation.

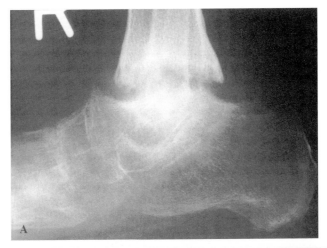

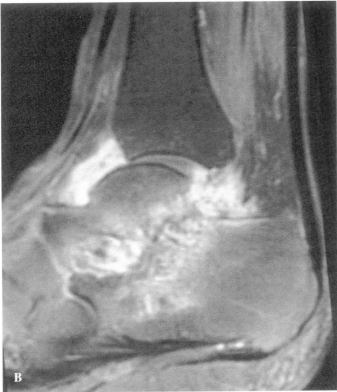

FIGURE 5. *A*, Rheumatoid arthritis. Lateral radiograph of the ankle shows advanced rheumatoid arthritis with generalized osteopenia and erosions at the ankle joint. Note the markedly narrowed joint spaces at the talonavicular, calcaneocuboid, and intertarsal joints. *B*, Contrast-enhanced sagittal T1-fat suppressed MR image of the ankle shows marked erosive changes at the posterior subtalar joint with enhancing marrow, sinus tarsi, and synovium. Subluxation at the ankle joint reflects ligamentous laxity.

dorsal joint margin. This limits mobility, especially dorsiflexion. Pressure upon the dorsal median cutaneous nerve, a branch of superficial peroneal nerve, by osteophytes might result in compression neuropathy. Lateral foot pain may be the presenting complaints if the patient is walking on the lateral foot to avoid pain at the first metatarsophalangeal joint.

RHEUMATOID ARTHRITIS

Rheumatoid arthritis (RA) manifests as inflammation of synovial joints typically in a bilateral, symmetric fashion. Increased blood flow to inflamed synovium manifests radiographically as periarticular osteoporosis. Diminished osteogenesis and disuse exaggerate osteopenia (Fig. 5). Earliest radiographic changes may be subtle, including periarticular soft tissue swelling and juxta-articular osteoporosis. Pannus formation (proliferative synovium) results in chondronecrosis, manifested radiographically as uniform joint space narrowing. Erosions first form at "bare areas" where intracapsular bony margins, unprotected by overlying hyaline cartilage, are most prone to destruction by proliferative synovium. Severe erosive changes may ultimately extend across the joint surface. Subchondral cysts, which typically lack a sclerotic margin, communicate with the synovium and can grow large.

The foot is a common site of rheumatoid involvement, typically involved early in the course of the disease. The ankle is less commonly affected. MTP joints are target areas, with erosions favoring the medial aspect of the metatarsal heads. Subtalar and midfoot involvement typically results in uniform intertarsal joint space narrowing. Ankylosis, although rare in the adult form of RA, may involve only the tarsus. Synovitis at the retrocalcaneal bursa may produce erosions of the underlying dorsal calcaneus. Progressive hallux valgus and hammer toe deformities, fibular deviation of the lesser toes, and MTP joint subluxations are commonly associated with RA.[1]

SERONEGATIVE SPONDYLARTHROPATHIES

The seronegative spondylarthropathies are characterized by a negative rheumatoid factor and an association with the HLA-B27 histocompatibility antigen. These include psoriatic arthritis, Reiter's syndrome, ankylosing spondylitis, and arthritis associated with inflammatory bowel disease.

Psoriatic Arthritis

The arthropathy develops in up to 7% of patients with psoriasis. Young adults are typically affected, with no gender predilection. Rarely, arthritis may precede skin changes. Associated nail changes (thickening, pitting, or discoloration) are very common and correlate with the severity of arthritis.

Psoriatic arthritis affects both the peripheral appendicular and the axial skeleton. In feet and hands, IP joints are affected to a greater degree than more proximal joints. Psoriasis specifically targets the IP joint of the great toe (Fig. 6). Bilateral, asymmetric involvement is common. Bone mineral density is typically preserved or increased; bone repair and periosteal new bone formation may lead to exaggerated sclerosis of an involved bone ("ivory phalanx"). Fluffy periostitis and enthesopathy (proliferative bone formed at tendon and ligament insertions) accompany erosive changes. Erosions initially form at the joint margin, but may rapidly progress across the articular surface leading to apparent early widening of the joint space. Ultimately, joint space narrowing and ankylosis may ensue. Flaring of the phalangeal

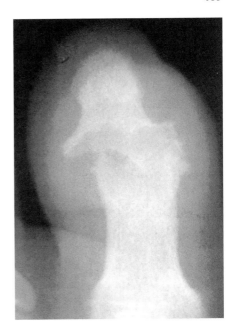

FIGURE 6. Psoriatic arthritis of the great toe. Central erosions are seen at the inter-phalangeal joint. There is fluffy periostitis near the joint margins. Note the associated soft tissue swelling.

bases together with erosion of the meatatarsal head may result in a "pencil in cup" deformity. Marked soft tissue swelling can affect an entire digit ("sausage digit"). Tuftal erosions cause acro-osteolysis. Psoriatic arthritis and Reiter's syndrome may be difficult to distinguish. Psoriasis tends to involve hands and feet equally, whereas Reiter's has a strong predilection for the lower extremities.[14]

Reiter's Syndrome

The arthritis primarily affects the distal and proximal IP joints. Similar to psoriasis, bilateral, asymmetric involvement is the rule, and all joints of a ray may be involved, resulting in a "sausage digit." Ankylosis is a less common feature of Reiter's disease. Calcaneal involvement is characteristic, often including erosive and proliferative changes ("whiskering") at the origin of the plantar aponeurosis. Retrocalcaneal bursitis and Achilles tendon thickening are common. The ankle is frequently affected, with soft tissue swelling and fluffy periostitis at the medial and lateral malleolus.

Ankylosing Spondylitis and Inflammatory Bowel Disease

Ankylosing spondylitis and inflammatory bowel disease cause arthritic changes that may be indistinguishable from one another, principally targeting the axial skeleton in a bilateral, symmetric fashion. If the foot is involved, the MTP joints, the first TMT joint, and IP joint of the great toe are primarily affected. Subluxations of the MTP joints may occur. Calcaneal involvement is similar to that seen with psoriasis and Reiter's disease. Clinical features and symmetric sacroiliac joint involvement suggest the correct diagnosis.

GOUT

Soft tissue swelling and nodular soft tissue masses are characteristic of but certainly not specific for gout. Eccentric soft tissue nodules of monosodium urate

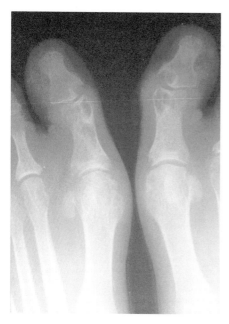

FIGURE 7.   Gouty arthritis. Characteristic "punched-out" erosions with overhanging edges. Note the preservation of joint spaces and prominent subchondral cysts.

crystal with surrounding inflammatory reaction (tophi) usually form near joints; less commonly, these can form either intra-articular or intra-osseous. Erosions, be they para- or intra-articular, are typically well defined with a sclerotic margin, and may demonstrate an overhanging edge formed by apposition of periosteal new bone (Fig. 7). As is the case with other forms of DJD, bone mineral is typically preserved, but unlike other forms of DJD, gout preserves joint spaces until late in the course of disease.

In the foot, gout targets the first MTP joint ("podagra"), although any of the MTP joints, especially the fifth, may be affected. The IP joints, mid- and hindfoot joints also may be involved. The ankle is usually affected only in association with foot involvement. Differential diagnosis of early gout includes both degenerative and inflammatory arthropathies and even infection. Pseudogout (the acute arthropathy of calcium pyrophosphate deposition disease, CPPD) may clinically mimic gout, but chondrocalcinosis (widespread and common in CPPD) helps distinguish the two. Multicentric reticulohistiocytosis is a rare condition most commonly affecting older women that can radiographically mimic gout, but distribution is typically bilaterally symmetric, targeting the distal IP joints.[9]

CALCIUM PYROPHOSPHATE DEPOSITION DISEASE (CPPD)

Calcium pyrophosphate crystals are usually deposited intraarticular, but may be, less commonly, periarticular. Unlike monosodium urate crystals, these demonstrate weak positive birefringence under polarized light microscopy. Radiographic features of CPPD arthropathy include chondrocalcinosis (affecting both hyaline and fibrocartilage) and DJD resembling osteoarthritis in an unusual distribution, often with very prominent subchondral pseudocyst formation. Clinical attacks of pseudogout are usually associated with physical inactivity.

CPPD may be idiopathic or familial, or can be associated with hemochromatosis, primary hyperparathyroidism, and gout. In the lower extremity, CPPD targets the patellofemoral compartment of the knee. Chondrocalcinosis may be present within meniscal fibrocartilage as well as articular hyaline cartilage. Involvement of the foot predominately affects the talonavicular joint, resulting in joint space narrowing, sclerosis, and fragmentation, mimicking neuropathic osteoarthropathy. The MTP and hindfoot joints may also be affected. Capsular, ligamentous, and tendinous calcifications (especially of the Achilles) are commonly seen.

HYDROXYAPATITE DEPOSITION DISEASE (HADD)

The crystals of HADD are of minute size and cannot be seen under light microscopy. Crystal deposition either intra-articularly or, more commonly, in a periarticular distribution in and about tendons or within bursae, results in acute arthritis, tendinitis, or bursitis. The middle-aged and elderly are typically affected with an equal male-female distribution. HADD may occur as a primary disorder or in association with collagen vascular disease, chronic renal disease, hypoparathyroidism, hypervitaminosis D, and other forms of soft tissue calcification. It often presents as a monoarticular arthropathy. Calcific deposits within the foot frequently affect the flexor hallucis brevis and longus as well as the peroneal tendons. Articular involvement of the first MTP joint may resemble gout.

THE DIABETIC FOOT

Neuropathic Osteoarthropathy (Neuroarthropathy)

Neuroarthropathy (NA) is a complication most frequently seen in diabetic patients, although tabes dorsalis, leprosy, syringomyelia, spina bifida, meningomyelocele,

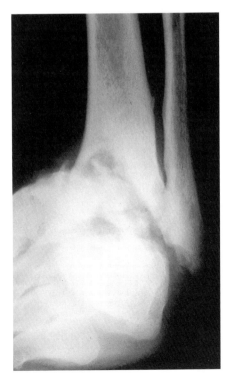

FIGURE 8. Neuropathic arthropathy of the ankle. Mortise view demonstrates disorganization and subluxation at the ankle joint. The talar dome is fragmented, and debris is in the joint space. The bones are dense owing to increased sclerosis.

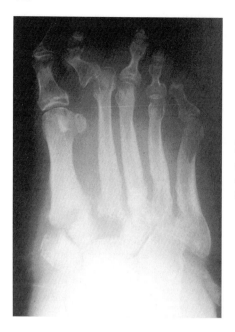

FIGURE 9. Neuropathic osteoarthropathy. There is a divergent Lisfranc fracture-dislocation with dislocation of the medial and middle cuneiform with respect to the talar head and first and second metatarsal base.

congenital insensitivity to pain, chronic alcoholism, and peripheral nerve injuries are known to be the causative conditions. It develops secondary to diabetic neuropathy with loss of pain sensation and proprioception, autonomic neuropathy, and other poorly understood mechanisms. The supporting soft tissue structures relax, causing instability, malalignment, and alteration of the normal biomechanical joint structure. Normal biomechanical stresses on an altered joint lead to fragmentation and disorganization. Reparative processes result in subchondral sclerosis.

The classic description includes the "five Ds": increased **d**ensity, joint **d**istention, **d**ebris, **d**islocation, and joint **d**isorganization (Fig. 8), although there are three different forms of neuropathic osteoarthropathy (hypertrophic, atrophic, and mixed). There are three stages of progression of neuropathic joints from a radiologic point of view. Stage I is described as the "stage of development." Stage II is the "stage of coalescence." Stage III is the "stage of reconstruction."

The five Ds describe the hypertrophic form that predominates in the foot and ankle, most commonly affecting the talonavicular and TMT joints. This resembles a Lisfranc fracture-dislocation (Fig. 9). Type 1 neuroarthropathic feet are those involving the tarsometatarsal and naviculocuneiform joints. Type 2 neuroarthropathic feet are those involving any or all triple hindfoot joints (subtalar, talonavicular, and calcaneocuboid). Type 3A neuroarthropathic feet involve the tibiotalar joint, and type 3B neuroarthropathic feet are those that develop a fracture of the posterior tubercle of the calcaneus.

Distinction between neuroarthropathy and osteomyelitis is particularly challenging in the diabetic foot and may require biopsy for accurate diagnosis.[13] CT may best demonstrate sharply marginated spicules or fragments of bone of neuroarthropathy, while indistinct osseous margins suggest superimposed infection. MR demonstrates marrow edema in the involved bones and can be very difficult or impossible to distinguish from osteomyelitis; cortical destruction and adjacent soft tissue abscess favor osteomyelitis. While pathologic contrast enhancement of bone and soft tissue may be seen in both progressive neuroarthropathy and infection, peripheral vascular disease may limit enhancement in the diabetic foot.[6] Ultimate diagnosis and treatment plan between the neuroarthropathy and osteomyelitis, however, are mostly clinical.

OSTEOMYELITIS

Osteomyelitis is caused by either hematogenous or contiguous spread of infection, be it from penetrating trauma, surgery, or, most frequently in diabetic patients, by direct extension from a foot ulcer. *Staphylococcus aureus* is the most common pathogen. Conventional radiographs are a first line screening tool, but bony changes may not be apparent for 1–2 weeks or until 30–50% of bone has been destroyed. Radiographic findings of osteomyelitis include obliteration of the soft tissue fat planes, focal osteopenia, cortical destruction, periostitis, and cortical sequestration. With chronic osteomyelitis, the infection persists 6 weeks or longer. The periosteum forms a peripheral shell of new bone, an "involucrum" in an attempt to contain the infection. Pus can tunnel through the cortex via "cloacae," and surrounding soft tissue abscesses and sinus tracts may form. Radiodense pieces of infected, necrotic bone within the medullary cavity or cortex (sequestra) must be removed to prevent re-infection. Small

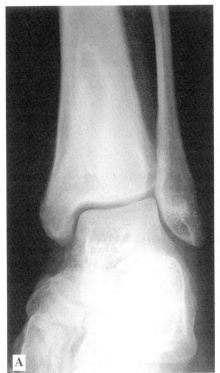
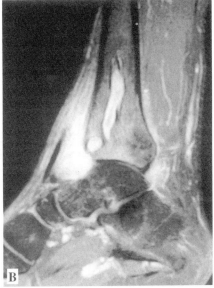

FIGURE 10. *A,* Chronic osteomyelitis of the distal tibia. An oblique radiograph of the ankle demonstrates a tubular radiolucency surrounded by increased sclerosis. *B,* Gadolinium-enhanced fat-suppressed sagittal T1-weighted MR image in the same patient demonstrates a tract within the distal tibia breaking through the anterior cortex (cloaca) with surrounding soft tissue inflammation. Note the marked marrow enhancement of the distal tibia.

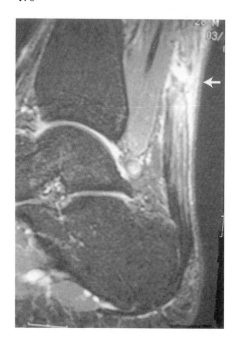

FIGURE 11. Achilles tendon rupture. Sagittal FSEIR-MR image demonstrates complete disruption of the Achilles tendon (arrow).

bony sequestra are best demonstrated using CT. MR can demonstrate marrow signal changes of early osteomyelitis, prior to detectable radiographic findings, and may delineate the true extent of disease. Similar to marrow edema regardless of etiology, marrow signal changes will appear dark on T1-weighted and bright on T2-weighted or inversion recovery sequences.[4,14] Intravenous gadolinium will enhance infected areas and better delineate soft tissue abscesses and sinus tracts (Fig. 10). In cases where MR is unavailable or is contraindicated, nuclear scintigraphy using white blood cells tagged with either Tc99[M] or indium[111] may be used. At other sites, only bone scintigraphy using Tc99[M] in conjunction with gallium[67] scans is available.[3,5]

ACHILLES TENDON INJURY

The Achilles tendon is the strongest and thickest tendon in the body and normally does not rupture without degeneration. Rheumatoid arthritis, collagen vascular diseases, and corticosteroids (injection or oral) predispose to tendon rupture. An injured Achilles tendon with longitudinal splitting of fibers, type I tear, is manifested as a thickened tendon that is of uniformly dark signal on MR. Increased signal within the thickened tendon is a more advanced (type II) tear. It may be difficult to distinguish high-grade partial tears from complete tears if tendon distraction is not present. The Achilles tendon typically ruptures 2–6 cm above its insertion where there is a hypovascular zone (Fig. 11). MR permits detection of the extent and level of tendon rupture as well as the size of the gap between fragments.[7] Conservative treatment with casting is commonly chosen in older or sedentary patients. Surgical repair is indicated in younger and athletically active patients, possibly reducing the risk of re-rupture.

FLEXOR TENDON INJURIES

The most frequently injured flexor tendon is the posterior tibial tendon (PTT) (Fig. 12). It tears, most typically in middle-aged and older women, as a result of

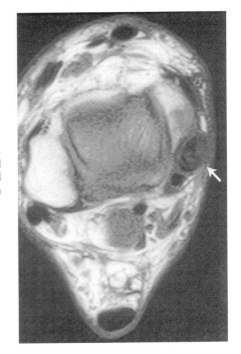

FIGURE 12. Posterior tibialis tendon tear. Axial SE T1-MR image shows marked enlargement, irregularity, and increased signal within the posterior tibialis tendon (arrow) consistent with a type II tear.

degeneration and repetitive microtrauma. The midportion of the PTT is the most vulnerable as a result of the poor blood supply and focal stress where the tendon curves under the medial malleolus. The posterior tibial muscle plantar-flexes the ankle and inverts the foot; its tendon supports the medial longitudinal arch, which collapses, usually following 1.5 years of symptoms, resulting in an acquired flatfoot deformity with posterior tibial insufficiency. Acquired deformities include hindfoot valgus and forefoot abduction with lateral subluxation of the navicular as a result of unopposed action by the peroneus brevis tendon. An accessory navicular is noted with increased frequency in association with PTT dysfunction.

Axial plane MR best depicts the ankle tendons. The PTT normally measures no greater than 2.5 times the transverse diameter of the flexor digitorum longus tendon (FDL). Tendons are of uniformly low signal intensity on all pulse sequences. A type I tear is characterized by tendon hypertrophy with or without increased intrasubstance signal, a type II tear demonstrates focal tendon thinning or contour defect, and a type III tear indicates complete tendon rupture. Fluid surrounding a tendon within the tendon sheath (tenosynovitis) often accompanies a tear. Peritendinitis implies inflammation of both a tendon and its tendon sheath. Injuries of the FDL or flexor hallucis longus tendon are less common but demonstrate similar MR characteristics.

PERONEAL TENDON INJURIES

On MR, peroneal tears often appear as longitudinal splitting with associated tenosynovitis. Tears might involve the peroneus longus, brevis, or both tendons. Repetitive peroneal tendon subluxation or dislocation predisposes to peroneal tendon tear; this may occur with laxity or prior injury of the peroneal retinaculum or a congenitally shallow or convex peroneal groove of the fibula.

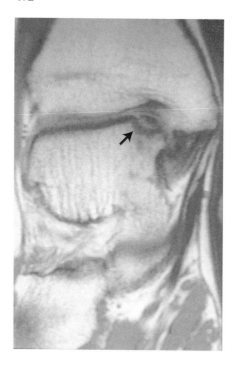

FIGURE 13. Osteochondritis dissecans (OCD). Coronal FSEIR-MR image demonstrates a small, non-displaced osteochondral fragment at the medial talar dome (arrow).

LIGAMENT INJURIES

Inversion injuries can damage the lateral collateral ligaments. Injury may be diagnosed using inversion stress radiographs, including comparison films of the uninjured side. MR may demonstrate grade I injuries (sprains, presenting as subtle increased signal or ligamentous thickening); grade II injuries (disruption of 50% of the fibers); and grade III injuries (complete tear with discontinuity of the fibers). The anterior talofibular ligament (ATFL) is the most commonly injured lateral ankle ligament; inury is usually treated conservatively. Calcaneofibular ligament injury, which results in ankle instability, is treated operatively.

Isolated deltoid ligament (medial collateral ligament) injury is rare and is caused by an ankle eversion mechanism. Syndesmotic (anterior inferior tibiofibular ligament) sprains, which result from a similar eversion or inversion mechanism, account for disabling ankle pain and "feeling of insecurity" in nearly 10% of ankle injuries.

OSTEOCHONDRAL DEFECTS

Osteochondral lesions of the talar dome result from osteochondral injury that involves either the medial (Fig. 13) or lateral corner of the talar dome. Medial lesions tend to be posterior, whereas lateral lesions tend to be anterior. Clinical management depends upon the status of the osteochondral fracture fragment. Stage I lesions (osteochondral compression fractures with intact articular cartilage) are radiographically occult. Stage II lesions involve a partially detached osteochondral fragment with a flap of articular cartilage. Stage III lesions (complete fractures with non-displaced in-situ fragment) and stage IV lesions (loose osteochondral fragment) may be evaluated using CT-arthrography, but are best evaluated using coronal MR or MR arthrography for detection of osseous and articular cartilage defects as well as possible associated collateral ligament injury. Subchondral cystic changes may

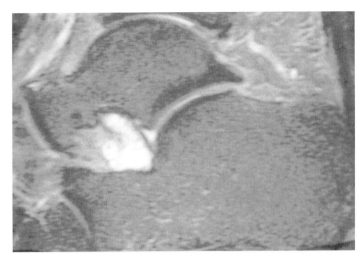

FIGURE 14. Sinus tarsi syndrome. Sagittal FSEIR-MR image demonstrates a multi-loculated ganglion cyst within the sinus tarsi. Note the ligament of the tarsal canal.

develop from synovial fluid entering through the osteochondral defect. Granulation tissue might fill these subchondral craters and may be indistinguishable from fluid using non-contrast enhanced MR.[10]

Stage I and II lesions are managed conservatively with casting. Stage III and IV lesions are treated surgically. Secondary osteoarthritis will complicate OCD in 50% of cases; prompt MR evaluation may permit earlier diagnosis and improve long-term outcome.

ENTRAPMENT NEUROPATHIES

Sinus Tarsi Syndrome

Sinus tarsi syndrome manifests as chronic lateral foot pain, which may be accompanied by minor subtalar instability. Approximately 70% of cases are associated with prior or recurrent inversion injury; there is a strong association of PTT or lateral collateral ligament injury. Less commonly, this may be associated with inflammatory arthropathy (Fig. 14).

MR has largely supplanted arthrography for evaluation of lateral collateral ligament injury. Sinus tarsi syndrome appears as replacement of the normal fatty signal within the sinus tarsi reflecting inflammation and fibrosis, often with obscuration of the sinus tarsi ligaments. Treatment usually includes local anesthetic and steroid injections and possible immobilization followed by rehabilitation. Rarely, surgical excision of the inflammatory tissue, ligamentous reconstruction, and even triple arthrodesis may be required to treat refractory symptoms.

Tarsal Tunnel Syndrome

Tarsal tunnel syndrome is entrapment neuropathy of the posterior tibial nerve within the tarsal tunnel. The **tarsal tunnel**, which contains the posterior tibial neurovascular bundle, starts at the ankle and extends into the foot, bordered superiorly and medially by the flexor retinaculum, inferiorly by the abductor hallucis muscle, and laterally by the talus and calcaneus. The most common etiologies include displaced

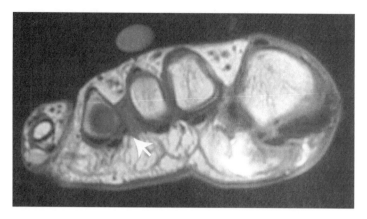

FIGURE 15.   Morton neuroma. Coronal SE T1-MR image demonstrates an ovoid mass in the third intermetatarsal space (arrow).

fracture fragments, ganglion cysts, scarring, varicosities, and accessory muscles. Associated paresthesias and burning pain that worsens with weight bearing occur along the plantar aspect of the foot and heel or proximally along the medial calf.[8,12]

Morton Neuritis (Neuroma)

A Morton neuritis represents either ischemic or post-traumatic, degenerative fibrosis entrapping the plantar digital nerve at the level of the metatarsal heads, most commonly in the third intermetatarsal space (Fig. 15). Morton neuromas are frequently asymptomatic; these incidental Morton neuromas tend to be less than 5 mm in size. Differential diagnoses include intermetatarsal bursitis, metatarsalgia, stress fractures, and osteonecrosis of the metatarsal heads; these are best differentiated using MR. Morton neuromas tend to be relatively low signal on both T1- and T2-weighted sequences and demonstrate avid contrast enhancement. Ultrasonography can effectively differentiate Morton neuroma from intermetatarsal bursitis.[2,16]

REFERENCES

1. Abdo RV, Iorio LJ: Rheumatoid arthritis of the foot and ankle. J Am Acad Orthop Surg 2:326–332, 1994.
2. Bencardino J, Rosenberg ZS, Beltran J, et al: Morton's neuroma: Is it always symptomatic? AJR 175:649–653, 2000.
3. Devillers A, Garin E, Polard JL, et al: Comparison of Tc-99m-labelled antileukocyte fragment Fab' and Tc-99m-HMPAO leukocyte scintigraphy in the diagnosis of bone and joint infections: A prospective study. Nucl Med Commun. 21:747–753, 2000.
4. Erickson SJ, Johnson JE: MR imaging of the ankle and foot. Radiol Clin North Am 35(1):163–192, 1997.
5. Jay PR, Michelson JD, Mizel MS, et al: Efficacy of three-phase bone scans in evaluating diabetic foot ulcers. Foot Ankle Int 20:347–355, 1999.
6. Kao PF, Davis BL, Hardy PA: Characterization of the calcaneal fat pad in diabetic and non-diabetic patients using magnetic resonance imaging. Magn Reson Imaging 17:851–857, 1999.
7. Maffulli N: Rupture of the Achilles tendon. J Bone Joint Surg Am 81:1019–1036, 1999.
8. Masciocchi C, Catalucci A, Barile A: Ankle impingement syndromes. Eur J Radiol 27(Suppl 1):S70–73, 1998.
9. Rand T, Trattnig S, Breitenseher M, et al: [Chronic diseases of the ankle joint.] Radiologe 39:52–59, 1999.
10. Rubin DA: Magnetic resonance imaging of chondral and osteochondral injuries. Top Magn Reson Imaging 9:348–359, 1998.

11. Shereff MJ, Baumhauer JF: Hallux rigidus and osteoarthrosis of the first metatarsophalangeal joint. J Bone Joint Surg Am 80:898–908, 1998.
12. Steinbach LS: Painful syndromes around the ankle and foot: Magnetic resonance imaging evaluation. Top Magn Reson Imaging 9:311–326, 1998.
13. Tomas MB, Patel M, Marwin SE, Palestro CJ: The diabetic foot. Br J Radiol 73:443–450, 2000.
14. Weishaupt D, Schweitzer ME, Alam F, et al: MR imaging of inflammatory joint diseases of the foot and ankle. Skeletal Radiol 28:663–669, 1999.
15. Wechsler RJ, Schweitzer ME, Deely DM, et al: Tarsal coalition: Depiction and characterization with CT and MR imaging. Radiology 193:447–452, 1994.
16. Zanetti M, Strehle JK, Kundert HP, et al: Morton neuroma: Effect of MR imaging findings on diagnostic thinking and therapeutic decisions. Radiology 213:583–588, 1999.

BARRY RODSTEIN, MD, MPH
MOOYEON OH-PARK, MD

HINDFOOT PAIN AND PLANTAR FASCIITIS

From Department of Rehabilitation
Medicine
Beth Israel Medical Center
New York, New York (BR)
and
Department of Rehabilitation
Medicine
Weiler Division, Montefiore Medical
Center
Bronx, New York (MO-P)

Reprint requests to:
Department of Rehabilitation
Medicine
Beth Israel Medical Center
1st Avenue at 16th Street
New York, NY 10003

In physiatric practice, heel pain is one of the most commonly encountered complaints of the lower extremity. It is a confusing complex of symptoms called by many different names such as heel spur syndrome, subcalcaneal pain syndrome, heel bursitis, proximal plantar fasciitis, and nerve entrapment syndrome. Clear distinction between these is controversial and often difficult. Given the multiple possible etiologies, it is not surprising that there are numerous methods used for treatment, with no single approach being consistently successful. In this chapter, we emphasize the differential diagnosis as well as treatment options and their appropriate application based on biomechanical principles.

KEY STRUCTURES THAT MAY CAUSE HINDFOOT PAIN

Heel spurs may occur in different parts of the calcaneus, although the plantar aspect is the most common. Plantar heel spurs detected in radiologic evaluation, however, are often not the cause of heel pain. According to Shmokler, the incidence of plantar heel spurs was 13% of the general population but only 39% of those with heel spurs reported any history of heel pain.[23] While there is a common misconception that plantar heel spurs originate from the plantar aponeurosis, they actually originate in the flexor digitorum brevis. Thus, the concept of a direct contribution of the heel spur to the plantar fascial pain has been disputed. The heel spur area, however, can become painful in situations of concurrent bursitis, spur fracture, or plantar fascial inflammation or rupture.

The **heel pad** is made up of fat globules enveloped by fibroelastic septa arranged in a closed-cell configuration. The fibrous septa are anchored together, deep to the calcaneus, and to the skin. The septa are reinforced internally with diagonal and transverse elastic fibers that connect the thicker walls and separate the fat into compartments. The tissue septa are U-shaped and filled with fat columns. This design is ideal for resisting compressive loads. In fat pad atrophy, the fat globules become partially collapsed and are therefore less effective in resisting these loads. The fat pad contains an ample nerve and blood supply, which is separate from those of the surrounding musculature and skin.[11] Pacinian corpuscles and free nerve endings are within the fat pad rather than in the dermis.

The **plantar fascia** along with the spring ligament, short plantar ligament, and long plantar ligament comprises the ligament system, which supports the longitudinal arch. It originates from the medial calcaneal tuberosity and inserts distally through several slips into the plantar plates of the metatarsophalangeal joints, the flexor tendon sheaths, and the bases of the proximal phalanges of the digits. Extension (dorsiflexion) of the toes and the metatarsophalangeal (MTP) joints tenses the plantar aponeurosis, raises the longitudinal arch of the foot, inverts the hindfoot, and externally rotates the leg as a part of supination response in closed chain motion. This mechanism, whereby the arch is raised and supported with dorsiflexion of the toe, increases stability of the foot, and has been termed the "**windlass mechanism.**"[10] This mechanism is passive and depends entirely on bony and ligamentous structures.

Entrapment of posterior tibial, inferior calcaneal (Baxter's), medial plantar, lateral plantar, sural, or saphenous nerves may all cause heel pain. Baxter's nerve branches off from the lateral plantar nerve or directly from the tibial nerve and passes between the ADQ and the medial margin of the quadratus plantae muscle. It supplies deep sensation to the heel and motor innervation to the abductor digiti quinti (ADQ).[21] Entrapment of the medial plantar nerve may occur under the navicular tuberosity, especially in the pronated foot.

PLANTAR FASCIITIS

Plantar fasciitis is probably the most common foot condition encountered in physiatric practice. It is considered a normal adaptive process to aging of the foot, although it can be caused or exacerbated by biomechanical deterioration or rheumatologic disorders. Some authors further classify this as distal or proximal plantar fasciitis, as the clinical presentation and response to therapy may vary accordingly. Distal plantar fasciitis may respond to stretching of the fascia requiring a foot orthosis designed for pronation control. On the other hand, these measures may not be as effective for proximal plantar fasciitis, which may respond to local relief. The natural history of plantar fasciitis appears to be self-limiting, and conservative treatment should be contemplated before invasive methods such as injection or surgery.[25] Often the injury will have occurred over time with chronic biomechanical derangement, and patients and physicians are often frustrated from the slow improvement in spite of the best possible treatment. Plantar fasciitis often presents as part of a complex of symptoms caused by underlying biomechanical abnormalities. In such cases, treatment should be designed to address these issues as well as to provide symptomatic relief. Cavus as well as pronated feet are vulnerable to the development of plantar fasciitis, although the underlying biomechanics are different.

Patients with obesity, bilateral symptoms, or symptoms for a prolonged period tend not to respond quickly to treatment. Often patients present to the office carrying a diagnosis of "recalcitrant plantar fasciitis" having had little improvement with a multitude of treatments including exercise, massage, ultrasound, iontophoresis, anti-inflammatory medications, injections, custom insoles, and shoe modifications. The following should be considered in these cases:

1. Conditions that can be misdiagnosed as plantar fasciitis include heel pad atrophy, Baxter's nerve entrapment, interdigital neuritis, peroneus longus tendinitis, and seronegative spondyloarthropathies.

2. Pathologic biomechanics such as excessive pronation with forefoot (FF) varus, heel cord tightness, or excessive supination (cavus foot) are often overlooked.

3. "Quick fixes" such as injection or a foot orthosis alone without other supplementary measures including night splinting, stretching exercises, or appropriate lifestyle modifications are often unsuccessful.

History Taking

Pain in plantar fasciitis is most severe early in the morning on initial weight bearing as a result of the acute stretching of the plantar fascia, which has contracted during the night. Fascial pain typically occurs from midstance to takeoff, while pain at initial heel contact suggests local heel pathology such as bursitis.

A burning or tingling sensation in addition to pain may suggest concurrent neurologic conditions such as tarsal tunnel syndrome, Baxter's nerve entrapment, medial plantar nerve entrapment (jogger's foot), or saphenous nerve entrapment. Other symptoms such as forefoot and knee pain may suggest underlying abnormal biomechanics or concurrent pathologies such as posterior tibial tendon insufficiency or peroneal tendinitis.

Heel pain that occurs in conjunction with skin lesions, conjunctivitis, arthritis, back pain, or abdominal complaints may suggest a seronegative spondyloarthopathy. Gout, Paget disease, or sarcoidosis rarely presents with isolated painful inflammation in the plantar heel.[18]

Clinicians should inquire about previous treatments including physical therapy, FOs, injections, and surgery. Previous exercise programs should be reviewed in detail for appropriateness before deciding that the physical therapy was "ineffective." Previously effective FOs may become ineffective as a result of deterioration of the materials, development of new biomechanical deficits, or the use of inappropriate footwear.

Physical Examination

In plantar fasciitis, the tenderness along the fascia is aggravated by palpation with simultaneous passive dorsiflexion of the toes (which tenses the fascia). The point of maximum tenderness is mostly located in the central portion of the midfoot. This can be differentiated from FHL tendinitis in which the tenderness occurs more medially (upon palpation of the FHL tendon) with slight dorsiflexion of the 1st MTP joint, specifically. Tenderness in peroneus longus (PL) tendinitis is along an oblique line connecting the cuboid and the 1st metatarsal base. The tenderness on palpation is aggravated by having the patient plantarflex the 1st ray against resistance. Tenderness in PL tendinitis may extend along the peroneal groove of the cuboid, behind the lateral malleolus, and even into the muscle at the proximal fibula. The plantar fascia should also be palpated for defects (rupture) or masses (plantar fibromatosis, cyst or hematoma). Occasionally the patient may walk with a supinated foot to avoid excessive stress to the medial strand of the plantar fascia, resulting in lateralization of the foot pain.

Patients with plantar fasciitis often have tight heel cords.[12] Tightness of the Achilles tendon should be evaluated in the subtalar neutral position, and when present should be addressed with stretching, heel lifts, or both. Often there is excessive pronation as well, which further stretches and thereby irritates the plantar fascia. In the cavus foot, on the other hand, poor shock absorption is probably the main contributing factor in addition to a tight Achilles tendon.

Footwear with a low heel or hard sole often aggravates the symptoms. Tight shoes prevent the foot from normal spreading for shock absorption, and may also aggravate plantar fasciitis.

Differential Diagnosis and Imaging Studies for Plantar Fasciitis

Plantar fasciitis is a clinical diagnosis rarely requiring expensive imaging studies. The differential diagnosis includes heel pad atrophy, bursitis, tendinitis of the peroneus longus, flexor hallucis longus, or tibialis posterior tendons, stress fracture of the calcaneus or metatarsals, and radicular pain.

Plain x-rays are useful when other bony lesions such as calcaneal stress fracture, spur fracture, or enthesopathies are suspected. An oblique view may allow visualization of a bony lesion of the calcaneal tuberosity or posterior calcaneal spurs, which are not always detected on the lateral view. MRI is rarely indicated, although it may be useful to define palpable soft tissue lesions such as plantar fibromatosis, cyst, hematoma, or rupture.

Treatment

More than 90% of patients with plantar fasciitis improve with conservative management and don't require surgical intervention.[3,4] As there is no clear consensus on the specifics of treatment, clinicians should develop their own approach, which may include night splinting, fascial taping, mobilization of the plantar fascia, lengthening exercises for the gastrocsoleus and plantar fascia, roomy footwear, soft materials to substitute for the fat pad, and heel elevation. Lifestyle modifications such as weight control, wearing soft-soled shoes, and avoiding prolonged standing are important components of conservative management. Abnormal biomechanics should be addressed and is discussed in depth in other chapters.

NIGHT SPLINTS

Though often omitted in the treatment of plantar fasciitis, night splinting should be included as a cornerstone of treatment in severe or recalcitrant cases. Plantar fasciitis is typically more painful in the morning as a result of the acute stretching of the fascia, which will have contracted during the night. Night splints with 5 degrees of ankle dorsiflexion and an extended footplate can be worn at night to maintain the fascia in an elongated position. Symptoms may subside about a week after initiating their use. Splinting should continue for about 3 months and then be weaned over a few week period.[24] The "DynaSlipper" is a simple and inexpensive alternative to the traditional night splint, particularly for less severe cases. Although it does not prevent plantarflexion, it is less cumbersome and may improve compliance as compared with traditional splinting.

FASCIAL TAPING

Fascial taping is useful in diagnosis and providing immediate pain relief in the acute painful stage. Although various taping methods are available, practitioners need to be proficient in only a few methods. Modified low-dye taping is a simple

FIGURE 1.   Low-Dye taping.

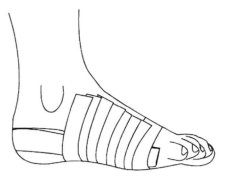

taping method with two components. A horizontal component around the heel substitutes for the function of the plantar fascia and should be below the posterior calcaneal protuberance to avoid undue pressure over the calcaneus on weight bearing. The circumferential component is designed to support the midfoot[6] (Fig. 1). Combining taping with a silicone heel cup results in a synergistic effect by providing cushioning and heel elevation. Heel elevation shortens the leverage for push-off and shifts the body weight toward the forefoot. It also reduces the need for pronation-resupination especially in patients with tight heel cords.

Low-dye taping is also used for other painful heel conditions such as heel spur bursitis (combined with a heel cup) and cuboid subluxation (with a cuboid pad). Appropriate patients can be educated in self-taping for the acute stage of plantar fasciitis.

Physical Therapy

Stretching of the plantar fascia and Achilles tendon alone can improve the symptoms in the majority of patients.[19] The Achilles tendon and plantar fascia function as one biomechanical unit, and stretching of the Achilles tendon naturally accompanies stretching of the plantar fascia. Actually, "Achilles tendon stretch" is probably a misnomer because tendons are not easily stretchable; a more appropriate term might be "lengthening of the gastrocsoleus muscle."

Gastrocsoleus muscle lengthening should be performed with the foot in slight supination to avoid stretching of the subtalar joint. Patients should maintain the stretch for 15–30 seconds without bouncing, to avoid triggering the stretch reflex. Patients frequently have difficulty with proper technique, and physicians should therefore have patients demonstrate the technique and re-instruct them on each visit if necessary. Patients with back or knee problems may perform this exercise without bending over by placing a wedge or book under the forefoot. The patient should be reminded that lengthening the gastrocsoleus muscle is a tedious process that may take several weeks to months.

Plantar fascia massage can be useful, and one easy method involves rolling progressively harder balls under the feet beginning with tennis balls and progressing to golf balls. Modalities including ultrasound, iontophoresis,[7] and phonophoresis have been used; however, their long-term effectiveness has not been established.

Proper Footwear

When the foot is confined in a tight shoe and not allowed to spread or pronate for shock absorption, the plantar fascia is exposed to excessive stress, frequently resulting in pain. Patients who have tight heel cords often compensate by pronating to achieve a plantigrade foot, particularly if they use low-heeled shoes. This will also place the plantar fascia under excessive stress. Thus, footwear with a mildly elevated heel is recommended in the acute stage to reduce the stress on the plantar fascia, whereas some athletic footwear, with its relatively low heel, may not be a good choice.

There is no universally effective FO for every patient with plantar fasciitis as a result of variability in degrees and types of biomechanical abnormalities. For example, plantar fasciitis can occur in diverse pathologic conditions including excessively pronated or supinated feet. The FO, therefore, should be designed to address the particular abnormal biomechanics and is discussed in depth in the chapter Use of Athletic Footwear, Therapeutic Shoes, and Foot Ortheses in Physiatric Practice.

OTHER TREATMENT OPTIONS

A new device, the OssaTron (HealthTronics Inc., Marietta, GA), was approved by the FDA for treatment of chronic plantar fasciitis. It is recommended for patients who have had plantar fasciitis for at least 6 months and in whom standard methods of treatment have failied. The OssaTron generates shock waves, which pass through a dome filled with water, to the heel. Treatment is performed as an outpatient procedure. The long-term benefit of this device remains to be investigated. Complications included mild sensory symptoms and plantar fascial tears.

Steroid injection should be reserved for refractory cases and should be deep to the plantar fascia so as not to damage the fat and fibroelastic septa of heel pad.[15] A medial approach allows the steroid to spread around the broad origin of the plantar fascia.[2] Repeated injection should be avoided because of potential complications of fat pad atrophy, fascial rupture, hematoma leading to abscess, or painful neuroma formation. The long-term benefit of injection is controversial.

OTHER PAINFUL HINDFOOT CONDITIONS

Rupture of the Plantar Fascia

An acute onset of proximal heel pain in patients with or without trauma (including steroid injection) may indicate an acute rupture of the plantar fascia.[22] There may be a history of acute hyperextension of the foot such as wedging the foot into a small pothole. On physical examination, ecchymosis, tenderness, or a palpable defect in the proximal plantar fascia may be noted. Conservative treatment includes footwear with elevated heels, medial wedges, supportive taping, crutch walking, and casting for the refractory cases.

Heel Pad Atrophy

Heel pad atrophy is frequently observed in the elderly as well as those with peripheral neuropathy, dysvascular feet, pes cavus, rheumatoid arthritis, and steroid use.[11] Hard-soled shoes, obesity, and prolonged standing often aggravate this condition. As compared with plantar fasciitis, the pain is diffuse around the whole heel with minimal focal tenderness. Heel pad atrophy should be suspected if the bone is palpable when pressing on the heel pad with the thumb.

Treatment includes heel elevation, containment of the heel pad, and use of insole material with superior shock absorption. In our experience, a trial of taping in conjunction with a silicone heel cup in the office often provides prompt symptomatic relief. Since this includes horizontal taping around the heel, it prevents the fat pad from spreading. The horizontal taping should be below the posterior calcaneal protuberance to avoid irritation of the calcaneus as previously mentioned in plantar fasciitis. For long-term benefit, an insole made of materials with good shock-absorption such as Poron, PPT, or Spenco can be used in footwear with a-strong heel counter and an elevated heel.[13]

Herniation of subcutaneous fat nodules through defects in the dermis is another rare cause of heel pain.[14] Larger nodules tend to be more painful, although smaller ones are more common. Local ischemia or inflammation is postulated as the mechanism of pain. This herniation usually occurs on the side of the heel, and local measures using padding around the painful point may provide relief.

Direct trauma to the heel can lead to cyst formation and separation of the fat pad from its anchor on the calcaneus. MRI is diagnostic. Management of heel pad separation consists of aspiration of the cyst, compressive dressing, and immobilization in a non–weight bearing cast to promote adherence of the heel pad to the calcaneus.

Bursitis Under a Heel Spur

Patients present with excruciating pain at heel contact, and careful examination may reveal local swelling and tenderness on the plantar aspect of the heel, especially at the distal medial quadrant. The differential diagnosis includes fracture of a calcaneal spur and rupture of the plantar fascia. When presenting bilaterally, seronegative enthesopathies should be considered. Conservative management includes heel elevation and a FO with local relief under the painful bursa. In recalcitrant cases, a steroid injection to the bursa can be effective.

Peroneal Tendinitis

This condition is often encountered in patients after inversion ankle injuries or fractures. Also, iatrogenic peroneal tendinitis can be caused by FOs with a high medial arch support if they lack lateral balancing (a vertical "ledge" to prevent lateral slippage of the foot). Footwear with a high and rigid heel counter may irritate the skin and peroneal tendons; this can be alleviated by elevation of the heel or wearing footwear of supramalleolar height. The differential diagnosis includes sural neuroma, talocrural joint pathology, os trigonum lesion, and plantar fasciitis.

Tenderness due to peroneus longus pathology can be elicited by palpation along the course of the muscle and tendon from the proximal fibula, posterior to the lateral malleolus, below the peroneal tubercle of the calcaneus, under the cuboid, and across the plantar aspect to the 1st metatarsal base. Since the pain and tenderness are often across the plantar surface, it can be confused with plantar fasciitis. Patients usually complain of pain from midstance to push-off. The tenderness in peroneus brevis pathology is usually along a course from the distal fibula, posterior to the lateral malleolus, and above the peroneal tubercle of the calcaneus to the 5th metatarsal base.

Edema control and immobilization are the mainstays of treatment. This can be achieved by applying a short Unna boot up to the distal calf while allowing limited ambulation. A lateral Barton wedge and footwear with a broad heel base can be added to place the peroneal tendon in a less stressed position. In patients with peroneal tendinitis related to poorly balanced FOs, lowering the medial arch and balancing the lateral border of the FO with reinforcement of the lateral counter of the shoe should be considered.

Flexor Hallucis Longus (FHL) Tendinitis

FHL tendinitis can result from ankle trauma such as a fracture, with maximum tenderness usually occurring posterior to the medial malleolus. In physiatric practice, however, "distal FHL tendinitis" is not uncommon in patients who wear FOs or AFOs as a result of irritation from a prominent FO arch or distal edge of the orthoses. In cavus foot with FF equinus or spastic ankle equinus, the distal edge of the orthoses frequently exerts undue pressure and discomfort to the tendon behind the 1st MT head. Lowering the arch of an FO or trimming the distal edge of an AFO should be considered in these cases.

Os Trigonum Lesion

Os trigonum refers to a non-united lateral tubercle on the posterior aspect of the talus and is usually asymptomatic. In dancers, the os trigonum or adjacent soft tissue can be caught between the posterior lip of the tibia and the calcaneus as a result of forceful plantar flexion of the foot beyond its range. This can also be seen in soccer or football punting.[9]

The tenderness is located posterolaterally behind the peroneus tendon instead of medially as in FHL tendinitis. Location of the pain and tenderness may be similar to that seen in peroneal tendinitis; however, forced plantar flexion of the ankle triggers the pain in an os trigonum lesion while resisted eversion precipitates pain in peroneal tendinitis. A lateral radiograph of the ankle is usually diagnostic.

Treatment is directed toward avoiding aggravating activities such as excessive plantar flexion of the ankle. Low-heeled shoes in addition to taping reduce pinching of the soft tissue and pain. Cortisone injections are usually not recommended, and surgery should be considered in recalcitrant cases.[8]

Tibialis Posterior Insufficiency

Although this is a rather common cause of posterior heel pain, it tends to be under-diagnosed. The point of maximum tenderness is usually between the navicular and medial malleolus, or behind the medial malleolus. In severe cases, pain and tenderness may be noted proximally in the posterior margin of the medial tibia. Early biomechanical treatments with a UCBL, SMO, or rear entry AFO are discussed in the chapter Conservative Management of Acquired Flatfoot.

In the acute painful stage, a short Unna boot can be used with a medial heel wedge in the shoe to reduce inflammation and edema, and to provide relative immobilization while allowing the patient to continue sedentary work. If necessary, a CAM-walker with an Unna boot can provide additional immobilization, and, in contrast to casting, allows for examination of the leg and is more convenient for the patient.

If the deformity is reducible to STJ-neutral without significant gastrocsoleus tightness, a medial heel to sole wedge combined with heel elevation may be tried prior to prescribing a formal FO, UCBL, or AFO.

Neurogenic Symptoms and Heel Pain

In patients with chronic heel pain, subtle symptoms of burning, tingling, or a feeling of "pins and needles" should be sought to identify possible neurologic conditions such as nerve entrapment syndromes. Differentiation among the entrapment syndromes is often difficult as a result of the variability in degree and location of nerve entrapment. The examiner should look for reproduction of the patient's symptoms by focal percussion or compression to localize the lesion.

In general, the role of electrodiagnosis in neurogenic lesions of the foot is limited owing to various factors including the wide range of normal values, difficulty in temperature control, edema, error of distance measurement, false-motor points, false-positive needle EMG of intrinsic foot muscles, and the effect of normal aging.[5,16] There are, however, a few conditions (e.g., tarsal tunnel syndrome, Baxter's nerve entrapment) for which electrophysiologic studies are the sole diagnostic tool. Various neurogenic conditions are summarized in Table 1.

Calcaneal Stress Fracture

This condition occurs mainly in patients with excessive stress to their heels such as military recruits. It can also occur in diabetic patients as a Charcot neuroarthropathy without any history of trauma. The pain is diffuse and usually not localized to the plantar aspect of the heel alone. Unlike most other heel pain syndromes, the "heel squeeze test" (simultaneous medial and lateral compression of the calcaneus) will usually be positive.[1] The lateral plain x-ray shows a vertical sclerotic band running from the posterior superior plateau into the cancellous region, although this finding may be delayed by a few weeks after the onset of symptoms. Technetium 99 bone scan or MRI may be required to detect early cases.

TABLE 1. Neurogenic Conditions of the Hindfoot

Condition	Presentation	Treatment
Tarsal tunnel syndrome	Uncommon condition, often over-diagnosed. Burning on variable locations of the plantar surface and the heel.	Address the contributing biomechanical factors (i.e., correction of pronation or supination). May need surgical intervention.
Entrapment: 1st branch of lateral plantar nerve to ADQ (Baxter's nerve, inferior calcaneal nerve)	Aching pain simulating plantar heel spur syndrome; tenderness is on medial side of the heel (between the abductor hallucis and quadratus plantae) rather than the plantar aspect of the heel.	Prevent excessive pronation and provide simultaneous pressure relief at the area of tenderness.
Jogger's foot (medial plantar nerve entrapment)	Pain under the navicular bone, burning sensation on the medial plantar surface.	Prevent excessive pronation and provide simultaneous pressure relief at the area of tenderness.[20]
Saphenous neuroma	Suspect with local trauma, including after arthroscopic surgery, bypass surgery or vein harvesting. Confusing pattern of pain anywhere from medial lower leg or ankle to medial hindfoot. Percussion reproduces the symptoms and eversion worsens the pain.	Trial of medial hindfoot wedge. Meticulous physical examination localizing the neuroma followed by local anesthetic injection (diagnostic and therapeutic).
Sural neuroma	Suspect with foot surgery, arthroscopic surgery, fracture, external fixation devices or irritation from lateral heel counter. Inversion worsens the pain.	Usually benefits from lateral wedge.
Calcaneal branch neurodynia (medial calcaneal neuritis)	Complication of injection or irritation from the footwear; especially with excessive pronation.	Treat with local nerve block and control pronation.

Patients are usually allowed to ambulate with crutches with or without casting for 6–8 weeks. Stress fractures of the calcaneus in diabetics should be treated very carefully because they may turn into full-blown neurogenic osteoarthropathy (Charcot foot).

Insertional Achilles Tendinitis, Retrocalcaneal Bursitis, Haglund Deformity

These entities are clinically confusing for the physician to differentiate. The principles of the conservative management of these conditions, however, are similar.

The Haglund deformity refers to a prominent posterior superior calcaneal protuberance, and can be identified on a lateral plain radiograph. The "parallel pitch line" is a line drawn from the posterior lip of the talar articular facet parallel to the base line along the medial tuberosity and the anterior tubercle of the calcaneus. The Haglund deformity (bursal prominence) is considered abnormal if it extends above this line.[17]

Symptoms can be relieved with roomy shoes to avoid irritation from the posterior heel-counter, a heel grip (relief) inside the posterior heel counter, and a heel lift. Measures for dampening excessive pronation should be tried. Lengthening exercises of the gastrocsoleus muscle are a mandatory part of treatment. Repeated injections should be avoided, owing to the risk of tendon rupture.

Sinus Tarsi Syndrome

This condition is a symptom complex characterized by a history of frequent ankle sprains, swelling of the sinus tarsi area with pain, and a feeling of instability. Prompt symptom relief usually occurs with local anesthetic injection and suggests this diagnosis, and steroid can be included to provide longer-term relief. This syndrome has been ascribed to disruption of interosseous ligaments in the subtalar joint with associated inflammation and soft tissue proliferation. Sinus tarsi syndrome may present as deep hindfoot pain and may be accompanied by retrocalcaneal swelling when communication between the tarsal sinus and retrocalcaneal space exists. Clinicians may attempt to control the subtalar joint by using a medial wedge in the office. If significant relief is noted after a few weeks, a UCBL or supramalleolar AFO can be prescribed for long-term benefit.

Persistent Pain and Instability After Ankle Injury

Lingering pain after an inversion injury is a somewhat common complaint encountered by the physiatrist. Talar dome injury, syndesmosis (anteroinferior tibiofibular ligament complex) injury, peroneal tendinitis, calcaneocuboid arthritis, peri-cuboidal tenosynovitis, sinus tarsi syndrome, Lisfranc joint injury, and fracture of lateral metatarsals including a Jones fracture should all be considered. Management of the above conditions is described in the chapter Physiatric Management of Sports-Related Foot and Ankle Injury. Patients with syndesmosis injury often complain pain and swelling at the anterior ankle. A "squeeze test of the proximal leg" or "foot abduction test" (see Problem-Oriented History Taking and Physical Examination of Patients with Foot Pain) is useful in differentiating between syndesmosis injuries and other soft tissue injuries because direct local palpation may not differentiate them. Proximal tibiofibular ligament pathology should be suspected when the patient complains of lateral knee pain in addition to the ankle pain. Orthopedic intervention may be necessary for severe syndesmosis injuries.

CONCLUSION

Plantar fasciitis and most other painful hindfoot conditions can usually be managed conservatively without surgical intervention. Precise diagnostic assessment followed by biomechanically oriented management usually yields a favorable outcome even when previous treatments were unsuccessful. A quick-fix approach such as an injection can be problematic in the long run. Treatment should be tailored to the individual patient utilizing available measures such as physical therapy, taping, splinting, footwear, FOs, and weight reduction.

REFERENCES

1. Alexander IJ: The Foot Examination and Diagnosis. New York, Churchill Livingstone, 1997, pp 118–122.
2. Dasgupta B, Bowles J: Scintigraphic localization of steroid injection site in plantar fasciitis. Lancet 346:1400–1401, 1995.
3. Davis PE, Severud E, Baxter DE: Painful heel syndrome: Results of nonoperative treatment. Foot Ankle Int 15:531–535, 1994.
4. Gill LH, Kiebzak GM: The outcome of nonsurgical treatment for plantar fasciitis. Foot Ankle Int 17:527–532, 1996.
5. Glennon P, Terrence OK: Electrodiagnosis of nerve entrapment syndromes that produce symptoms in the foot and ankle. In Myerson M (ed): Foot and Ankle Disorders, Philadelphia, WB Saunders, 2000, pp 800–807.
6. Goslin R, Tollafield DR, Rome K: Mechanical therapeutics in the clinic. In Tollafield DR (ed): Clinical Skills in Treating the Foot. New York, Churchill Livingstone, 1997, pp 187–216.
7. Gudeman SD, Eisele SA, Heidt RS, et al: Treatment of plantar fasciitis by iontophoresis of 0.4% dexamethansone; a randomized, double-blind, placebo-controlled study. Am J Sports Med 25:312–316, 1997.
8. Hamilton WG: Stenosing tenosynovitis of the flexor hallucis longus tendon and posterior impingement upon the os trigonum in ballet dancers. Foot Ankle 3:74–80, 1982.
9. Hardaker WT Jr: Foot and ankle injuries in classical ballet dancers. Orthop Clin North Am 20:621–627, 1989.
10. Hicks JH: The mechanics of the foot: The plantar aponeurosis and the arch. J Anat 88:25–31, 1954.
11. Jahss MH, Michelson JD, Desai P, et al: Investigations into the fat pads of sole of the foot: Anatomy and histology. Foot Ankle 13(5):233–242, 1992.
12. Kibler WB, Goldberg C, Chandler TJ: Functional biomechanical deficits in running athletes with plantar fasciitis. Am J Sports Med 19:66–71, 1991.
13. Kim D, Oh-Park M: Foot and ankle disoders associated with functional impairment in the elderly. J Musculoskeletal Rehab Med 12:7–24, 1999.
14. Lin E, Ronen M, Stamper D, et al: Painful piezogenic heel papules. J Bone Joint Surg Am 67:640–641, 1985.
15. Miller RA, Torres J, McGuire M: Efficacy of first-time steroid injection for painful heel syndrome. Foot Ankle Int 16:610–612, 1995.
16. Park TA, Del Toro DR: Electrodiagnostic evaluation of the foot. Phys Med Rehabil Clin North Am 9:871–896, 1998.
17. Pavlov H, Heneghan MA, Vigorita V: The Haglund syndrome: Initial and differential diagnosis. Radiology 144(1):83–88, 1982.
18. Pfeffer GB: Plantar heel pain. In Myerson (ed): Foot and Ankle Disorders. Philadelphia, WB Saunders, 2000, pp 834–850.
19. Pfeffer GB, Bacchetti P, Deland J, et al: The non-operative treatment of proximal plantar fasciitis. Foot Ankle Int 20:214–221, 1999.
20. Rask MR: Medial plantar neurapraxia (jogger's foot): Report of 3 cases. Clin Orthop 134:193–195, 1978.
21. Rondhuis JJ, Huson A: The first branch of the lateral plantar nerve and heel pain. Acta Morphol Neerland-Scand 24(4):269–279, 1986.
22. Sellman JR: Plantar fascia rupture associated with corticosteroid injection. Foot Ankle Int 15:376–381, 1994.
23. Shmokler RL, Bravo AA, Lynch FR, et al: A new use of instrumentation in fluoroscopy controlled heel spur surgery. J Am Podiatr Med Assoc 78(4):194–197, 1988.
24. Wapner K, Shrakey PF: Use of night splint for treatment of recalcitrant plantar fasciitis, Foot and Ankle 12(3):135–137, 1991.
25. Wolgin M, Cook C, Graham C, Mauldin D: Conservative treatment of plantar heel pain: Long-term follow-up. Foot Ankle 15(3):97–102, 1994.

NANCY E. STRAUSS, MD
DUDLEY K. ANGELL, MD

FOOT CONDITIONS RELATED TO NEUROMUSCULAR DISORDERS IN ADULTS

Department of Rehabilitation
Medicine
Columbia University College of
Physicians & Surgeons
New York Presbyterian Hospital
New York, New York

Reprint requests to:
Department of Rehabilitation
Medicine
Columbia Presbyterian Hospital
Harkness Pavilion HP 184
180 Fort Washington Avenue
New York, NY 10032-3710

The functional foot is a vital part of the mobility in the neurologically impaired patient. The function of the foot is to bear weight and support the body in the upright position during standing and walking. Body weight is transmitted through the lower extremities to the talus, which serves as a pivot point from which forces are directed posteriorly into the os calcaneus and anteriorly into the forefoot. The forefoot varies its position to provide a broad base of support to aid in stability and balance.[16] The foot is continuously changing its position relative to the rest of the body to achieve the goal of upright posture, as are the various parts of the foot itself. To avoid losing balance, adaptations are made when environmental challenges are encountered. Subtle changes in foot position during standing and walking occur as a result of complex neurologic pathways. Visual, cutaneous, and proprioceptive impulses provide information to determine preferred posture and position.

Muscle imbalance produces foot deformity. Muscle imbalance can result from selective neurologic impairment of different groups of muscles, and can be further exaggerated by spasticity, if present. Ligamentous laxity will worsen any deformity. Immobility without adequate joint range of motion will result in contracture. If sensation is impaired, skin and joint breakdown become a concern. In the denervated foot, other manifestations include osteoporosis, fracture, pathologic fractures, and osteoarthritis.[16]

The physiatrist is often the first clinician called upon to evaluate a patient with a chief complaint of foot dysfunction and foot pain. It is important to remember that the foot cannot be examined in isolation to the rest of the lower extremity. The patient should be fully disrobed and gowned, since foot problems are often the initial complaint in the patients with neuromuscular disease. A thorough history and comprehensive physical examination of the neurologic and musculoskeletal systems may lead to the correct diagnosis.

The physiatrist should not hesitate to consult other experts in treating problems of the foot. Neurologists, orthopedic surgeons, podiatrists, orthotists, and physical therapists are often called upon for their diagnostic and operative expertise, patient education, long-term foot care, advising the technologic detail in foot orthoses, and assessment of functional status of the patient. Finally, patients themselves should be active participants in the decision making process. It is only the patient who can truly evaluate if his or her feet are providing the functional stability and support required for daily activities.

SPECIAL CONSIDERATIONS REGARDING SHOES

It is not uncommon for a physician to prescribe a pair of shoes that provide stability, support, and alignment, only to find that the patient comes to the next appointment wearing a pair of least expensive, thin, flexible, lightweight shoes. The reason for this is that the patient self-selects the treatment that meets his or her main functional goals: energy conservation and remaining upright without falling.

When a patient with a neuromuscular problem chooses a pair of shoes for walking, he or she often seeks the following features: (1) **Lightweight**. (2) **Ability to facilitate sensory feedback**. A **thin-soled** shoe will allow sensory input better than a thick-soled shoe. The patient needs to feel changes in the terrain so that he or she can correct the posture and prevent falling. (3) **Desirable coefficient of friction**. A sole with a high coefficient of friction will provide more stability, although it may become more difficult to advance the foot. A sole with a lower coefficient of friction is easier to advance, but may increase risk of sliding.

Choosing shoes is a complex process for the patient with neuromuscular diseases. Factors that play a role in choosing desirable safe shoes are muscle strength and tone, ligamentous integrity, contracture, and skin integrity. Impaired cognition may interfere with this process. The most reliable way for patients to decide which shoe will help them meet their goals is by trying them on and testing them out on different ground surfaces. Ideally, they would do so for an amount of time that simulates their pattern of daily use. When patients find shoes that meet their needs, it is recommended that they purchase more than one pair. When a patient becomes accustomed to a certain pair of shoes, his or her gait accommodates, and a new posture is assumed. At the time of change, the patient must pay close attention to balance and posture to prevent falls.

SPECIAL CONSIDERATIONS REGARDING ORTHOSES

As discussed earlier regarding shoe preferences, special considerations must be made when considering orthoses as well. Distribution of weakness must be fully evaluated before an orthosis is prescribed to ensure that adequate strength is present. The angle of the ankle joint will have a significant influence on the biomechanics of the knee. Therefore, quadriceps strength as well as proximal muscle strength must be adequately determined. In a patient with muscle weakness, the weight of the brace becomes a critical factor. A trial with a prefabricated orthosis may provide information of the patient's capability to adjust his or her biomechanics to the use of the custom made orthoses.

SPECIAL CONSIDERATIONS REGARDING SURGERY

There are many surgical procedures available to aid in correcting or minimizing foot deformities and providing stabilization in the patients with neuromuscular diseases. Careful attention to the benefits and risks of surgery must be considered. Goals of surgery must be realistic in terms of functional gains. The anesthesiologist must be made aware of the patient's neurologic condition, and any risk of adverse reaction to anesthetic agents must be addressed. The physiatrist should be involved in the postoperative treatment plan as the patient adjusts to a change in foot position, posture, and foot biomechanics.

PHYSICAL EXAMINATION OF THE FOOT AND ANKLE IN NEUROMUSCULAR DISEASE

The complete examination including neurologic examination of the foot and ankle is covered elsewhere in this volume and is beyond the scope of this chapter.

A systematic examination of the hindfoot, midfoot, and forefoot, including the morphology of the toes, is essential. It should be noted whether the hindfoot is in a varus or a valgus position. The hindfoot may also exhibit a cavus position, in which the **calcaneus pitch angle** is greater than 30 degrees. The calcaneus pitch angle is measured by comparing the inclination of the inferior calcaneus to the fifth metatarsal on a standing lateral radiograph of the foot and ankle. The average angle is 24.5 degrees. Moderate deformity is an angle of 31–40 degrees, and an angle greater than 40 degrees is considered severe pes cavus.[29] The midfoot should be examined for **pronation, supination**, or **collapse**, the rocker-bottom deformity. The forefoot should be examined for adduction and abduction, as well as valgus, typified by a depressed first metatarsal, and varus, which shows an elevated first metatarsal. Forefoot valgus, varus, and equines in relation to the hindfoot should be delineated. The toes are examined for hammer toe or claw toe deformities.

Special consideration should be given to the evaluation of the subtalar joint, which provides the main axis of inversion and eversion of the foot. While viewing the patient from behind, a heel position of eversion is noted. Having the patient stand on the ball of the foot causes the heel to assume an inverted position if there is normal motion in the subtalar joint and, to a lesser degree, the transverse tarsal joint. Any failure to invert the heel should be noted and evaluated.

Disorders of Central Origin (Upper Motor Neuron Disorders)

Upper motor neuron disorders, including stroke, traumatic brain injury, multiple sclerosis, and cerebral palsy, usually have the clinical features of hypertonicity, increased deep tendon reflexes, and muscle weakness. Generally, these disorders cause similar deformity in the foot and ankle, and are therefore treated in a similar manner. It is the hypertonicity, or spasticity in particular, that causes foot deformity. Muscle weakness is usually more amenable to treatment with orthotics.

Equinus or equinovarus deformities are a common feature in the patients who suffer from lower extremity spasticity. This occurs because of the static or dynamic contracture of the gastrocnemius and soleus complex combined with spasticity of the tibialis anterior and/or tibialis posterior muscles.[20] In addition, spastic toe flexors can occur and cause disability, especially in the mildly affected patient.[27]

In the patient with **stroke**, equinus deformity in combination with weakness of the anterior muscle group causes toe walking. In order to compensate for the increased functional length of the leg, the patient must exhibit increased flexion at the hip or circumduction of the leg. Dynamic electromyography during the gait cycle has shown that throughout stance phase the patients exhibit equinus deformity at the ankle, hyperextension of the knee in the most severely spastic patients, and increased flexion of the hip.[37] Conservative treatment for the spastic equinus/equinovarus foot in the patient with stroke focuses on reducing the spastic deforming forces in the ankle and the subtalar joint. Although passive stretching, casting and bracing, and oral antispasticity medications[24] can be prescribed and attempted, none have been found to be effective in all patients.

Local nerve blocks have the advantage over oral antispasticity medication in that the problematic area can be targeted without systemic effect. Phenol block of the tibial nerve has been shown to eliminate ankle clonus as well as resistance to passive stretch, thus achieving functional gains neurologic examination without serious complications.[36] This has also been shown in patients following head injury and spinal cord injury.[31] Diagnostic blocks of the tibial nerve using fast-acting local anesthetics can help differentiate between a dynamic equinus foot and a fixed contracture.[3]

Botulinum toxin, type A, has been used for the spasticity in post-stroke patients. Kirazli et al.,[26] compared phenol block of the tibial nerve and botulinum toxin type A motor point injections in the treatment of ankle plantar flexion and foot inverter spasticity post-stroke. The researchers concluded that both treatments were effective in reducing spasticity, but changes were more significant in the group that received botulinum toxin at weeks 2 and 4, whereas there was not a significant difference between the two groups at weeks 8 and 12. A surgical long-term treatment is neurotomy of the tibial nerve. Gait was analyzed in nine hemiplegic patients before and 6 months after selective tibial neurotomy, and it was found that after the procedure triceps surae spasticity decreased, passive motion of the ankle increased, claw toes disappeared, and patient perception of gait comfort was improved.[9]

In the patient with flexible spastic foot drop a rigid AFO will aid in providing foot and ankle stability, foot clearance and knee control, and better balanced gait pattern with enhanced functional activation of the vastus lateralis muscle. A flexible PLSO (posterior leaf spring orthosis) may, initially, satisfy the patient's need of dorsiflexion, although it may allow a disabling equinovarus deformity to develop once the patient's limb becomes spastic. Although AFO may compensate for instability of the ankle and knee, it does not compensate for the dysfunction of the central nervous system after stroke.[30]

Functional electrical stimulation has a role in foot drop in the hemiparetic limb by increasing dorsiflexion and reciprocally decreasing plantar flexor spastic reflexes.[33] Granat et al.[18] studied the orthotic and therapeutic value of the peroneal stimulator in adult hemiplegic patients. They found a significant improvement in foot inversion during stance on all ground surfaces tested, as well as improvement in symmetry of gait. The Odstock drop foot stimulator has been studied in patients with central nervous system disorders and is perceived by its users to be of considerable benefit related to a decrease in the effort of walking,[43] and has been found to have a high patient compliance.[7] Electromyographic biofeedback technique has been shown to increase muscle strength and improve recovery of functional locomotion in patients with hemiparesis and foot drop after cerebral hemorrhage.[22] Electromyographic biofeedback and peroneal nerve stimulator technique are likely to have a common mechanism in the improvement of gait pattern in the treatment of post-stroke foot drop.[42]

Surgical treatment to reduce the deforming force of spasticity may be considered if significant functional deficit remains after conservative treatment. Surgical procedures include tendon transfers, tendon lengthenings, tenotomies, and arthrodeses.[20]

The most common procedure, the split anterior tibial tendon transfer (SPLATT), involves rerouting $\frac{1}{2}$ of the tibialis anterior tendon posterolaterally to the cuboid. Division of the tibialis anterior tendon decreases the inversion force generated by the spastic muscle. Recently a combined SPLATT and lengthening of the posterior tibial tendon has been recommended for equinovarus deformity associated with forefoot adduction.[5] The split posterior tibial tendon transfer, in which $\frac{1}{2}$ of the tibialis posterior tendon is rerouted posteriorly to the peroneus brevis, is also often performed. It is indicated when there are weak evertors and is usually combined with a heel cord lengthening. Yamamoto[48] studied 104 stroke patients in an average postoperative follow-up period of 6.4 years, who had the following corrective surgical procedures: tenotomy of the toe flexors for hammer toe deformity; lengthening of the aponeurosis of the gastrocnemius for equinus deformity; or transfer of the anterior tibial tendon, posterior tibial tendon, or long toe flexors for varus deformity. Of significant interest is that 76% of the patients were satisfied with the results, 79% of the patients did not use an orthosis, and in 74% of the patients the correction was maintained.

In patients with **traumatic brain injury** (TBI), the foot must be examined and if there is any suspicion of pain or deformity, direct injury must be excluded by radiographic studies. The treatment plan of the foot conditions due to intracranial injury of TBI follows the same course as those due to stroke. The split anterior tibialis tendon procedure in hemiplegic, triplegic, and quadriplegic TBI patients has been shown to be effective in correcting deformity, allowing for improved shoewear, and wheelchair positioning in the non-ambulatory patient, and improved ambulation with decreased bracewear in the more functional patient.[25,45] Young[49] describes the peroneus longus muscle to be the major deforming force in the spastic plano-valgus foot in the neurologically impaired adult, and release, transfer, or tenodesis of the peroneus longus was effective in correcting the deformity.

The types of foot deformities in patients with **multiple sclerosis** will depend on the distribution of weakness and muscle imbalance and the amount of spasticity. For example, complications of severe spasms of the anterior tibialis muscle include pes cavus and claw toes.[38] Superimposed impairments in sensation, endurance, and coordination will further contribute to foot dysfunction. Orthotic management must include close attention to the weight of the orthosis, as fatigue and endurance are problematic. Owing to this disease having a variable course, it is difficult to predict function based on current physical examination. For this reason, surgical intervention should be used as a last option and only if realistic goals are identified. Design of the AFO should be as adjustable as possible to be utilized when the patient's neurologic status changes (i.e., an articulated AFO).

Foot deformities in patients with **spinal cord injury** may vary with the level and completeness of the lesion. Equinovarus deformities can develop, as can claw toe deformities, which are more common in incomplete lesions. Incomplete spinal cord injured patients with weak ankle dorsiflexors but sufficiently strong knee extensors may be candidates for use of a peroneal stimulator as an orthotic device.[43]

Pressure sores may develop over bony prominences, including the malleoli, base of the fifth metatarsal, and heels. Protective footwear can be prescribed to minimize the pressure from the footplate of the wheel chair. Ingrown toenails may lead to repeated episodes of autonomic hyperreflexia, in which case ablation of the nailbed may be required.[27]

When treating the adult patient with **cerebral palsy**, the physician must remember that this is not a new condition; the patient has lived with the impairment for many years and has adapted accordingly. If the patient is not complaining about the foot deformity or pain in the region, treatment is usually not indicated.

The common ankle and foot deformities in cerebral palsy are equinus, equino-valgus, equinovarus, calcaneus, and hallux valgus.[4] Once structural ankle equino-varus deformity develops, the patient utilizes compensatory subtalar joint pronation to accomplish dorsiflexion of the foot, in order to clear the ground. Any attempts to correct the planus foot (i.e., bracing) without the proper correction or accommodation of the ankle equinus will fail.

A report of split anterior tendon transfer for spastic equinovarus foot deformity in a population of patients, which included patients with cerebral palsy, described good long-term results with minimal complications.[45] The long-term results of triple arthrodesis in patients with cerebral palsy were studied with respect to patient satis-faction. The investigators concluded that patient satisfaction was predominantly re-lated to persistent pain and to residual deformity. Persistent pain and distance limitations were strongly correlated with residual planovalgus deformity.[44]

Disorders of the Motor Neuron

In **amyotrophic lateral sclerosis**, there are findings of muscle spasticity as well as muscle weakness/atrophy. The distribution of weakness is patchy, but com-monly affects distal muscles first.[14] One study found that the clinical feature that best correlated with walking performance was lower extremity muscle strength.[17] The physician must be aware of the poor prognosis as well as the endurance limita-tions when formulating a conservative treatment plan. The goal in treating foot drop is to prevent it from limiting mobility and to prevent falls. The lightest and least re-strictive AFO is our choice, since energy conservation is a factor. This is usually ac-complished by a PLSO.

In patients with **poliomyelitis**, owing to the extreme variation and location and number of lost motor units, the pattern of weakness is quite variable with lower ex-tremities being more affected than upper extremities. The sacral nerve roots are usu-ally spared, resulting in characteristic sparing of the intrinsic muscles of the foot.[14] The muscles most frequently affected are the tibialis anterior, quadriceps, and tib-ialis posterior muscles. The most common deformities are the valgus foot, knee flex-ion contracture, and hip flexion abduction contracture.[41]

Since there are a large number of patients with a history of poliomyelitis who have new musculoskeletal and neuromuscular complaints, often several decades after the acute illness has been studied, post-polio clinics have been established. The most prevalent new health-related complaints are fatigue, muscle or joint pain, and weakness.[1] The need for changes in orthotic and footwear prescriptions must be carefully assessed.

When faced with any new complaint in a patient with a preexisting neurologic condition, a new diagnosis must be excluded before attributing the complaint to the preexisting condition. History taking must include all prior surgeries so that the physician can gain an awareness of the patient's baseline deformity.

Drennen[14] discussed two widely used surgical techniques for the treatment of foot deformities in patients with poliomyelitis. The first is tendon transfers to pro-vide active motor power to replace the function of paralyzed muscles, to eliminate the deforming effect of a muscle when its antagonist is paralyzed, and to produce stability through better muscle balance. The second procedure is **triple arthrodesis** (fusion of the subtalar, calcaneo-cuboid, and talo-navicular joints). The goals of triple arthrodesis are to (1) create a stable and static realignment of the foot; (2)

remove deforming forces; (3) arrest progression of deformity; (4) eliminate pain; (5) improve brace and shoe fitting, or eliminate the need for a brace; and (6) improve cosmesis.

Disorders of the Nerve

In the patients with **peripheral polyneuropathies**, the combination of distal motor weakness, autonomic dysfunction, foot deformity, and impaired sensation can have severe effects on foot integrity. Foot problems may be the first manifestation (foot drop, foot deformity, plantar ulcer, etc.) of such disorders. The patients with **Charcot-Marie-Tooth disease** (CMT) may have a characteristic pes cavus deformity, which, given the prevalence of this deformity, warrants a detailed discussion here.[2,21,29]

The three most important elements of the cavus foot deformity are **forefoot (FF) valgus**; **cavus deformity** in the midfoot, hindfoot, or forefoot; and **hindfoot (HF) varus**, resulting from muscle imbalance.

FF valgus is primarily the result of overpull of the peroneus longus muscle. On examination, this can be noted by viewing the foot in the unloaded position with the hindfoot (calcaneus) held in the neutral position. The medial forefoot is more plantar flexed in relation to the lateral forefoot. In CMT, the peroneus brevis becomes weakened out of proportion to its antagonist, the tibialis posterior, which increases the high arch of the cavus foot and increases inversion of the hindfoot (HF). HF varus, present in approximately 25% of CMT patients, can be either flexible or fixed. The lateral block test described by Coleman[11] is used to determine the flexibility of the subtalar joint and hindfoot, as well as the contribution of forefoot valgus to the cavus deformity. This can be used to guide surgical management, i.e., if the deformity is rigid, (the hindfoot remained varus on the block), surgical correction of the plantar flexed first ray alone will not correct the deformity.

The patient's initial complaints are related to general foot weakness and unsteady gait often presenting with frequent ankle sprains. Other foot complaints include pain under the metatarsal heads, claw toes, foot fatigue, and difficulty with shoe fitting. Muscle wasting usually occurs first in the foot intrinsics, then the peroneals, and next the anterior tibialis muscle, with the posterior tibialis and gastrocsoleus muscles the last to be atrophic.

In planning treatment of the cavus foot, a sequential approach to evaluation is important. As outlined by Mizel, et al.,[29] several issues should be addressed: (1) Is the cavus deformity primarily hindfoot or forefoot? In the patient with CMT, cavus usually is anterior in nature. (2) Are the deformities fixed or flexible? Fixed deformity may require bony realignment to produce a neutral calcaneus. In the forefoot, if passive dorsiflexion of the metatarsals is not possible, the deformity is fixed. (3) What are the deforming forces? (4) Is there ankle instability? (5) What are the patient's goals?

The patient and physician should remember that CMT is a progressive condition and thus one-time success by a particular approach would not necessarily lead to permanent solution.

Conservative management consists of proper footwear, extra depth shoes with support to unload the metatarsal heads, and, in some cases, custom molded shoes may be needed. A high-top foot wear with lateral flare may be prescribed in patients who have a history of frequent ankle inversion injury. A running sneaker with antipronation medial support may not be appropriate in these instances because the antipronation feature may increase the tendency of inversion. Ankle-foot orthoses

(AFO) can be used when foot drop is present. The FF cavus, FF valgus, and prominent MTP may require custom-molded AFO. Fasciotomy, tendon lengthening, transfer, and tenotomies can eliminate deforming forces to balance the foot, but osteotomies and arthrodeses may be necessary to correct alignment and eliminate pain.[2] The triple arthrodesis is used in patients with severe rigid cavus deformity with very limited subtalar mobility.

Friedreich's ataxia is a progressive familial form of spinal cerebellar degeneration. The most common foot deformity is bilateral symmetric claw foot with marked elevation of the longitudinal arch, prominent metatarsal heads, widening of the forepart of the foot, and hyperextension and clawing of the lesser toes.[27] As the disease progresses, the foot deformity becomes fixed and the feet assume a broad, stumpy, foreshortened, high-arched appearance. Since the patient's functional capacity is hampered largely as a result of ataxia rather than foot deformity itself, orthotic treatment has limited success.

Entrapments occurring at any location from the lumbosacral nerve roots to their terminal branches can present with foot pain or dysfunction as the patient's initial complaint.[28] The site of entrapment can be located by the distribution of weakness, sensory loss, and also by electrodiagnostic studies in some instances.

There are multiple sites of entrapment in the tibial nerve that produce distinct entities: proximal tibial neuropathy, tarsal tunnel syndrome, medial plantar neuropathy, lateral plantar neuropathy, interdigital neuritis (Morton's neuritis), medial plantar proper digit neuropathy (Joblin's neuroma), calcaneal neuropathy, and sural neuropathy.[35]

Tarsal tunnel syndrome is the result of entrapment of the posterior tibial nerve beneath the flexor retinaculum at the ankle, with symptoms of burning pain and numbness and tingling in the sole of the foot and the toes.[13] The distribution of symptoms is dependent upon the particular branch of the tibial nerve involved. The helpful diagnostic signs are Tinel's sign at the tarsal tunnel and sensory loss in the territory of the terminal branches of the tibial nerve.[35] Electrodiagnosis aids in distinguishing between L5 or S1 radiculopathy and sensory peripheral neuropathy. The treatment of tarsal tunnel syndrome depends on the cause. The treatment may include rest, anti-inflammatory agents, orthotic device use, biomechanical analysis and retraining, and local anesthetic injection (both for therapeutic as well as diagnostic use). A medial heel wedge may be used in an attempt to remove traction on the nerve by inverting the heel. Surgical decompression may be indicated in patients who do not respond to conservative treatment.[13]

Peroneal neuropathy is the most common entrapment neuropathy of the lower extremity and the most common cause of foot drop. The deep peroneal branches are more affected than the superficial branches. The nerve can also be injured as a result of direct trauma, stretch injury, extrinsic mass, compression, or intrinsic nerve sheath tumors.[23] Treatment depends on the nature and severity. Lightweight AFOs are usually sufficient for foot drop correction and for ankle stability.

Surgical intervention may be appropriate in cases of complete laceration of nerve, complete axonal lesion with no evidence of recovery, and when a mass (tumor, ganglion cyst) is present. Ninkovic's[34] technique involves transposition of the lateral head of the gastrocnemius to the anterior side of the lower leg and suturing the proximal end of the deep branch of the peroneal nerve to the motor branch of the tibial nerve. This allows the lateral head of the gastrocnemius to be innervated by the deep branch of the peroneal nerve, thus taking over the function of the paralytic muscles. This differs from the more widely used technique of posterior tibial tendon transfer, which has not been uniformly successful, probably owing to short range of the tendon excursion and being a flexor-phased muscle.

The "**anterior tarsal tunnel syndrome**" results from compromise of the deep peroneal nerve as it passes beneath the extensor retinaculum at the ankle. It can affect either the motor, sensory, or both.[15] Patients present with numbness or paresthesias in the region between the first two toes. Patients can also complain of vague pain about the ankle, especially at night. The etiology of this syndrome is unclear but seems to occur more often in patients who assume a position of plantar flexion at the ankle with dorsiflexion of the toes, as in the case of women who wear high-heeled shoes. Since most patients respond to a change in footwear, surgical exploration is rarely needed.[15]

Saphenous neuropathy: The saphenous nerve can be injured during sports activities, automobile accidents, fracture, external fixation devices, harvesting saphenous veins for vascular procedures, operation around the foot and ankle, sprain of the ankle, and arthroscopic surgeries.[8]

Some of the patient's complaints may be vague medial knee, ankle, or plantar pain, or simply aching of the whole ankle on weight bearing. Careful history, high level of suspicion, and pinpoint palpation with a "sharpened pencil eraser tip" can localize the neuroma or injured site with reproduction of the symptom. Treatment is mostly conservative by utilizing the protection, minimizing pronation to reduce tension from the nerve on weight bearing, and assurance.[8]

Compartment syndrome is the dysfunction of muscles, nerves, and blood vessels within a tightly closed space as a result of increased pressure. The compromise in perfusion, circulation, and function of the contents of the space will vary with the amount of excessive pressure and the duration of that pressure. Compartment syndrome should be suspected in the presence of limb pain out of proportion to that anticipated from a clinical situation, weakness of muscles within the compartment, **pain on passive stretch of the compartment muscles**, and tenderness of compartment fascia.[40] The leg has four compartments separated by tight fascia: (1) The anterior compartment contains the deep peroneal nerve, anterior tibialis muscle, extensor hallucis muscle, and extensor digitorum longus muscle. (2) The lateral compartment contains the superficial peroneal nerve and the peroneal muscles. (3) The superficial posterior compartment contains the gastrocsoleus muscle. (4) The deep posterior compartment contains the tibial nerve, the posterior tibialis muscle, and the flexor digitorum longus muscle.[47] Most serious consequences result when the anterior or deep posterior compartments are affected. Compartment syndromes involving the foot can also occur and cause impairment and disability and require early diagnosis and prompt intervention to prevent acquired cavus deformities or even amputations, especially in the diabetic patients.[32]

Acute compartment syndrome is a medical emergency that may require emergent fasciotomy. Post-fasciotomy rehabilitation involves early standing and ambulation to prevent contracture that can be the most serious disabling permanent consequence. There are no or few contraindications of early standing and ambulation after fasciotomy, although the operated limb may appear grotesque. This should be discussed with surgeons who may be reluctant to allow early ambulation after the fasciotomy. Surgical interventions to treat residual nerve compression and refractory problematic deformities include (1) release of nerve compression; (2) release of fixed contractures (using infarct excision, myotendinous lengthening, muscle resection, or tenotomy); (3) tendon transfers or arthrodesis to increase function; and (4) osteotomy or amputation for severe non-salvageable deformities.[6,39] David et al.[12]

studied 40 patients with post-traumatic compartment syndrome of the lower leg who developed talipes equinovarus adductus foot deformity and were treated with surgical procedures and found patient satisfaction to be high.

Disorders of Muscle

Most myopathies are usually static and non-progressive disorders of muscle, generally causing a proximal muscle weakness; however, associated foot deformities have been described.[14] When orthoses are needed in this population, the lightest weight material is essential.[19]

Dystrophies are progressive disorders of muscle and commonly have associated foot deformities that result from muscle imbalance. The disorder that has been most studied is **Duchenne's muscular dystrophy** (DMD), and although it is primarily a pediatric neuromuscular disease, we will make mention of it in this chapter. The equinus deformity of the ankle is one of the most serious orthopedic problems associated with DMD. Equinus of the forefoot can develop in severely affected young patients as a result of tight plantar structures (medial fascia). Equinovarus deformity occurs when equinus contractures are accompanied by varus deformity at the heel.[14] Night splints and aggressive range of motion exercises can minimize the equinus deformity. As the condition progresses and the patient is still ambulatory, toe walking is required to compensate for increasing quadriceps weakness, allowing the weight line to pass in front of the knee joint. Bracing for ambulation at this stage may result in the patient losing his or her compensatory mechanism to remain upright. As plantar flexion becomes fixed, remaining upright becomes precarious. Forefoot and hindfoot inversion develops as peroneal strength diminishes.[14] Surgical correction of the equinus deformity, along with postoperative bracing, may prolong ambulation thus secondarily retarding the development of contractures.[46] The goals of surgery should be clearly stated because the energy cost of ambulation is high and the overall progression of the disease is not halted. Anesthesia risks must also be addressed. The posterior tibial muscle retains good function despite progression of muscle weakness in other areas. Tendon transfer and lengthening procedures have been compared regarding recurrence of deformity.[46] In the advanced non-ambulatory patient with DMD, the degree of equinus deformity may limit the footwear options. In severe cases, custom-made shoes may be required. Although sensation is intact, special attention must be made to skin integrity as well as toenail care.

Becker's dystrophy is similar to DMD in clinical appearance and distribution of weakness. Progressive equinus deformity develops in the forefoot as well as the hindfoot. It is rare to develop hindfoot varus. Development of foot deformities and muscle weakness can be asymmetric, with early contracture of the tendo-Achilles.[14] Management is similar to that of DMD. However, the onset of the condition, as well as the age of loss of ambulation, is later.[10]

Myotonic dystrophy, **fascioscapulohumeral dystrophy**, **distal muscular dystrophy**, and **scapulohumeral dystrophy** are some of the myopathies that affect distal lower extremity muscles in addition to the proximal muscles. Various foot deformities and dysfunction may occur in these patients. Treatment should be individualized and mostly by conservative means.

CONCLUSION

It is clear from the broad range of diseases covered in this chapter that insult to any part of the neurologic or neuromuscular system may result in foot dysfunction and foot deformity. The physiatrist must not examine the foot in isolation. Foot complaints may be the first hint that a more generalized condition exists. The physiatrist must go forth and explore the cause of the dysfunction, and create a unique and individualized treatment plan to minimize this dysfunction.

REFERENCES

1. Agre JC, Matthews DJ: Rehabilitation concepts in motor neuron diseases. In Braddom RL (ed): Physical Medicine and Rehabilitation. Philadelphia, WB Saunders, 1996, pp 955–971.
2. Alexander IJ, Johnson KA: Assessment and management of pes cavus in Charcot-Marie-Tooth disease. Clin Orthop Rel Res (246):273–281, 1989.
3. Arendzen JH, van Duijn J, Beckmann MK, et al: Diagnostic blocks of the tibial nerve in spastic hemiparesis. Effects on clinical, electrophysiological and gait parameters. Scand J Rehab Med 24(2):75–81, 1992.
4. Banks HH: The management of spastic deformities of the foot and ankle. Clin Orthop Rel Res (122):70–76, 1977.
5. Barnes MJ; Herring JA: Combined split anterior tibial-tendon transfer and intramuscular lengthening of the posterior tibial tendon. Results in patients who have a varus deformity of the foot due to spastic cerebral palsy. J Bone Joint Surg (Am) 73(5):734–738, 1991.
6. Botte MJ, Santi MD, Prestianni CA, Abrams RA: Ischemic contracture of the foot and ankle: Principles of management and prevention. [Review] Orthopedics (Thorofare, NJ) 19(3):235–244, 1996.
7. Burridge J, Taylor P, Hagan S, Swain I: Experience of clinical use of the Odstock dropped foot stimulator. Artif Organs 21(3):254–260, 1997.
8. Busis, NA: Femoral and obturator neuropathies. Neurol Clin 17(3):633–653, 1999.
9. Calliet F, Mertens P, Rabaseda S, Boisson D: The development of gait in the hemiplegic patient after selective tibial neurotomy [French]. Neuro-Chirurgie 44(3):183–191, 1998.
10. Cohen-Sobel E, Darmochwal V, Caselli M, et al: Atypical case of Becker's muscular dystrophy. Early identification and management. J Am Podiatr Med Assn 84(4):181–188, 1994.
11. Coleman SS, Chestnut WJ: A simple test for hindfoot flexibility in the cavovarus foot. Clin Orthop (123):60–62, 1977.
12. David A, Lewandrowski KU, Josten C, et al: Surgical correction of talipes equinovarus following foot and leg compartment syndrome. Foot Ankle Int 17(6):334–339, 1996.
13. DeLisa JA, Saeed MA: The tarsal tunnel syndrome. Muscle Nerve 6(9):664–670, 1983.
14. Drennan JC: Orthopaedic Management of Neuromuscular Disorders. Philadelphia, JB Lippincott, 1983.
15. Dumitru D: Electrodiagnostic Medicine. Philadelphia, Hanley & Belfus, 1995, pp 903–904.
16. Enna CD: Peripheral Denervation of the Foot. New York, Alan R. Liss, 1988.
17. Goldfarb BJ, Simon SR: Gait patterns in patients with amyotrophic lateral sclerosis. Arch Phys Med Rehabil 65(2):61–65, 1984.
18. Granat MH, Maxwell DJ, Ferguson AC, et al: Peroneal stimulator; evaluation for the correction of spastic drop foot in hemiplegia. Arch Phys Med Rehab 77(1):19–24, 1996.
19. Granata C, De Lollis A, Campo G, et al: Analysis, design and development of a carbon fibre reinforced plastic knee-ankle-foot orthosis prototype for myopathic patients. Proceedings of the Institution of Mechanical Engineers. Part H—Journal of Engineering in Medicine 204(2):91–96, 1990.
20. Harkless LB, Bembo, GP: Stroke and its manifestations in the foot. A case report. Clin Podiatr Med Surg 11(4):635–645, 1994.
21. Holmes JR, Hansen ST Jr: Foot and ankle manifestations of Charcot-Marie-Tooth disease. [Review] Foot Ankle 14(8):476–486, 1993.
22. Intiso D, Santilli V, Grasso MG, et al: Rehabilitation of walking with electromyographic biofeedback in foot-drop after stroke. Stroke 25(6):1189–1192, 1994.
23. Katirji B: Peroneal neuropathy. [Review] Neurol Clin 17(3):567–591, vii, 1999.
24. Katz RT, Dewald JPA, Schmitt BD: Spasticity. In Braddom RL (ed): Physical Medicine & Rehabilitation, 2nd ed. New York, WB Saunders, 2000, pp 601–602.
25. Keenan MA, Creighton J, Garland DE, Moore T: Surgical correction of spastic equinovarus deformity in the adult head trauma patient. Foot Ankle 5(1):35–41, 1984.
26. Kirazli Y, On AY, Kismali B, Aksit R: Comparison of phenol block and botulinus toxin type A in the treatment of spastic foot after stroke: A randomized, double-blind trial. Am J Phys Med& Rehab 77(6):510–515. 1998.
27. Klenerman L, Fixsen JA: Common neurologic disorders affecting the foot. In Klenerman L (ed): The Foot and Its Disorders, 3rd ed. Boston, Blackwell Scientific Publications, 1991, pp 155–160.
28. McCluskey LF, Webb LB: Compression and entrapment neuropathies of the lower extremity. [Review] Clin Podiatr Med Surg 16(1):97–125, vii, 1999.

29. Mizel MS, Miller RA, Scioli MW (eds): Orthopaedic Knowledge Update Foot and Ankle 2. Illinois, American Academy of Orthopaedic Surgeons, 1998, pp 88–100.

30. Mojica JA, Nakamura R, Kobayashi T, et al: Effect of ankle-foot orthosis (AFO) on body sway and walking capacity of hemiparetic stroke patients. Tohoku J Exp Med 156(4):395–401, 1988

31. Moore TJ, Anderson RB: The use of open phenol blocks to the motor branches of the tibial nerve in adult acquired spasticity. Foot Ankle 11(4):219–221, 1991.

32. Myerson MS: Management of compartment syndromes of the foot. Clin Orthop Rel Res 271:239–248, 1991.

33. Mysiw WJ, Jackson RD: Electrical stimulation. In Braddom RL (ed): Physical Medicine & Rehabilitation. Philadelphia, WB Saunders, 1996, pp 464–492.

34. Ninkovic M, Sucur D, Starovic B, Markovic S: A new approach to persistent traumatic peroneal nerve palsy. Br J Plast Surg 47(3):185–189, 1994.

35. Oh SJ, Meyer RD: Entrapment neuropathies of the tibial (posterior tibial) nerve. [Review] Neurol Clin 17(3):593–617, vii, 1999.

36. Petrillo CR, Knoploch S: Phenol block of the tibial nerve for spasticity: A long-term follow study. Internat Disabil Stud 10(3):97–100, 1988.

37. Pinzur MS, Sherman R, DiMonte-Levine P, et al: Adult-onset hemiplegia: Changes in gait after muscle-balancing procedures to correct the equinus deformity. J Bone Joint Surg (Am.) 68(8):1249–1257, 1986.

38. Rivera-Dominguez M, DiBenedetto M, Frisbie JH, Rossier AB: Pes cavus and claw toes deformity in patients with spinal cord injury and multiple sclerosis. Paraplegia 16(4):375–382, 1979.

39. Santi MD, Botte MJ: Volkmann's ischemic contracture of the foot and ankle: Evaluation and treatment of established deformity. [Review] Foot Ankle Internat 16(6):368–377, 1995.

40. Seiler R, Guziec G: Chronic compartment syndrome of the feet. A case report. J Am Podiatr Med Assn 84(2):91–94, 1994.

41. Sharma JC, Gupta SP, Sankhala SS, Mehta N: Residual poliomyelitis of lower limb-pattern and deformities. Indian J Pediatr 58(2):233–238, 1991.

42. Takebe K, Basmajian JV: Gait analysis in stroke patients to assess treatments of foot-drop. Arch Phys Med Rehab 57(1):305–310, 1976.

43. Taylor PN, Burridge JH, Dunkerley AL, et al: Patient's perceptions of the Odstock Dropped Foot Stimulator (ODFS). Clin Rehabil 13(5):439–446, 1999.

44. Tenuta J, Shelton YA, Miller F: Long-term follow-up of triple arthrodesis in patients with cerebral palsy. J Pediatr Orthop 13(6):713–716, 1993.

45. Vogt JC: Split anterior tibial transfer for spastic equinovarus foot deformity: Retrospective study of 73 operated feet. J Foot Ankle Surg 37(1):2–7, 1998.

46. Williams EA, Read L, Ellis A, et al: The management of equinus deformity in Duchenne muscular dystrophy. J Bone Joint Surg (Br) 66(4):546–550, 1984.

47. Winkel D, Matthijs O, Phelps V: Diagnosis and Treatment of the Lower Extremities: Nonoperative Orthopaedic Medicine and Manual Therapy. Gaithersburg, MD, Aspen, 1997.

48. Yamamoto H, Okumura S, Morita S, et al: Surgical correction of foot deformities after stroke. Clin Orthop Rel Res (282):213–218, 1992.

49. Young S, Keenan MA, Stone LR: The treatment of spastic planovalgus foot deformity in the neurologically impaired adult. Foot Ankle 10(6):317–324, 1990.

SIREEN M. GOPAL, MD
LILA BARTKOWSKI-ABBATE, MA, PT

FUNCTION OF THE ACHILLES AND OTHER TENDONS IN NORMAL AND PATHOLOGIC CONDITIONS

Assistant Professor
Department of Rehabilitation
  Medicine
Montefiore Medical Center
Bronx, New York

Reprint requests to:
Department of Rehabilitation
  Medicine
Montefiore Medical Park
1500 Blondell Avenue
Bronx, NY 10461

The clinical problems related to the Achilles tendon (AT) and other tendons of the foot including the posterior tibialis (PTT), peroneal longus (PLT)/brevis (PBT), and tibialis anterior (TAT) tendons in physiatric practice are more common than often recognized. These tendon disorders may be the cause or effect in relationship to biomechanical pathology of the foot. Clear understanding of normal and deviated biomechanics of these tendons in pathologic conditions is crucial in diagnosis and management of musculoskeletal and neuromuscular pathologies of the foot.[15] This chapter emphasizes functional consequences of these tendon abnormalities and their relationship to common clinical conditions. *In this chapter, the term "tendon" refers to the muscle tendon unit.*

ANATOMY

Fiber Arrangement

The Achilles tendon is the thickest and strongest tendon of the body, capable of accepting up to 7000 N of force. The gastrocnemius (medial and lateral heads) and soleus muscle tendons join in their distal portions to form the conjoint Achilles tendon. Although the two muscles share a common tendon sheath, their functions must be considered individually, as the tendons remain separate during a spiral course down towards their calcaneal attachment. The gastrocnemius heads starts more superficial than the soleus; however, 12–14 cm proximal to the insertion, the gastrocnemius fibers rotate 90° in a medial-to-lateral direction, through 90° of rotation. This arrangement results in the soleus fibers lying more medial, whereas the medial gastrocnemius fibers assume a more posterior position[9] and extend more distally, which may have implications for the subsequent development of Achilles tendinopathy.

Blood Supply

Vascular studies have demonstrated that there is an area of relative avascularity in the AT 2–6 cm above its insertion.[8] Schmidt-Rohlfing et al. dispute the direct relationship between blood supply and incidence of rupture.[27] Although they found paucity of blood vessels in the typical rupture location, they also demonstrated a marked diminution in vessels at the tendon-bone interface. Because the Achilles tendon rarely ruptures near its insertion, they concluded that the anatomic variations in blood supply do not correlate with rupture site. Their supposition, however, failed to consider differences in tensile strength between the tendon proper and that at its insertion site. The Achilles tendon insertion site may be less prone to rupture secondary to its fibrocartilage structure and its greater tensile strength compared with the tendon's tensile strength at the common rupture zone.

Functional Anatomy

The gastrocnemius supplies power for propulsion in walking, running, and jumping. In contrast, the soleus, which consists primarily of type I (slow-twitch oxidative) fibers, is more important for posture, stabilizing the leg on the foot. The soleus muscle is postulated to respond early to immobilization by disuse atrophy and functional disability.[21,30] EMG studies indicate that the medial head of the gastrocnemius is the most active during running activities.[21]

The posterior tibialis tendon (PTT) courses behind the medial malleolus, posterior to the axis to the ankle and medial to the axis of the subtalar joint. It inserts into the medial-plantar aspect of the navicular bone, plantar aspects of the three cuneiforms, and the bases of the 2nd, 3rd and 4th metatarsals. Due to the short excursion of the PTT, even slight elongation of tendon makes it ineffective as the primary dynamic restraint to the longitudinal arch. (*It is therefore advisable to treat PTT insufficiency aggressively, prior to the occurrence of permanent elongation. Refer to Chapter 13 for details on pathological biomechanics and treatment.*) The PTT works as a functional antagonistic pair with the peroneus brevis tendon (PBT). It is hypothesized that stress applied to the PTT as it passes under the medial malleolus may compromise its vascularity in this area.

The peroneus longus muscle originates from the lateral fibula and intermuscular septum, its musculotendinous junction terminates proximal to the lateral malleolus. In contrast, the peroneus brevis originates from the distal two thirds of the fibula and intermuscular septum. Its musculotendinous junction may extend 2–3 cm below the level of the lateral malleolus.[24] The PBT inserts on the styloid of the fifth metatarsal and is the strongest abductor of the foot as well as a secondary ankle plantarflexor and foot evertor. The PLT and PBT share a common synovial sheath 2–3 cm proximal to the tip of the lateral malleolus. The PLT lies posterior and lateral to the PBT. Distally, the tendons pass into separate synovial compartments. The PBT usually passes superior to the peroneal tubercle of the lateral calcaneus and the PLT passes below. The PLT curls beneath the cuboid, crosses the undersurface of the foot, and inserts at the base of the 1st metatarsal and medial cuneiform. The PLT plantarflexes the first metatarsal and also serves as a secondary ankle plantarflexor and foot evertor. The PLT works with the Tibialis anterior tendon (TAT), which dorsiflexes and inverts the 1st ray, as a functional antagonist pair.[1]

TABLE 1. Pronation and Supination Response

Joint	Sagittal	Frontal	Transverse
Pronation Response			
STJ/MTJ	Dorsiflexion	Eversion	Abduction
Ankle	Dorsiflexion	—	—
Knee	Flexion	Valgus	Internal rotation
Hip	Flexion	Adduct	Internal rotation
L5–S1	Extension	Side-bending (T)	Rotation (A)
Resultant functional leg length discrepancy: Shorter[20]			
Supination Response			
STJ/MTJ	Plantarflexion	Inversion	Adduction
Ankle	Plantarflexion	—	—
Knee	Extension	Varus	External rotation
Hip	Extension	Abduct	External rotation
L5–S1	Flexion	Side-bending (A)	Rotation (T)
Resultant functional leg length discrepancy: Longer[20]			

STJ, subtalar joint; MTJ, midtarsal joint.

FUNCTION OF TENDONS RELATED TO BIOMECHANICS OF GAIT

The function of the lower extremities during gait is progression of the body via a kinetic chain reaction in response to ground reaction forces on weight bearing. The **subtalar joint (STJ) complex** (talocalcaneal, talonavicular, calcaneocuboidal joints) serves a key function in achieving this, being a mitered hinge joint connecting the tibia and the foot. It works as a torque converter, transferring the rotational movement of the leg to that of the foot and vice versa in a closed kinetic chain. Each joint in the lower extremity compensates for others in three planes—sagittal, frontal, and transverse. Transverse and sagittal plane motions in the closed kinetic chain are manifested with motions of equal but opposite direction occurring proximal to the STJ. This is because of restrictions placed on the foot by the ground in closed kinetic chain.

Pronation of the STJ is a normal and essential movement consisting of *eversion, abduction,* and *dorsiflexion* in the frontal, transverse, and sagittal planes, respectively. The **pronation response** is a closed chain of movements occurring throughout the lower extremity and trunk (Table 1). In normal gait, after heel strike, the STJ begins to pronate with unlocking of the MTJ along with knee flexion and internal rotation of tibia, femur and pelvis. When the hindfoot (HF) is everted, the midtarsal joints (MTJ) are unlocked and parallel to each other. This allows the hindfoot joint to remain supple to absorb shock and to adapt to uneven terrain. The pronation response continues until the center of gravity passes over the foot when both patellae are in line as viewed from the side.[3] This moment coincides with positions of maximal foot pronation, internal limb rotation, and knee flexion.

When the center of gravity passes over the support limb at midstance, external pelvic rotation is transmitted down the leg, resulting in the initiation of STJ supination and the **supination response**. When the hindfoot is inverted, the axes of MTJ become divergent and the foot is transformed from a shock-absorbing adapter into a rigid lever for propulsion (see Fig. 1 on page 506).

The subtalar and midtarsal joints are interdependent in function. Manter has described the STJ and MTJ as dual screws connected to the talonavicular in opposite directions.[17] During subtalar pronation, the midtarsal joint turns in the opposite direction along its longitudinal axis. Although the direction of motion at the midtarsal joint is opposite to that of subtalar pronation, the authors will describe this as "midtarsal pronation" in this chapter to avoid confusion. The same principle is applied to midtarsal supination.

While the insertion site of Achilles tendon to the calcaneus does not change, the instantaneous axis of STJ is changing throughout its range. The function of the Achilles tendon, therefore, varies accordingly as the axis of STJ changes during gait in normal and abnormal biomechancis.[7,9] It can produce a supinatory moment when positioned relatively medial to the STJ axis. This helps the locking of MTJ, thereby creating a rigid lever to propel the body weight over the metatarsal heads for push-off. It can produce a pronatory moment when positioned lateral to the STJ axis which can unlock the MTJ. Continuous change of HF position during gait will influence the orientation of forces generated by the Achilles tendon and can produce abnormal areas of tension within the tendon complex.

When the pronatory moment is excessive and prolonged, the AT moves from the medial to the lateral aspect of the heel with significant force, producing a whipping or bowstring effect in different stages during gait.[7] In addition, excessive torsional forces prior to toe-off are postulated to "wring out" the relatively avascular area of the tendon proximal to its insertion, adding to the degenerative forces in play.

The PLT courses around the stable cuboid to insert into the plantar-medial aspect of the base of the 1st ray. Contraction of the peroneus longus muscle exerts an abduction force on the forefoot and plantarflexion of the 1st ray, which stabilizes the 1st ray against the lesser tarsus. (The lesser tarsus is referred to the tarsal bones with the exception of the talus and the calcaneus bones) This plays a role in deceleration of pronation at the subtalar joint. The peroneus brevis stabilizes the fifth ray against the cuboid. It creates lateral stability by eccentrically decelerating the midtarsal joint pronation response.

Contraction of the PTT exerts an adduction force on the lesser tarsus. The simultaneous contraction of the PTT and PLT stabilizes the lesser tarsus transversely by compressing the lesser tarsal bones against one another providing a rigid lever.[23] In the clinical setting, failure of this midfoot stabilization is exemplified in PTT insufficiency. These patients are unable to perform single heel rise due to failure to lock the MTJ and provide a rigid lever for heel rise. The PTT also decelerates STJ pronation by contracting eccentrically during early stance. During midstance and late stance the PTT along with the soleus and long digital flexors assists with deceleration of the forward momentum of the tibia, resulting in an extension moment at the knee.

Walking and running gaits produce different effects and influences. In the normal individual, the running gait will produce a significantly increased varus attitude of the leg to the ground as the angle and base of gait both decrease and the feet plant more closely along the line of progression. This necessitates additional STJ pronation.

BIOMECHANICAL COMPENSATION AND ASSOCIATED PATHOLOGIES

In a balanced plantigrade foot, the STJ reaches the neutral position by midstance and requires little or no muscle activity to support weight. In many individuals, however, the STJ may not function in this ideal position due to various biomechanical factors such as a tight Achilles tendon, structural deformities, muscle dysfunction, and torsional abnormalities of the lower limb.

TABLE 2. Biomechanical Factors and Their Planes of Compensation

Biomechanical Factor	Plane of Deforming Force	Plane of Compensation
Tight Achilles tendon	Progressive dorsiflexion of FF on HF	Pronation with sagittal plane dominance at MTJ & STJ
Forefoot varus	FF inversion relative to HF	Pronation with frontal plane dominance at STJ
Internal femoral torsion	Transverse plane movements of calcaneus on the talus	Pronation with transverse plane dominance at STJ

FF, forefoot; HF, hindfoot; MTJ, midtarsal joint; STJ, subtalar joint.

During gait, joints of the lower extremity, especially the STJ and MTJ, compensate for these abnormal biomechanics to achieve a plantigrade foot as a stable weight bearing base (Table 2). This compensation can be in amount, speed and timing during gait cycle. The abnormal compensation can lead to overuse/stress of musculoskeletal structures, especially soft tissue muscles, fascia, and tendons (Table 3). For example, in abnormal HF positions the Achilles tendon can be placed under undue strain.

In forefoot (FF) varus (a common developmental or acquired foot deformity), the STJ and MTJ pronate until late stance phase to allow push-off with a plantigrade foot. The pronation continues well into late stance, when normal supination (joint locking) should be present (Fig. 2). This abnormal timing of pronation may place increased stress on joints and soft tissues that may be implicated in various clinical syndromes. Ideally, these factors can be identified by a keen physician before they become symptomatic and then often can be treated non-surgically with long lasting results.

EFFECT OF ACHILLES TENDON ON DISORDERS OF THE LOWER EXTREMITY

Tight Achilles Tendon

A tight Achilles tendon affects other pathologic conditions of lower extremity and their management (Table 4). Clinicians, therefore, should be able to analyze the

TABLE 3. Pathologic Conditions Implicated with Biomechanical Compensation

Joint of Compensatory Motion	Pathologic Conditions Implicated
Subtalar joint (most frequent compensation site)	Plantar fasciitis, metatarsalgia, stress fracture of 2nd metatarsal head, hallux abductovalgus
Midtarsal joint (responsible for adjustment between fore and hindfoot)	defomity/bunion, metatarsal head callus, pinch callus on the medial aspect of 1st MTP, posterior tibialis tendinitis, peroneus longus tendinitis, shin splints, periostitis, tibial stress fracture
Ankle joint	Anterior impingement in FF equinus, excessive stretching of Achilles tendon
Knee joint	Pes anserine bursitis, patellofemoral and patella maltracking knee pain, patellar tendinitis, valgus (pronation) or varus stress on knee
Hip joint	Greater trochanter bursitis, ilio-tibial band syndrome, piriformis syndrome
Sacroiliac & lumbosacral spine	Sacroiliac joint dysfunction, functional leg length discrepancy, back pain

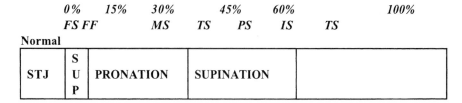

FIGURE 1.   Normal and abnormal timing of pronation.

FS-Foot Strike; FF — Foot flat; MS — Midstance; TS — Terminal Stance
PS — Preswing; IS- Initial Swing; TS — Terminal Swing, SUP - Supination

Note: Pronation at subtalar joint continuing well into the midstance and terminal stance in the patients with FF varus — a common developmental or acquired foot deformity where the FF is stuck in varus.

FIGURE 2.   Abnormal timing of compensation in forefoot varus.

biomechanical relationship between the tight AT and other disorders and incorporate this in their management.

ACHILLES TENDINITIS, RETROCALCANEAL BURSITIS, INSERTIONAL TENDINITIS

Disorders of the Achilles tendon are frequently encountered in physiatric practice. The incidence can be as high as 18% among the running population.[14] A tight AT may be the underlying biomechanical factor predisposing towards Achilles tendinopathy or pathology of other surrounding structures. On weight bearing, the tight AT does not allow dorsiflexion range of the HF, which necessitates compensatory pronation at the STJ-MTJ complex. This in turn allows for relative dorsiflexion of the FF compared with the HF (Table 2).

Intrinsic factors such as excessive subtalar motion, tibia varum, femoral anteversion, or functional overpronation can predispose to Achilles tendinitis. Twisting stress on the AT results from internal rotatory force on the tibia imparted from the

TABLE 4.   Conditions Predisposed Secondary To Tight Achilles Tendon

Achilles tendinopathy, pericalcaneal bursitis
Posterior tibialis myositis/tendinitis (runners shin splints)
Plantar fasciitis
Metarsalgia, seasmoiditis
Diabetic Charcot neuropathic osteoarthropathy with midfoot collapse

hyperpronated foot and external rotatory force on the knee accompanied with knee extension. From midstance to toe-off, the Achilles tendon is brought from an excessive lateral position relative to STJ to a medial position. This results in heel inversion thereby locking the transverse tarsal joint and creates a "whipping action" over the calcaneus combined with previously mentioned rotational forces on the tendon. Vascular blanching may result in a hypovascular zone, although the direct relationship between blood supply and incidence of rupture is unclear.[18]

Orthoses can be designed to dampen the speed and degree of the excessive pronatory moment, and are often the mainstay in treatment and prevention of recurrence. The AT has been shown to exhibit significantly less whipping and bowstringing with the use of a proper orthosis, as the tendon remains more medial to the subtalar joint axis. This reduces the pronatory influence of the AT and minimizes the tension on the tendon. The resultant wringing action of the AT that is implicated in both vascular impairment and development of subsequent degenerative changes likewise can be minimized.

An oversupinated foot can also contribute to Achilles tendon and surrounding soft tissue pathologies. For example, in cavus foot the calcaneus is more varus and vertical in attitude, which will make the bursal projection relatively more prominent posteriorly leading to irritation of these soft tissue structures.[11,29] Charcot-Marie-Tooth disease (CMT) patients typically develop a supinated and cavus foot. Patients develop FF valgus and equinus due to a plantarflexed 1st ray. HF varus may result at the STJ to compensate for the rigid plantarflexed 1st ray. This predisposes to pathologies of the Achilles tendon and surrounding structures due to the above mentioned mechanisms.[29]

FUNCTION OF ACHILLES TENDON IN POSTERIOR TIBIAL TENDON INSUFFICIENCY

PTT insufficiency is usually associated with pronation deformity. The AT may function as an evertor since the STJ axis is no longer lateral to the Achilles insertion. The AT becomes progressively shortened as the foot remains in a prolonged pronated position. Attempts to correct the STJ to a neutral position are rarely successful without restoring the flexibility of the Achilles tendon. This is often difficult, if not impossible, due to the already altered STJ axis as encountered in later stages of PTT insufficiency. Patients often complain of pain in the navicular area with footwear, foot orthoses, or ankle foot orthoses unless the Achilles shortening has been accommodated by a heel lift.

FUNCTION OF ACHILLES TENDON IN PLANTAR FASCIITIS

In addition to bony and ligamentous structures, the plantar fascia provides adjunctive support to maintain the arch. A tight AT is associated with pronation of the STJ and MTJ and subsequent flattening of arch. This can subject the plantar fascia to excessive stress resulting in pain and inflammation. Plantar fasciitis occurs as a result of micro-tears and fractures of the fibers and the subsequent painful inflammatory responses. Lengthening exercises of gastrocsoleus muscle unit are the mainstay of conservative management of plantar fasciitis. Since the Achilles tendon and plantar fascia function as one unit, gastrocsoleus lengthening exercises naturally stretch the plantar fascia as well. This is described in detail later in this chapter. Footwear with an elevated heel to accommodate the tight Achilles tendon reduces stress on the plantar fascia and may provide symptomatic relief.

The rehabilitation specialist should be careful in maintaining a fine balance between the use of heel accommodation and Achilles stretching exercises, which act in an essentially opposite manner, and the treatment approach should be specific to each patient.

FUNCTION OF ACHILLES TENDON IN FOREFOOT DISORDERS

FF pain that clinically presents as metatarsalgia, sesamoiditis, or interdigital neuritis is frequently aggravated by a tight AT which can cause an excessive shift of weight bearing from the HF to the FF. In addition, the plantarflexed ankle demands excessive dorsiflexion of the metatarsophalangeal joints during the push-off period in late mid stance. Management of forefoot pain should include a mild accommodating heel lift with gradual gastrocsoleus lengthening exercises. Higher heel lifts should be avoided in these patients as it can aggravate forefoot symptoms.

CHRONIC VENOUS ULCER

Patients with chronic venous ulcer around the ankle area have limited mobility secondary to pain and swelling. This can often result in a functional AT contracture. In our clinical practice, we have encountered many patients with venous ulcers, sickle cell anemia, compartment syndrome, and burns with longstanding gait disorders secondary to a shortened AT. In venous ulcer patients, once an equinus deformity develops, the effectiveness of the calf muscle venous-pump is significantly reduced. To prevent an equinus deformity, these patients should be instructed that the heels should be in contact with the ground during the weight-bearing phase of ambulation and when standing. Patients should avoid use of high-heeled shoes for relief of pain.

UPPER MOTOR NEURON DISEASE (STROKE, CEREBRAL PALSY, TBI)

Spasticity of the gastrocsoleus muscle often leads to knee recurvatum with pronation of the STJ to compensate for ankle equinus and the functional leg length discrepancy. Patients that are especially active and ambulate often develop low back pain, greater trochanteric bursitis or tendinitis, iliotibial band stress syndrome, or metatarsalgia. For knee pain in this population, clinicians should be on the lookout for knee pathologies related to hyperextension such as an overstretched posterior capsule, popliteus muscle dysfunction, ligamentous instability, or anterior fat pad impingement.

Management includes Achilles lengthening exercises, treatment of spasticity with nerve or neuromuscular blocks (phenol or botulinum toxin) or accommodation with a heel lift and the use of ankle foot orthoses (AFO). When prescribing an AFO in early upper motor neuron disorders, the rehabilitation specialist should consider the natural history of spasticity and take steps to prevent the development of a spastic equinus deformity. Flexible dorsiflexion assist AFOs without plantarflexion stops such as a posterior leaflet spring orthosis (PLSO) may serve the purpose initially but turn out to be an inappropriate choice. An AFO with adjustable ankle range can be useful in these patients, as it has a plantarflexion stop to help control spasticity related equinus. The adjustable ankle range also allows for therapeutic stretching of the tight AT during ambulation.

FRACTURES OF ANKLE

Patients may develop AT and long toe flexor tightness simultaneously in the months after management of distal tibia and/or ankle fractures. Patients with ankle fractures commonly have associated tethering of the long toe flexors. On weight bearing and subsequently stretching of the AT, patients may present with curling of the toes, pain on the distal tip of the toes, and hallux limitus. Prevention of this complication can be achieved with early mobilization of Achilles tendon as well as the long toe flexors. In prescribing an ankle splint for these patients, the foot plate of splint should be extended to include the toes. Mobilization exercises of the toe flexors should be performed simultaneously with range of motion exercises of the ankle. This can significantly lessen future gait related problems.

ELDERLY WITH DIFFICULTY OF GAIT

A tight AT is common in the elderly and may contribute to gait abnormalities. In the elderly, the center of gravity is located more posterior and the tight AT can easily throw the body weight backward.[10] These patients complain of a feeling of falling backwards or may have difficulty in getting up from a chair. This symptom can be aggravated further in patients with underlying central nervous system disorders such as normal pressure hydrocephalus, parkinsonism or cervical spondylotic myelopathy.

The elderly may complain of calf pain and tenderness from acute stretching of the gastrocsoleus muscle on weight bearing after prolonged bed rest or after changing to footwear with lower heels. Because stretching exercises of the gastrocsoleus muscle can be an arduous and often impossible task, an accommodative heel lift can dramatically improve the gait pattern of these patients.

Footwear prescriptions for these patients should include some heel accommodation. Most sneakers have a limited heel height differential (the height difference between the forefoot and hindfoot) of less than $\frac{1}{2}$ inch as compared to that of common footwear ($\frac{3}{4}$ inch). Sneakers with lower heel heights force the STJ to hyperpronate to compensate for the tight AT. In our practice we provide $\frac{1}{4}$ inch heel lifts inside sneakers to accommodate the tight AT.

CAVUS FOOT

In cavus foot, the calcaneus is more varus and vertical (tilting more posteriorly), which will make the bursal projection relatively more prominent posteriorly. This leads to irritation of Achilles tendon and surrounding structures.[11,29] Depending on the etiology and underlying biomechanical abnormalities, the Achilles tendon length can be variable in a cavus foot. In most instances patients with cavus foot have associated tight ATs and lengthening exercises are therefore an appropriate management strategy.

In some patients with cavus foot, however, rigid FF equinus (excessive plantarflexion of FF) is more prominent than the equinus deformity of the ankle. For these patients, heel lifts would be the mainstay of conservative management rather than stretching of the gastrocsoleus muscle complex.

Over-Lengthened Achilles Tendon

CONDITIONS ASSOCIATED WITH OVER-LENGTHENED ACHILLES TENDON

The gait of patients with AT insufficiency and over-lengthening is described as a calcaneal gait. The calcaneal gait lacks push-off, has a shorter stride length, and patients weight-bear on the heel during ambulation. The gait may appear as if a patient is stepping into a pothole. Patients with calcaneal deformity typically have difficulty in knee control (buckling of the knees) because the dorsiflexed ankle generates a flexion momentum at the knee. The calcaneal gait may be present in patients with ruptured Achilles tendon, poliomyelitis, or meningomyelocele. It can be observed in patients after tendo Achilles lengthening (TAL) for spastic-equinus conditions. Patients receiving TAL surgery are placed in a cast with the ankle in relative plantarflexion to prevent this disabling deformity.

Conservative management of this deformity with footwear and orthoses is challenging and often more difficult than management of an equinus deformity.

In the patient with flexible calcaneal deformity, high top shoes with slightly elevated heel would be a simple and rather effective option. Further extensive bracing with a dorsiflexion stop is difficult since the dorsal skin of the foot may not be sturdy enough for such a bulky brace. Fixed calcaneus deformities are even harder to manage than flexible ones. Placing a sole lift in the footwear under the FF may bring the ground reaction force up to the patient's FF and reduces the flexion momentum of the knee. This is opposite to the principle of managing the fixed ankle equinus deformity with heel elevation.

FOREFOOT EQUINUS

As briefly discussed above, FF equinus usually occurs in the cavus foot (e.g., Charcot-Marie-Tooth disease), although it can be seen in other congenital or acquired disorders. A patient with FF-equinus will achieve heel contact on the ground by compensatory mechanisms in the sagittal plane. In contrast, to the compensation for ankle equinus deformity which occur at the STJ and MTJ, the compensation for forefoot equinus in cavus foot mainly occurs in the ankle and knee joints. This is secondary to the associated limited mobility of the STJ and MTJ. The Achilles tendon is often over-stretched since the tibio-talar (ankle) joint must utilize its full dorsiflexion range to compensation for FF equinus. Practicing clinicians often fail to recognize the above biomechanical significance of the FF-equinus and prescribe gastrocsoleus stretching exercise under the erroneous assumption of a tight AT in these patients. In this instance, a surgical correction of the FF-equinus deformity or accommodation of the FF-equinus with heel lifts would be appropriate.

EFFECT OF PTT ON DISORDERS OF THE LOWER EXTREMITY

The anterior tibialis functions as an antagonistic pair with the PLT, while the PTT works functionally with the PBT. These musculotendinous complexes work as functional antagonists as their insertions are on opposite sides of the same bones (ATT-PLT) or have opposite anatomic function (PTT-PBT). The ATT-PLT complex inserts on opposite aspects of the 1st ray with the PLT functioning as a 1st ray depressor. The PTT inverts while the PBT functions as an evertor of the hindfoot. These four muscles, especially the PTT and PL, are the primary dynamic stabilizers providing the locking mechanism of the hindfoot and midfoot. The secondary restraints to the longitudinal arch include the FHL, FDL, plantar fascia, spring ligament, and capsule of the talonavicular joint.

Without the function of PTT (primary dynamic stabilizer), the foot cannot be transformed into a rigid lever. The unopposed forward propulsive force of the gastrocsoleus muscle complex, therefore, acts at the midfoot instead of the metatarsal heads, creating excessive midfoot stress. Since the secondary restraints are weaker and have less mechanical advantage than the PTT, symptoms related to their compromise, such as plantar fasciitis, pericuboidal pain, and medial midfoot pain under the talonavicular articulation, can occur.[4]

The loss of PTT function with progression in the stages of PTT insufficiency[28] also results in the peroneus brevis muscle acting unopposed in a dynamic abduction eversion force. This can result in the development of HF and FF abduction. As the heel assumes an increased valgus alignment, the AT becomes positioned lateral to the axis of rotation of the STJ. The AT, therefore, assumes a role as an evertor instead of as an invertor of the calcaneus. Over time this shortened position of the AT becomes rigid and makes conservative management of PTT difficult. Excessive eversion of the calcaneus results in arthritic changes in the STJ and a lateral impingement between the calcaneus and fibula, creating significant pain and discomfort at the subfibular and lateral aspect of sinus tarsi area.

EFFECT OF PERONEAL TENDONS ON THE DISORDERS OF LOWER EXTREMITY

Peroneal Tendon Insufficiency

Peroneal tendon insufficiency is commonly seen after ankle trauma such as fracture or sprain. Patients may develop chronic and recurrent pain and swelling around the posterior malleolus, extending proximally to the shin. Initial edema control with Unna boots and footwear with a lateral flare or a lateral wedge in the shoe are commonly utilized to reduce the stress on the peroneal tendons.

Symptoms Related to Peroneal Tendon Overuse

Peroneal tendon overuse can occur in a biomechanically disadvantaged foot. Two clinical scenarios have been commonly noticed in our practice. When the patient's footwear has excessive lateral wear of the heel, the foot tends to slide laterally. This places excessive varus stress to the foot and can lead to PLT overuse. A similar situation may occur with the use a pronation control foot orthosis when the medial arch support is aggressive and lacks appropriate lateral balancing; this is particularly likely when the footwear has weak lateral counter. Early on, local tenderness may be noted on physical examination at the proximal lateral shin where the main muscle belly of the PL is located. Subjective pain in the area usually follows. Management includes avoidance of an excessively worn lateral heel and reducing medial arch of the foot orthosis (FO) while providing appropriate lateral balance.

Peroneal Tendons in Charcot-Marie-Tooth (CMT) Disease

The tibialis anterior muscle (1st ray elevator) is involved early in the disease while PLT (1st ray depressor and functional antagonist of tibialis anterior) remains strong. The imbalance of these two muscle groups can cause progressive 1st ray plantarflexion secondary to the unopposed action of the PLT leading to the development of FF valgus.

Early in the disease process the PBT is involved, while its functional antagonist the PTT along with the gastrocnemius-soleus are usually unaffected. Relative unopposed action of the PTT against the PBT actively induces HF varus, which may already occur as a compensatory mechanism for FF valgus. It is postulated that the above concept of dynamic pairing and unopposed muscle imbalance may be responsible for the characteristic FF valgus with HF varus in these patients, although the exact mechanism is not clearly understood.[1]

Peroneal Tendons and Cuboido-Metatarsal Instability/Pain

Chronic idiopathic or post-traumatic lateral midfoot pain is not uncommon. Patients may complain of vague lateral midfoot pain, and it is often difficult to identify the exact location of the pathology. Many patients have a history of previous and recurrent ankle sprains or trauma to the foot. The symptoms may emanate from

pathology of the ligaments, tendons, synovium, or other articulating structures surrounding the cuboid bone (calcaneoocuboidal, metatarsocuboidal, cuboid-cuneiform,
and cuboidonavicular joints). The above constellation of symptoms is termed "pericuboidal arthritis/synovitis pain" by some authors. The exact role of the midfoot stabilizers (tendons) and the AT is not clearly understood; however, treatment of this
condition should address the dysfunction related to these tendons. Management principles include cuboid support (for the instability) with pronation control as the mainstay.
A cuboid pad and midfoot taping should be used only in sturdy footwear. Pronation
control can be provided with an insole foot orthosis or with a UCBL with an incorporated cuboid pad for additional control of FF abduction and calcaneal eversion.

Acute subluxation of the cuboid and derangement of the cuboid at the base of
the 4th and 5th metatarsals may occur during sports activities.[16] This condition is
seen more often in patients with hyperpronated feet. The pulling of the PLT against
ankle inversion is implicated to be the mechanism of the cuboid subluxation. Manual
reduction followed by cuboid padding and taping provides symptomatic relief. An
FO may be required for some patients to treat the underlying biomechanics.

Lateral Ankle Instability

The peroneal tendons are secondary stabilizers of the lateral ankle in addition
to the ligament. Patients with chronic peroneus brevis insufficiency may complain
of pain, swelling, and instability of lateral ankle.[2,5,12,19,26,31] Conversely, the longer
ankle instability is present, the greater the risk of a peroneus brevis tear.[25]

INFLUENCE OF THE TENDONS IN THE CARE OF THE DIABETIC FOOT AND PARTIAL FOOT AMPUTATIONS

Most diabetic foot care literature focuses on wound care, footwear, or orthosis
management. Abnormal biomechanics in the diabetic foot are rather common and
need to be addressed, as they may play a rather important role in the development of
deformities and non-healing wounds. Non-enzymatic glycation of soft tissue structures in diabetes can result in AT inflexibility. The tight AT does not allow the tibia
to roll over the foot during stance phase, placing excessive stress and shear on the
midfoot and forefoot. This contributes to aggravation of midfoot Charcot neuroarthropathy, forefoot ulcers, and wound recurrence after partial foot amputation.
Since weight bearing gastrocsoleus muscle lengthening exercises can be precarious
and may frequently aggravate the problems, surgical lengthening may be the treatment option for these patients.

In partial foot amputation, the peroneus longus and long toe extensors are usually lost while the AT, PTT, and anterior tibialis are functionally preserved depending on the level of the amputation. These patients frequently develop inversion or
inversion-equinus deformity of the HF and MF. As a result, the patients can develop
recurrent ulcers at the stump unless appropriate reconstructive tendon transfer procedures are performed, possibly at the time of surgery. In addition, Achilles tendon
lengthening (TAL) and capsulotomy of the ankle and STJ may be required.[6]

THERAPEUTIC EXERCISES

Achilles Tendon Lengthening Exercise

As we recognize the biomechanical role of the Achilles tendon and importance
of maintaining the proper strength and length, the rehabilitation medicine specialist
should be familiar with the AT lengthening exercises and its pitfalls.

The practitioner must not only be able to differentiate between a tight gastrocnemius vs. soleus, but also be familiar with the end-feel and understand if there is a tight capsule that is preventing full ankle range of motion. During overpressure, at the end point of the patient's passive range of motion (with the muscles relaxed), only inert structures are being stressed. If the end-feel is firm, but one is not at the end of normal passive range of the ankle joint, this end-feel may be related to related to stretching of the joint capsule or ligaments.[13]

Most functional demands on the ankle and foot occur in weight-bearing postures. Kinesthetic input from skin, joint, and muscle receptors and the resulting joint and muscle responses are different in open and closed kinematic chain activities. As the gastroc-soleus muscle tendon complex can accept up to 7000 N of force, its lengthening is best achieved in weight bearing rather than with open chain exercises. The assist of gravity during weight bearing can quickly increase the length of the gastrocsoleus complex, but it is important that the subtalar joint is positioned in neutral or in slight supination to lock the midfoot by partially rotating the leg inwards. This should help stretch the gastrocsoleus complex, instead of stretching the midfoot and plantar fascia. The patient strides forward with one foot, keeping the heel of the other foot flat on the floor. He then shifts his body weight forward on to the front foot. The patient should keep the knee of the hind leg extended for lengthening of the gastrocnemius muscle, and flexed for lengthening of the soleus muscle.

Patients who have difficulty in performing above techniques may try an alternative lengthening technique by standing on an inclined board with FF pointing upward and heels downward. A small pocket book may be used as an alternative to the wedge. A greater stretch will occur if the patient leans forward.[13]

It is important for patients to have appropriate biofeedback during the lengthening exercise. Patients need to be educated that they should feel the sensation of a stretch, not pain, in the area of the gastrocsoleus muscle belly instead of Achilles tendon area. The stretch should be maintained for an extended period of time (at least 30 seconds), without bouncing, and be performed as many times as possible (at least 6 times per day).[22]

Since patients frequently use an incorrect technique, practitioners should ask them to demonstrate and correct their technique during each visit, as necessary.[22] Practitioners as well as patients should be patient about the result of lengthening exercises since the process of AT lengthening is tedious, often requiring several weeks to months before results are noted. Accommodation with a heel lift may be used as a temporary measure until satisfactory lengthening is achieved.

As discussed earlier, patients with capsular contractures of the ankle and STJ will not respond to stretching exercises. In earlier stages, joint mobilization by an experienced physical therapist in the non-diabetic foot can be attempted. Also, patients with diabetic Charcot neuropathic osteoarthropathy of the midfoot are not candidates for Achilles lengthening exercise, as weight bearing exercises may in fact further damage midfoot structures by the so called nutcracker effect. Patients with a short partial foot amputation and short lever arm of the foot exert excessive pressure to the amputation stump. The better approach may be surgical lengthening in these cases.

Posterior Tibialis Strengthening

Posterior tibialis strengthening can be effectively achieved with the patient trying to eccentrically control forces as he moves from lateral to medial in the weight bearing position. Have the barefoot patient weight-bear more on the involved lower extremity, moving the foot more into pronation along with hip and knee internal rotation followed by moving patient into foot supination. Further eccentric strengthening can be stimulated by single leg standing, using a wobble board, a half inch foam roller with flat side down, then flat side up or on a decline slant board. PTT strengthening should be initiated in early PTT dysfunction as pain subsides. In later stages of PTT insufficiency, strengthening may not only be ineffective but possibly detrimental.

Dorsal Intrinsic Strengthening

Dorsal intrinsic strengthening is usually indicated to support the medial arch. In sitting, have the patient place her foot on the floor on top of a towel then scrunch her toes in order to move the towel proximally. Increase the difficulty by having the patient complete this activity in weight bearing. Lastly, move patient into the heel off position with the contralateral limb forward while the patient again tries to scrunch at the towel. This will strengthen the intrinsic foot muscles during the push-off position of gait.

SUMMARY

It is important to develop an understanding of the anatomy and function of the key tendons of the foot in normal and pathologic conditions. The role of these muscles and tendons in the biomechanics of the foot should be considered in regards to the lower extremity response to pronation/supination in weight bearing and locomotion.

In managing these tendon pathologies, identification of the underlying biomechanical factors and related proximal kinematics is crucial. Specific soft tissue symptoms and signs in the lower extremity can be correlated to these biomechanical factors. Biomechanical orthotic management, therapeutic exercises, non-surgical and surgical management should be targeted to address these biomechanical factors. These factors should be evaluated and managed along with the clinically presenting tendon dysfunction (cause and effect relationship) for effective and long lasting results.

REFERENCES

1. Alexander IJ, Fleissner PR Jr: Pes cavus: Pediatric orthopedic problems. Foot Ankle Clin 3(4):723–735, 1998.
2. Bassett FH, Speer KP: Longitudinal rupture of the peroneal tendons. Am J Sports Med 21:354, 1993.
3. Bates BT, Osternig LR, Mason B, et al: Foot orthotic devices to modify selected aspects of lower extremity mechanics. Am J Sports Med 7:338–342, 1979.
4. Baumhauer JF: Pathologic anatomy. Foot Ankle Clin 2(2):217–225, 1997.
5. Bonnin M, Tavernier T, Bouysset M: Split lesions of the peroneus brevis tendon in chronic ankle laxity. Am J Sports Med 25:699, 1997.
6. Brodsky JW: Amputation and prostheses of the foot and ankle. In Coughlin MJ, Mann RA (eds): Surgery of the Foot and Ankle, 7th ed. St. Louis, Mosby, 1999, pp 970–1006.
7. Clement DB, Taunton JE, Smart GW: Achilles tendinitis and peritendinitis: Etiology and treatment. Am J Sports Med 12:182, 1980.
8. Clement DB, Taunton JE, Smart GW: Achilles tendinitis and peritendinitis: Etiology and treatment. Am J Sports Med 12:182, 1980.
9. Cummings JE, Anson JB, Carr WB, et al: The structure of the calcaneal tendon in relation to orthopedic surgery with additional observations on the plantaris muscle. Surg Gynecol Obstet 83:107, 1946.
10. Elble RJ: Changes in gait with normal aging. Gait disorders of aging. Falls and therapeutic strategies. (Ed: Masedeu JC, Sudarsky L, Wolfson L: Chapter 6.) Philadelphia, Lippincott-Raven, 1997, pp 93–105.
11. Fuglsang F, Torup B: Bursitis retrocalcanearis. Acta Orthop Scand 30:315, 1961.
12. Krause J, Brodsky J: Peroneus brevis tendon tears: Pathophysiology, surgical reconstruction and clinical results. Foot Ankle 9:271, 1998.

13. Kisner C, Colby LA: Therapeutic Exercise, Foundation and Techniques, 2nd ed. Philadelphia, FA Davis, 1990, pp 5, 396.
14. Krissoff WB, Ferris WD: Runner's injuries. Physician Sport Med 7:55–64, 1979.
15. Mann RA: Biomechanical approach to the treatment of foot problems. Foot Ankle 2:205–212, 1982.
16. Mann RA: Acquired flatfoot in adults. Clin Orthop 181:46–51, 1983.
17. Manter JT: Movements of subtalar and transverse tarsal joints. Anat Rec 80:397–409, 1941.
18. Marks RM: Achilles tendinopathy. Peritendinitis, pantendinitis and insertional disorders. Foot Ankle Clin 4(4):789–809, 1994.
19. Mason R, Henderson I: Traumatic peroneal tendon instability. Am J Sports Med 24:652, 1996.
20. Minkowsky JM, Minkowsky R: The spine, an integral part of the lower extremity. (Chapter 4: Clinical biomechanics of the lower extremities. Ed: Valmassy RL.) St. Louis, Mosby, 1996, pp 95–112.
21. Myerson MS, Mandelbaum BR: Disorders of Achilles tendon and retrocalcaneal region. Foot and Ankle Disorder. (Ed: Myerson MS) Philadelphia, WB Saunders, 2000, pp 1367–1398.
22. Riley MA: The Gastrocnemius Stretch. Guidelines for Foot Orthotics. Thorofare, NJ, Slack, 1995, pp 26–27.
23. Root M, Weed J, Orien W: Clinical Biomechanics, Vol II. Normal and Abnormal Function of the Foot, Los Angeles, 10–17, 1977.
24. Sammarco GJ: Injuries to the tibialis anterior, peroneal tendons, and long flexors and extensors of the toes. In Baxter D (ed): The Foot and Ankle in Sport. St. Louis, Mosby, 1995, p 53.
25. Sammarco GJ, DiRaimondo C: Chronic peroneus brevis tendon lesions. Foot Ankle 9:163, 1989.
26. Sammarco GJ: Peroneal tendon injuries. Orthop Clin North Am 25:135, 1994.
27. Schmidt-Rohlfing B, Graf J, et al: The blood supply of the Achilles tendon. Int Orthop 16(1):29–31, 1992.
28. Sferra JJ, Rosenberg GA: Nonoperative treatment of posterior tibial tendon pathology. Foot Ankle Clin 2(2):261–273, 1997.
29. Stephens MM: Haglund's deformity and retrocalcaneal bursitis. Orthop Clin North Am 25(1):41–46, 1994.
30. Soma CA, Mandelbaum BR: Achilles tendon disorders. Clin Sports Med 13:811–823, 1994.
31. Yodlowski M, Mizel M: Reconstruction of peroneus brevis pathology. Techniques Orthop Surg 4:146, 1994.

PHALA A. HELM, MD
GEETHA PANDIAN, MD

PHYSIATRIC MANAGEMENT OF THE DIABETIC FOOT AND FOOT ULCERS

From Department of Physical
  Medicine and Rehabilitation
University of Texas Southwestern
  Medical Center
Dallas, Texas

Reprint requests to:
Department of Physical Medicine
  and Rehabilitation
University of Texas Southwestern
  Medical Center
5323 Harry Hines Boulevard
Dallas, TX 75390-9055

In the specialty of physical medicine and rehabilitation, we frequently see patients with complications secondary to diabetes mellitus. We are able to treat complications such as cerebral vascular accidents, amputations, peripheral neuropathy, peripheral vascular disease, and others effectively. However, we are not as effective in recognizing and managing diabetic foot problems that lead to amputation. Prevention of amputations in diabetics has not been an area our specialty has emphasized. Since the diabetic population represents a large percentage of our practice, we must learn how to care for their feet, thereby preventing further complications of this undertreated area. Table 1 shows important statistics for ulcers and amputation that support our reasoning of why physical medicine should be more involved in diabetic foot care. Proper patient evaluation is necessary to develop a successful treatment plan. Table 2 outlines an assessment guide for diabetic foot patients.

RISK FACTORS FOR FOOT ULCERATION

A recent study of pathways leading to diabetic foot ulcers identified peripheral neuropathy as the *most common component* cause and was present in 78% of the ulcer pathways.[29] Dr. Paul Brand's statements about sensory loss still holds true. He said, "The truth is that when sensation is lost, even intelligent people lose all sense of identity with their insensate parts. An insensitive limb feels like a wooden block fastened to a body and is treated as such. It is a deep rejection of a 'dead'

TABLE 1.   Important Statistics for Diabetics

5.9% prevalence of diabetes in the United States[9]

15% will develop foot ulcer[23]

14–24% of people will require amputation[3]

50% of all non-tramautic lower extremity amputations are diabetics[23]

50% of the amputations are toes[23]

43–65% of the amputations are transtibial or transfemoral[23]

85% of all amputations are preceded by a non-healing foot ulcer[23]

2–4 fold increase in ulcers and amputations with age and duration of diabetes[23]

1.6 increased risk of ulcers in males[23]

25% of all diabetic hospital admissions are for diabetic foot problems[9]

Average admission for foot infection 22 days[18]

60–70% of diabetics with foot ulcers have neuropathy without vascular disease[18]

15–20% have neuropathy and vascular disease[18]

5% with diabetes < 20 years reported current or past foot ulcer[23]

30–40% of foot ulcers recurred in people who returned to their original footwear[23]

11-fold increase in risk of ulcers in patients with calluses[23]

TABLE 2.   Guidelines for Assessment of Diabetic Foot Patients

Proper patient evaluation is necessary to develop a treatment plan.

Medical History
- Duration of wound
- Initiating trauma
- Prior treatment
- Previous wounds
- Previous surgeries on foot
- Revascularization, venous surgery

Neurologic Examination
- Deep tendon reflexes.
- Protective sensation—test with 10-g 5.07 Semmes Weinstein monofilament. Test plantar surface of toes and metatarsal heads. One to three of six sites better define an insensitive foot.
- Dry scaly skin and fissuring can be caused by autonomic neuropathy that leads to abnormalities of regulation of skin temperature and sweating.
- Intrinsic muscle weakness of the feet (motor neuropathy) can cause clawing of the toes.

Vascular Examination
- Examine for pulses—dorsalis pedis and posterior tibialis. Check ankle arm index (AAI) or ankle brachial index (ABI) if pulses are absent. Lower normal limit 0.94–0.97. Critical ischemia ABI < 0.5.
- Toe pressures are not routinely needed. May be more accurate reflection of blood supply to the foot.
- Toe pressures 45 mm Hg indicates better chance of ulcer healing.
- Transcutaneous pressure of oxygen (TcpO$_2$) also not routinely indicated. TcpO$_2$ values < 30 mm Hg are a high risk factor associated with foot ulcer.

Musculoskeletal
- Gait evaluation
- Range of motion assessment of hip, knee, ankle, and foot.
- Check for bony deformities of the foot.

Soft Tissue Examination
- Examine for corns, calluses, plantar warts, fungal infections.
- Check toenails for fungal infections, length and roughness.
- Evaluate skin for dryness, fissures and suppleness.

part".[7] Considering all of the potential risk factors patients with a neuropathy have, the chance of developing a foot ulcer without proper care and patient education is overwhelming.

Bony Abnormalities

HALLUX VALGUS (BUNION)

A bunion is a lateral deviation of the great toe at the metatarsophalangeal (MT) joint that may lead to a prominence of the medial aspect of this joint. There can be swelling of the area aggravated by shoe wear. The great toe may slide over or under the second toe, creating a high pressure area. High pressure areas can occur over the medial aspect of the MT joint, dorsal 2nd toe, and between the great toe and 2nd toe leading to ulceration.

BUNIONETTE (TAYLOR'S BUNION)

This is a deformity of the fifth metatarsophalangeal joint. There is prominence of the 5th metatarsal head and medial deviation of the small toe. There is often an overlying hard callus created by pressure from narrow-toed shoes.

HALLUX RIGIDUS

This deformity is caused by degenerative arthritis of the metatarsophalangeal (MT) joint of the great toe. This causes stiffness in extension (dorsiflexion). Lack of extension increases the pressure on the plantar aspect of the great toe at push off and can lead to ulceration.

MALLET TOE

A mallet toe is a flexion deformity of the distal interphalangeal (DIP) joint. The second toe is the one most commonly involved. A callus can develop that could progress to an ulcer.

CLAWTOES

This deformity is characterized by extension at the metatarsophalangeal (MT) joint, flexion of the proximal interphalangeal joint (PIP), and sometimes the distal interphalangeal joint (DIP). It is caused by intrinsic muscle weakness and affects all the toes. It also results in a high arched cavus foot. High pressure areas are created over the dorsal aspect of the toes (PIP joint), the tips of the toes, and over the metatarsal heads. Calluses can form in these areas. Fat pad subluxation distally over the metatarsal heads can also occur, exposing the metatarsal heads to increased pressure (Fig. 1).

CHARCOT DEFORMITIES

The current theory is that following the development of autonomic neuropathy there is increased blood flow to the extremity resulting in osteopenia. In view of abnormal stresses on the extremity, there is often profound osseous destruction resulting in collapse and bony prominences that create high pressure areas and possible skin breakdown. This will be discussed in more detail later in the chapter.

HINDFOOT VARUS

This deformity can cause increased pressure under the lateral border of the foot at the base of the fifth metatarsal.

Table 3 describes treatment protocols for bony abnormalities.

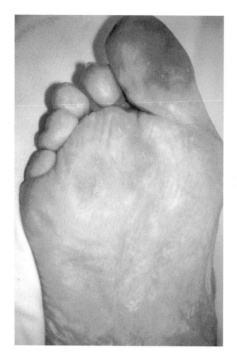

FIGURE 1. Fat pad subluxation over metatarsal heads resulting in high pressure areas.

Soft Tissue Problems

CALLUSES (HYPERKERATOTIC TISSUE)

Hard calluses develop in areas of the foot subjected to increased pressures, particularly the metatarsal heads. The callus causes an increase of forces on the underlying

TABLE 3. Treatment of Bony Abnormalities

Hallux valgus (bunion)	1. Shoe with wide/deep toe box.
	2. Passively stretch great toe in medial direction, stabilizing the remainder of the foot.
	3. Splint great toe in medial direction for night wear if patient has sensation.
	4. Surgery for severe deformities and persistent ulcers.
Bunionette	1. Soft shoe that has roomy toe box.
	2. Callus trimming.
	3. Digipad (silicone pad) that fits over fifth toe.
Hallux rigidus	1. A rigid sole shoe will help prevent additional pressure on the great toe at push off.
Mallet toe	1. Callus trimming.
	2. Soft custom insoles.
	3. Surgery to straighten toe if persistent ulcers.
Hindfoot varus	1. Lateral heel wedge.
Clawtoes	1. Deep roomy toe box as seen in extra depth shoes.
	2. Custom molded insole.
	3. Callus trimming.
	4. Passive stretching of the toes.
	5. Surgical correction if ulceration persists.
Charcot joints	1. May need custom made shoes.

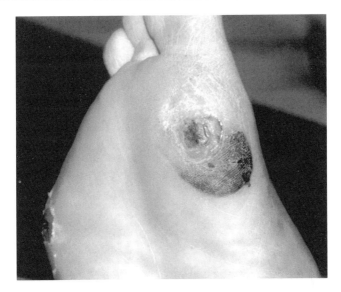

FIGURE 2.   A hematoma has developed as a result of shear forces, and when debrided an ulcer will be visible.

tissues. The callus is like a "rock" in the shoe that cannot be felt by a person with an insensate foot. The subcutaneous tissue becomes trapped between bone and thick skin below and is subjected to shear force with walking. The increased forces lead to tissue breakdown, and a sterile deep hematoma develops (Fig. 2). Neuropathic ulcers begin deep to the skin. One may see underlying hemorrhage with above skin callus intact. When the callus is trimmed, an ulcer is discovered.[22]

CORNS

Hard corns occur over bony prominences of the toes, and soft corns occur most commonly between the fourth and fifth toes. Soft corns are usually caused by tight shoes that result in pressure between the condyle of a phalanx of one toe and the condyle of the head of the adjacent metatarsal.

PLANTAR WARTS

Plantar warts develop any place a wart virus has infected. There are three types: single, mother-daughter, and mosaic. Usually the single type occurs under bony prominences. It is a small horny lesion that may be as large as 7 mm in diameter. Callus surrounds it, and the papillary lines diverge around it. Shaving the hyperkeratotic tissue reveals a sharply outlined, horny margin with visible capillary tips. The mother-daughter type may also occur under a pressure point. The mother wart is surrounded by small satellites (daughters). Shaving the keratotic tissue reveals a large lesion that looks like the single wart and the satellites with a central capillary tip. The mosaic type resembles a callus because of a granular keratotic surface. It may reach a size of 5 cm in diameter. Warts are usually tender if pinched from side to side. The skin lines cross the calluses, while they go around the plantar warts.

INGROWN TOENAILS

An ingrown toenail occurs because of improper nail trimming, tight shoes, thickened nail, congenital deformity of the nail, hereditary predisposition, or trauma.

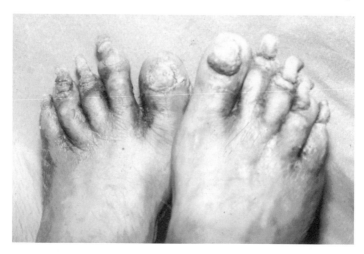

FIGURE 3. Fungal infection of the toenails causes toenails to thicken, resulting in increased pressure inside footwear.

There are three types of ingrown nails: (1) normal nail plate—with improper trimming, develops spur that grows into nailfold; (2) lateral nail margin grows inward; (3) soft tissue hypertrophy over normal nail plate.[26] If the skin breaks down, bacteria or fungus can cause an infection.

ONYCHOMYCOSIS

Fungal infections of the toenails are the most common skin condition affecting diabetics (Fig. 3). Etiology of the infection is unclear; however, some believe that diabetic neuropathy may predispose the patient to subungual hemorrhage, increasing the chance of infection. The fungus lifts the nail plate dorsally, and as the nail becomes thicker, pressure from shoes may lead to subungual hematoma and ulceration.[19]

LIMITED JOINT MOBILITY

Studies have shown that stiffness of the hands and skin thickening are commonly seen in diabetics.[23] As a result, patients have limited joint mobility, a condition referred to as cheiroarthropathy. It has been shown that non-enzymatic glycosylation of collagen is accelerated in diabetics and results in abnormally cross-linked collagens that are usually resistant to degradation.[10] Others have shown that the joints of the foot can also be affected, and that limited joint mobility may predispose to foot ulceration[10,13] (Fig. 4). Fernando showed in his study that limited joint mobility may be a major factor in causing abnormally high plantar foot pressures.[15] A tight Achilles tendon often seen in diabetics can cause increased forefoot pressure.

GAIT ABNORMALITIES

People with neuropathy are more likely to have gait abnormalities of postural instability and sway. This may have clinical significance and increase the risk of minor trauma and ulcerations.[20]

TOE AMPUTATIONS

Studies have shown that amputations of the toes of a foot increase the risk of ulcerations on other parts of the foot. Diabetic patients with amputation of the great

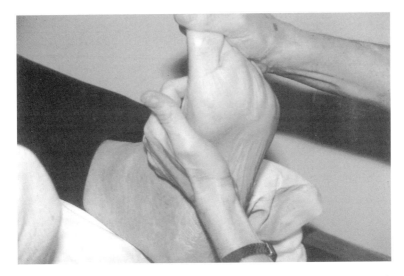

FIGURE 4.   Mobilization of a diabetic's stiff foot can aid in pressure redistribution.

toe develop deformities of the remaining toes and metatarsophalangeal joints. This results in high foot pressures and subsequent ulceration. It has been suggested that stability provided by the great toe is transferred laterally to the lesser toes and in order to stabilize the foot, the lateral toes contract.[28]

Table 4 describes treatment protocols of soft tissue problems.

Miscellaneous High Risk Factors

- Smoking impedes blood flow by multiple harmful mechanisms including vasospasm.
- Poor vision impairs patients' ability for self-exam. One study found 71% of the patients in a high risk foot clinic had poor vision.[12]
- Obesity can increase plantar pressures and prevent the patient from reaching the feet to examine them or deliver foot care.
- Poor glycemic control is reported to delay wound healing.
- Cognitive problems, living alone, poor compliance to treatments, and denial of existing problems all interfere with care of the patient.
- Alcohol consumption has been associated with an increased risk of foot ulcers.
- Tight footwear can cause increased pressure on medial and lateral foot.
- TED hose may strangulate toes, causing skin breakdown.

Patient Education

Basic foot care and recognition of impending foot problems are information with which the entire foot team should be aware. This should be taught to the patient, the family, and friends and reviewed on an "as needed" basis, which is usually several times a year. We need to emphasize to our patients about "neglect" and "subconscious rejection" of their foot problems.[7] Dr. Brand says, "education and reinforcement must be done with sympathy, understanding and good humor if it is to succeed."[7]

TABLE 4.   Treatment of Soft Tissue Problems

Callus	1. Callus shaving—soak feet several minutes before shaving. Place blade tangential to the lesion. When shaved flat, callus has a waxy appearance with no visible blood vessels, and normal papillary lines. 2. Removal of callus can reduce peak plantar pressure by 29%.[35]
Corn	1. Separate involved toes with digipad or lambswool. 2. Change footwear to a wider toe box shoe. 3. Surgical excision of condyle if problem persists.
Plantar warts	1. Surgery is contraindicated because of scarring. 2. Most lesions resolve in 5–6 months. 3. Shave the wart down to flat surface.
Ingrown toenails	1. Proper nail trimming (trim to contour of toe, not straight across) and extend 2 mm from nail bed. 2. Insert waxed dental floss beneath nail bed with blunt instrument and lift nail edge and pack the area.[9] 3. If purulent drainage, begin broad spectrum antibiotics. 4. Surgical ablation may be necessary.
Onychomycosis	1. Trim mycotic nail with a bone cutting tool (double action rongeur). Trim in multiple small bites and smooth with an electric sander. Protect eyes and wear a mask. 2. Paint nails with gentian violet. This can cause some thinning of the nail. 3. Oral medications with culture cure rates 70–80% are itraconazole and terbinafine. The medications are expensive, and there is a high recurrence rate of infection.[23]
Limited joint mobility	1. Paraffin (cooled to 118°F) to the feet followed by massage and mobilization. 2. Passive range of motion of the feet following paraffin. 3. Baps board with patient standing for additional active range of motion of feet and ankles. 4. Heel cord stretching for tight Achilles tendon.

FOOT ULCERATION

The most common sites of foot ulcerations are under the metatarsal heads, the medial sesamoid, dorsum of the interphalangeal joints of the toes, navicular tuberosity, and base of the fifth metatarsal.[9] Foot ulcerations in the diabetic patient are chronic wounds and appear to be "stuck" in the inflammatory, proliferative process, allowing for repeated injury, infection, and inflammation, thus impairing wound closure.[3] Fibrin that accumulates at the base of an ulcer may retard granulation. Callus may grow around the periphery of a healing ulcer, and it may grow over the ulcer, preventing full epithelialization.[18] Peripheral neuropathy is the most consistent factor associated with foot ulcerations, and trauma during ambulation may keep the wound in a chronic inflammatory phase. Ischemia may contribute to 30–40% of foot ulcers.[3] Ulcers of the heel are thought to be predominantly vascular in origin and do not respond to traditional treatment as total contact casting. Classification of a foot wound could facilitate appropriate treatment and monitor wound healing. Several classification systems are available, but none have been validated prospectively.

Assessment of Diabetic Foot Ulcers
- Measure size and depth of wound and record location.
- Check wound for undermining and sinus tracts.
- Probe depth of wound. If bone is visual or palpated, there is an 89% chance of osteomyelitis.

- Check for appearance, temperature, odor, edema, drainage, and necrotic tissue.
- Culture for aerobic and anaerobic organisms if wound is clinically infected. Take culture by curettage from ulcer base. Swab cultures are generally not useful and can add to the confusion.
- X-ray the foot (standing) in patients with a deep or long standing ulceration to exclude osteomyelitis. If the first x-ray is negative, take another in 2 weeks. If the x-ray remains negative, osteomyelitis is unlikely.

Ulcer Treatment

- Sharp debridement of devitalized tissue is highly recommended. The validity of enzymatic or other debridement strategies is not supported by studies.[3] The efficacy of hydrotherapy for cleansing and soaking a foot ulcer has not been supported by data.[3]
- Creating a moist wound environment is important for wound healing. There is limited evidence that specific types of dressings speed up healing of chronic foot ulcers.[3]
- Becaplermin (recombinant platelet-derived growth factor), if used with off loading, wound debridement, and infection control, shows modest benefit as a topical treatment.[3]
- Off loading is the removal of pressure on the injured extremity; this is essential for wound healing.[3]

In ulcer management, it is unforgivable and poor medical practice to put a foot with an ulcer into the patient's regular footwear and allow full weight bearing. Since the ulcer is not painful, the patient will continue to walk on it unless taught not to. Most clinics approach ulcer management with similar basic protocols:

1. Have the patient remove footwear and do not bear weight until the extremity can be off loaded.
2. Treat with antibiotics for wound infection and wait 2–3 days before casting.
3. Wound debridement and cleansing by trained personnel.
4. Off loading until healing occurs.

Off Loading

There are numerous methods described for off loading, but only a few have proven to be effective. The most extensively studied is the total contact cast (TCC), which has been found to be effective in ulcer healing (Fig. 5). The cast assists wound healing by:

1. Distributing weight bearing pressures evenly over the foot
2. Decreasing edema by pump action of the cast
3. Protecting the wound from additional trauma
4. Protecting the tissues from stretching, which can retard healing
5. Ensuring compliance
6. Maintaining ambulatory walking status

It has been shown that TCC reduces peak plantar pressures by as much as 75–84% at the first and third metatarsal heads compared with walking in normal shoes.[6]

Indications/Contraindications for Casting

Casting is beneficial in ulcer healing for both superficial and full thickness ulcers on the plantar aspect of the foot. It is also recommended for open wounds

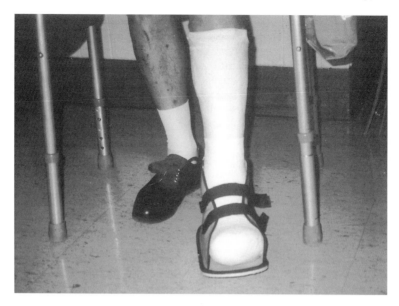

FIGURE 5.   Total contact walking cast distributes weight bearing pressures evenly over the foot. (From Helm PA, Pandian G: Prevention of amputation. Physical Medicine and Rehabilitation: State of the Art Reviews 8(1):21, 1994.)

after amputation. It has not been found to be effective for heel or leg ulcers. Patients with ulcers on ischemic extremities should not be casted, nor should patients with wound infection or osteomyelitis. If a patient has excessive drainage from the wound, casting is contraindicated. When there is fluctuating edema of the extremity as seen in patients on dialysis, a cast should not be applied because of the cast becoming too loose or tight. Those patients that are considered unsafe such as the visually impaired, elderly, morbidly obese, and those with gait abnormalities also should not be casted. The original method of total contact casting was described by Brand.[7]

1. Patient positioned prone with knee and ankle flexed to 90 degrees.
2. Ulcer cleansed and covered with ⅛" thick gauze pad held in place with surgical tape.
3. Lambswool placed between toes to prevent maceration.
4. Stockinette placed over foot and leg to knee level.
5. Felt pads applied over foot and leg to knee level.
6. Toes covered with soft spongy foam pad.
7. Plaster is applied directly to stockinette covering leg, ankle, and foot (toes enclosed). The cast should conform intimately to all surfaces.
8. After inner cast has set, medial, lateral, and anterior posterior plaster splints are applied and wrapped circumferentially with more rolls of plaster.
9. A rubber walking heel is applied over a thin plywood sole held on with plaster.
10. No weight bearing for 24 hours.
11. Change the first cast at 1 week and repeat cast changes every 2–3 weeks until wound healing is achieved.

Plaster is the preferred casting material because it can wick off the drainage from the wound into the cast. After the single layer of plaster, some use two layers of fiberglass casting tape. It is best to always enclose the toes in the cast, since this will protect the toes from trauma. If the cast is finished at the metatarsal heads, pressure is increased on the dorsal foot at toe off and this may cause ulceration. Leaving a window over the ulcerated area is definitely not advisable because this can cause additional pressure around the ulcer site and can cause tissue to bulge through the window. Another common mistake seen in cast application is applying a thick dressing over the wound. This only increases pressure over the wound instead of evenly distributing pressure over the plantar foot. Healing times with TCC have been reported anywhere from 37 to 65 days.[32] Following ulcer healing, it is imperative that the patient be fitted with proper footwear.

ALTERNATIVES TO TOTAL CONTACT CASTING

• Bed rest
• Bivalved total contact cast
• Healing shoes
• Crow brace–bivalved AFO walker
• DH pressure relief walkers

CHARCOT JOINT

Neuropathic osteoarthropathy or Charcot arthropathy is an accepted risk factor for progressive joint deformity, ulceration, and amputation in long standing diabetics. Prompt recognition and institution of immediate appropriate aggressive treatment are imperative to prevent progression to a profoundly debilitating limb threatening deformity. However, Charcot arthropathy frequently goes unrecognized, misdiagnosed, and, even when diagnosed, improperly treated.

Clinical Picture and Pathophysiology

Incidence of Charcot arthropathy has been reported to be around 0.3–7.5% in long standing diabetics.[14,31] The majority of patients are in their fifth and sixth decade at the time of diagnosis, although the range can be from the early twenties to late seventies. High incidence has been reported in patients with diabetes greater than 15 years' duration. Almost invariably, the diabetes is poorly controlled. Men and women are equally affected, and 5.9–39.3% of patients have bilateral involvement.[21]

The exact pathophysiology of Charcot arthropathy is not well understood; however, it does require the presence of peripheral neuropathy, which involves motor, sensory, and autonomic nerves. Altered vasomotor tone caused by autonomic neuropathy results in "sympathetic failure" leading to hypervascularity, bone arteriovenous shunting, and demineralization.[16] The bone becomes susceptible to fracture even with minor trauma. Loss of protective sensation and muscle weakness caused by the neuropathy predispose the joints to abnormal and extreme range of motion, resulting in capsular stretching, joint dislocation, subluxation and fatigue fractures of cartilage and bone. Thus Charcot arthropathy can develop through either a fracture or dislocation or, most commonly, a combination of both.

The patient usually presents with a markedly swollen, red, hot foot, with or without history of recent trauma or deviation from normal activity. Frequently, pain and discomfort are reported even though to a lesser degree than might be expected from the clinical picture.[16] The foot presents with pounding pulses and signs of anhidrosis. In the acute stages, the skin temperature over the affected area is often 6–8°C higher than the corresponding area on the contralateral foot.[14] Mild deformity with a prominent medial border or gross deformity with rocker bottom subluxation of the midfoot may be found along with crepitus and increased range of motion.[16] If a foot ulcer is present, it should be determined whether the ulcer developed as a consequence of the deformity or Charcot arthropathy resulted from pre-existing infected ulceration.

Sanders described five typical anatomic patterns of bone and joint destruction with Charcot arthropathy.[31]

Pattern I: Involves phalanges, metatarsophalangeal joints, and distal metatarsals. X-ray may reveal atrophic findings of "pencil pointing" of metatarsal heads and/or "hourglass resorption" of phalangeal joints. Frequently associated with amputation of great toe. Usually causes less morbidity.

Pattern II: Involves tarsometatarsal joints (Lisfranc joint). Most common presentation in diabetics. Frequently starts as subtle subluxation of second metatarsal and progresses to midfoot collapse.

Pattern III: Involves talonavicular and calcaneocuboid (Chopart joints) or naviculocuneiform joint.

Pattern IV: Involves ankle joint. Frequently leads to aggressive osteolysis with instability of ankle and subtalar joints.

Pattern V: Involves body or posterior process of calcaneus. With appropriate management, minimal deformity is the rule.

Differential Diagnosis

This includes cellulitis, infection, septic arthritis, gout, other arthritides, and osteomyelitis. Osteomyelitis is probably the most difficult diagnosis to rule out, especially when bony destruction and fragmentation are noted with radiologic examination. Sedimentation rate and white blood count may be increased with osteomyelitis and infection. However, even in presence of infection, white blood cell count may not be elevated as a result of the limited immune response in diabetics. As a rule, if there is no break in skin integrity, infection is probably unlikely. Brodsky describes a test to distinguish Charcot foot from infection.[8] The patient is instructed to lie down with affected leg elevated for 5 to 10 minutes. If swelling and rubor resolves, Charcot foot is more likely. With infection, erythema tends to persist even with leg elevation. It is important to realize that plain radiographs may be initially negative in early Charcot. Therefore, serial x-rays are recommended. Johnson recommends a modification of the Schauwecker technique using a combination of indium and technetium scans.[25] In this technique, indium labeled white blood cells (WBC) are injected on day 1. On day 2, the scan is performed. If there is no uptake, it can be assumed that infection is not present either in soft tissue or in bone. If increased uptake is noted in the suspected area of concern, an injection of technetium is administered and a three-phase bone scan is performed immediately, so that technetium and labeled WBC are in the foot at the same time. The indium labeled WBC will localize in the areas of infection (osteomyelitis or soft tissue), but not in a neuropathic fracture. Thus, if the area of uptake of labeled WBC and technetium correlates, it is more consistent with osteomyelitis. With this technique, Johnson reports 91% accuracy.[25] However, this combined scan approach is time consuming; because of its relative ease of use, magnetic resonance imaging (MRI) has become more popular recently. MRI scan is useful to distinguish cellulitis from abscess and soft tissue infection from bone marrow disease. However, any disease process affecting the bone or adjacent tissue can cause a change in the bone signal because of marrow edema.[9] Thus, abnormal MRI can be seen with osteomyelitis, trauma, or fracture. Therefore, its role in distinguishing osteomyelitis from neuroarthropathy is not clear.

Management

Early diagnosis of Charcot arthropathy is critical because final outcome is dependent upon the amount of destruction that occurs during the initial phases. If the problem is misdiagnosed and the patient is allowed to weight bear and ambulate, irreversible bone and joint destruction occurs. The goal is to prevent further trauma, promote bone and joint stability, and heal with minimal deformity. Eichenholtz divided the disease into different stages radiographically. Although originally three stages were described, a Stage 0 has been added to describe the pre-arthropathic phase[2] (see Table 5). Treatment protocols are based on the different stages to which the patient has progressed.

Conservative Treatment Protocol

Stage 0 and Stage I (stage of dissolution):
Total contact casting for 2–3 months. No weight bearing allowed until swelling and redness resolve.
Charcot restraint walker (a bivalved walking ankle foot orthosis) if patient is unable to tolerate cast and if there is no excessive shift in edema.
Change cast within 1 week initially and every 2–3 weeks following.
Stage II (stage of coalescence):
Total contact cast for 3 months.
Begin partial to full weight bearing.
Change cast every 2–3 weeks.
Stage III (stage of resolution):
Skin temperature gradient stabilized within 1°C of contralateral limb for 2 consecutive weeks.[4]
Bivalve ankle foot orthosis (AFO) or bivalved cast for 3–6 months.
Charcot restraint walker is another option.
Full weight bearing in orthosis. No weight bearing allowed without orthosis.
Chronic phase
Extra depth shoe with AFO.
Full weight bearing.

Eventually, an extra depth shoe with extended steel shank and rocker sole is used.[1] This transition from orthosis to shoe should occur gradually to prevent recurrence. Recently, there has been an interest in use of biphosphonates to alter the reduction in bone mineral density seen in neuroarthropathy, but controlled studies are

TABLE 5. Eichenholz Classification of the Neuropathic Process

Stage	Radiographic	Clinical
Stage 0: Foot at risk	Negative	Exaggerated inflammatory response: thrombophlebitis, cellulitis; no deformity
Stage I: Dissolution	Demineralization Periarticular fragmentation Subluxation and dislocation	Exaggerated inflammatory ± instability
Stage II: Coalescence	Callus formation Coalescence of fracture fragments	Reduction of inflammation and swelling More evident deformity
Stage III: Resolution	Healed fracture Sclerosis of fracture fragments	Minimal inflammation Fixed deformity Bony prominence Rocker foot deformity

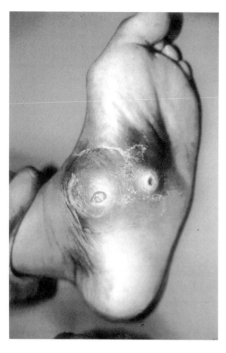

FIGURE 6.   Charcot foot with midfoot collapse and recurrent infected foot ulcers over bony prominences.

lacking.[16] Surgery is indicated in Charcot arthropathy patients only in the following conditions[1]: (1) recurrent infected foot ulcers due to bony prominence (Fig. 6); (2) unstable ankle and foot that are not shoeable or braceable; (3) acute displaced fracture in a neuropathic patient with good circulation. During surgery, coexistent contractures of the Achilles tendon, which might be causing accentuation of the deformity and plantar pressure, may require lengthening.

DIABETIC FOOT INFECTIONS

Diabetic foot infections account for 20% of all hospitalizations in diabetics.[24] They lead to limb and life threatening events if improperly treated. Diabetics with long standing disease with multiple secondary complications are more prone to develop serious infection. Bacterial invasion of a foot ulceration is the most common pathway for lower extremity infection. Malnutrition, hyperglycemia, vascular insufficiency, anaerobic metabolism, and abnormalities in function of neutrophils, macrophages, and fibroblasts have all been implicated as reasons for diabetic patient's inability to ward off infection.[3,30] Most diabetic infections are polymicrobial, and on average three to five organisms can be cultured from moderate to severely infected wounds.[30] Superficial swab cultures from non-inflamed wounds are rarely of any value, as virtually all foot ulcers are colonized with a variety of bacterial flora. Antibiotic therapy is not advocated for non-inflamed neuropathic wounds.[3] Classifying diabetic foot infections as mild (non-limb-threatening) or moderate to severe infection (limb-threatening) provides a useful guide for treatment based on aggressiveness of infection in the limb.[3] Non-limb-threatening infections occur in patients with superficial ulcerations. The extent of cellulitis is usually limited to less than 2 cm. As a rule, ischemia, systemic toxicity, osteomyelitis, and poor metabolic control are absent.

Microbiology of non-limb-threatening infection is usually predictable and usually caused by gram-positive cocci including *Staphylococcus aureus* and group B *Streptococcus*. Recommended antibiotic regimen is any one of the following as a single agent for 7–14 days: first-generation cephalosporin, amoxicillin–clavulanate, clindamycin, or dicloxacillin.[11] Fluoroquinolones such as ciprofloxacin and levofloxacin are not recommended as a single agent for treatment of these infections. Ciprofloxacin has suboptimal gram-positive activity, and though levofloxacin has a comparatively better gram-positive activity, it has not been studied specifically in diabetic foot infections. Treatment with antibiotics should be done in conjunction with wound debridement, and pressure relief of the ulcer site. Careful close follow-up to see whether infection resolves is necessary. It is important to remember that diabetics may not have fever or leukocytosis, owing to immunosuppression, even in the presence of significant infection.

Limb threatening infection is characterized by abscess, extensive cellulitis, osteomyelitis, septicemia, or gangrene. These patients require urgent hospitalization, parenteral antibiotics, and possible surgical evaluation.[3,11] Pittet et al. reports success without amputation in a large proportion of diabetic patients admitted with skin ulcer and suspected osteomyelitis. He treats conservatively with prolonged culture guided parenteral and oral antibiotics.[27]

OSTEOMYELITIS

Definitive diagnosis of osteomyelitis is difficult, especially in the presence of Charcot arthropathy and foot ulcer. Patients with deep or long standing ulcers should have plain x-rays to rule out osteomyelitis at their initial visit. Plain radiographs and the "bedside probe to bone" test with a sterile ophthalmologic probe remain the most accurate initial screening for osteomyelitis. Grayson et al. reports palpating bone on probing the foot ulcer has a sensitivity of 66%, a specificity of 85%, and a positive predictive value of 89% for osteomyelitis and a negative predictive value of 56%.[17] Most authors report plain radiographs have sensitivity of 43–75% and specificity of 69–83% for diagnosing osteomyelitis. If either one of these tests is positive, Caputo recommends a 4–6 week course of oral or intravenous antibiotics based on a deep culture specimen, especially if the patient is clinically stable without necrotizing infection and limited or absent bony destruction noted on plain radiographs.[11] Venkatesan et al. recommends a 12-week course of antibiotics.[34] If clinical deterioration occurs or repeat x-rays in 2–4 weeks shows progressive bony destruction, surgical debridement of infected bone should be considered. MRI or indium labeled leukocyte scans are reserved for patients in whom the diagnosis remain uncertain. The management of osteomyelitis still remains controversial. In selected patients, there is some evidence that cure may be achieved with a prolonged course of antibiotics without surgery, but obviously treatment must be individualized.

NEWER TECHNOLOGIES

Hyperbaric oxygen therapy (HBO_2) in management of diabetic wounds is based upon the physiologic role of oxygen in wound healing. Limited evidence shows that in selected groups of patients with severe wounds, HBO_2 therapy resulted in a decreased rate of amputation when compared with the control group.[33] The American Diabetic Association consensus development conference on diabetic wound care recommends use of HBO_2 therapy in severe ischemic wounds that have not responded to other treatments, particularly if ischemia cannot be corrected by vascular procedures.[3] However, additional randomized clinical trails are needed before this costly modality can be recommended on a regular basis. Use of electrical stimulation in patients with diabetic foot ulcers is still under investigation. Baker et al. reported 60% enhanced healing rate in 80 patients with diabetic ulcers with use of asymmetric biphasic square wave pulse electrical stimulation.[5]

Growth factors are polypeptide molecules that play an integral part in wound healing. Growth factors stimulate chemotaxis, cellular proliferation and migration, enzyme production, and angiogenesis. Several growth factors have been studied for their role in wound healing. However, becaplermin is the only growth factor approved by the Food and Drug Administration for topical use in the treatment of diabetic neuropathic foot ulcers, in conjunction with adequate off loading, debridement, and treatment of infection.

Bioengineered human dermis developed from culturing neonatal dermal fibroblasts and granulocyte colony stimulating factors are two other new therapies that are currently under investigation for their role in treatment of diabetic foot problems. Both seem to show some promise in accelerating wound healing and resolution of cellulitis respectively.

TEAM APPROACH TO DIABETIC FOOT CARE

It has been shown that diabetic foot care programs can decrease rate of ulcers and amputations 44–55%.[23] Management of the diabetic foot is complex and therefore requires combined skills of several disciplines. The aim of the team approach to care is to coordinate resources to better deliver health care.

REFERENCES

 1. Alvarez RG, Trevino SG: Surgical treatment of the Charcot foot and ankle. In Kelikian AS (ed): Operative Treatment of the Foot and Ankle. Connecticut, Appleton & Lange, 1999, pp 147–177.
 2. Alvarez RG: Charcot foot: Guidelines for treatment of great toe, midfoot, and hindfoot deformities. In Pfeffier GB, Frey CC (eds): Current Practice in Foot and Ankle Surgery. New York, McGraw-Hill, 1994, Vol 2, pp 257–289.
 3. American Diabetes Association: Consensus development conference on diabetic foot wound care. Diabetes Care 22:1354–1360, 1999.
 4. Armstrong DG, Todd WF, Lavery LA, et al: The natural history of acute Charcot's arthropathy in a diabetic foot specialty clinic. Diabetic Med 14:357–363, 1997.
 5. Baker LL, Demeith SK, Chambers R, et al: Effects of electrical stimulatio on wound healing patients with diabetic ulcers. Diabetes Care 20(3):405–412, 1997.
 6. Birke JA, Sims S, Buford WL: Walking casts: Effect on plantar foot pressure. K Rehab Res Ser 22:18–22, 1985.
 7. Brand PW: The diabetic foot. In Ellenberg M, Rifkin H (eds): Diabetes Mellitus. New York, Medical Examination Publishing Co, 1983, pp 829–849.
 8. Brodsky JW: Outpatient diagnosis and care of the diabetic foot. In Heckman JD (ed): Instructional Course Lectures. Rosemont, IL, American Academy of Orthopaedic Surgeons, 42:121–139, 1993.
 9. Brodsky JW: Evaluation of the diabetic foot. In Zuckerman JD (ed): Instructional Course Lectures. Rosemont, IL, American Academy of Orthopaedic Surgeons, 48:289–303, 1999.
10. Campbell RR, Hawkins SI, Maddison PJ: Limited joint mobility in diabetes mellitus. Ann Rheum Dis 44:93–97, 1985.
11. Caputo GM: The rational use of antimicrobial agents in diabetic foot infection. In Coulton AIM, Connor H, Cavanagh PR (eds): The Foot in Diabetes. West Sussex, John Wiley & Sons, 2000, pp 143–151.
12. Crausaz FM, Clovel S, Liniger C: Additional factors associated with plantar ulcers in diabetic neuropathy. Diabetes Med 5:771–775, 1988.
13. Delbridge L, Perry P, Marr S: Limited joint mobility in the diabetic foot: Relationship to neuropathy ulceration. Diabetes Med 5:333–337, 1988.
14. Fabrin J, Larsen K, Holstein PE: Long-term follow up in diabetic Charcot feet with spontaneous onset. Diabetes Care 23(6):796–800, 2000.
15. Fernando DIS, Masson EA, Veves A: Relationship of limited joint mobility to abnormal foot pressures and diabetic foot ulceration. Diabetes Care 14:8–11, 1991.

16. Frykberg RG: Charcot foot: An update on pathogenesis and management. In Boulton ATM, Connor H, Cavanagh PR (eds): The Foot in Diabetes. West Sussex, John Wiley & Sons, 2000, pp 235–260.
17. Grayson LM, Gibbons GW, Balogh KB, et al: Probing to bone in infected pedal ulcers: A clinical sign of underlying osteomyelitis in diabetic patients. JAMA 273(9):720–721, 1995.
18. Grunfeld C: Diabetic foot ulcers: Etiology, treatment, and prevention. Adv Intern Med 37:103–130, 1991.
19. Harkless LB, Higgins KR: Evaluation of the diabetic foot and leg. In Frykberg RG (ed): The High Risk Foot in Diabetes Mellitus. New York, Chruchill Livingstone, 1991, pp 61–77.
20. Katoulis EC, Ebdon-Parry M, Hollis S: Postural instability in diabetic neuropathic patients at risk of foot ulceration. Diabetic Med 14:296–307, 1997.
21. Klenerman L: The Charcot joint in diabetes. Diabetic Med 13:552–554, 1996.
22. Laing P, Klenerman L: The foot in diabetes. In Klenerman L (ed): The Foot and Its Disorders. London, Blackwell Scientific Publications, 1991, pp 139–152.
23. Mayfield JA, Reiber GE, Sanders LJ: Preventive foot care in people with diabetes. Diabetes Care 21:216–217, 1998.
24. Mulder GD: Diabetic ulcers: Evaluating and managing the diabetic foot: An overview. Adv Skin Wound Care 13(1):33–36, 2000.
25. Myerson MS, Alvarez RG, Brodsky JW, et al: Symposium: Neuroarthropathy of the foot. Contemp Orthop 26(1):43–46, 1993.
26. Pfeffer GB, Clain MR, Frey C: Foot and ankle. In Snider RK (ed): Essentials of Musculoskeletal Care. Rosemont, IL, American Academy of Orthopaedic Surgeons, 1997, pp 368–471.
27. Pittet D, Wyssa B, Herter-Clavel C, et al: Outcome of diabetic foot infections. Treated conservatively. Arch Intern Med 159:851–856, 1999.
28. Quebedeaux TL, Lavery LA, Lavery DC: The development of foot deformities and ulcers after great toe amputation in diabetes. Diabetes Care 19(2):165–167, 1996.
29. Reiber G, Vileikyte L, Boydo EJ: Causal pathways for incident lower extremity ulcers in patients with diabetes from two settings. Diabetes Care 22:157–162, 1999.
30. Saltzman CL, Pedowitz WJ: Diabetic foot infections. In Zuckerman JD (ed): Instructional Course Lectures. Rosemont, IL, American Academy of Orthopaedic Surgeons, 48:317–320, 1999.
31. Sanders JL, Frykberg RG: Diabetic neuropathic osteoarthropathy: The Charcot foot. In Frykberg RG (ed): The High Risk Foot in Diabetes Mellitus. New York, Churchill Livingstone, 1991, pp 297–338.
32. Sinacore DR, Mueller MI, Diamond JE: Diabetic plantar ulcers treated by total contact casting. Phys Therapy 67:1543–1549, 1987.
33. Stone JA, Cianie P: The adjunctive role of hyperbaric oxygen therapy in the treatment of lower extremity wounds in patients with diabetes. Diabetes Spectrum 10(2):118–122, 1997.
34. Venkatesan P, Lawn S, Macfarlane RM, et al: Conservative management of osteomyelitis in the feet of diabetic patients. Diabetic Med 14(6):487–490, 1997.
35. Young MJ, Cavanagh PR, Thomas G: Effect of callus removal on dynamic foot pressure in diabetic patients. Diabetes Med 9:75–77, 1992.

ALBERTO ESQUENAZI, MD

PARTIAL FOOT AMPUTATION: SURGERY AND REHABILITATION

Director, MossRehab Regional
    Amputee Center
and Gait & Motion Analysis
    Laboratory
Philadelphia, Pennsylvania

Associate Professor
Department of Rehabilitation
Jefferson College of Medicine
Philadelphia, Pennsylvania

Reprint requests to:
MossRehab Regional Amputee
    Center
and Gait & Motion Analysis
    Laboratory
1200 W. Tabor Road
Philadelphia, PA 19141

The ideal goal of surgical treatment is to remove as little tissue as is possible. In the case of partial foot amputations, this should be done with a clear understanding of the potential functional outcome for the patient. The selection of the surgical level of amputation is probably one of the most important decisions that must be made for the amputee. The viability of the soft tissues will usually determine the most distal possible level for amputation. The surgeon commonly does this at the time of surgery, when skin bleeding will be determined and in combination with skin oxygen tension, likelihood wound healing can be determined. More sophisticated predictive techniques to optimize the level of amputation are in use, but their reliability is limited.[2,18,28,29] After surgery, the patient with an amputation will use the residual limb as a weight bearing structure, ideally for full body weight. Bony prominences, adherent skin scars, grafted insensate skin, traction, shear, and perspiration will complicate this function. For this reason, the residual limb must be planed and surgically constructed with care to maintain muscle balance, optimize the transfer of loads, and assume the stresses necessary to meet its new function.[11,22] Greater bone and muscle lost as result of amputation will generally mean a greater loss of the normal locomotor mechanisms and therefore the greater the energy cost of ambulation as well as the degree of impairment.[29,31,35] As a general rule, the greater the anatomic loss of the foot, the more involved will be the rehabilitation and if needed the prosthetic restoration.

The skin is the crucial interface between the residual limb and the footwear or prosthesis. For this reason, outmost care in the management of the skin is essential for a pain free extremity that can tolerate weight bearing, have enough sensation to provide protective feedback, and have a durable soft tissue cover.[3,13]

Distal metatarsal and toe amputations should only be considered when full skin thickness coverage could be provided. Mid foot amputations (Lisfranc's tarsometatarsal and Chopart's tarsotarsal) should be contemplated only when primary skin coverage can be obtained.[24,29] Insensate skin graft coverage is an inadequate interface surface that will have a propensity to become adherent and have frequent breakdowns: additionally, foot deformities frequently caused by muscle imbalance may further increase disability.

Syme's amputation when correctly performed will provide an excellent weight bearing surface that permits short distance ambulation without the use of prosthesis (helpful for the unavoidable middle of the night bathroom trip).[7,13–15]

SURGICAL TECHNIQUE

Toe

A toe amputation is best performed with side-to-side or plantar to dorsal flaps to utilize the best available soft tissue for closure without tension. In great toe amputation, if the entire proximal phalanx is removed, often the sesamoids retract exposing the keel-shaped plantar surface of the first metatarsal to weight bearing. This often leads to high local pressures, callus formation, or ulceration. The sesamoids can be stabilized in position for weight bearing by leaving the base of the proximal phalanx intact or performing tenodesis of the flexor hallucis brevis tendon.

Isolated second toe amputations should be avoided, as a hallux valgus deformity frequently will occur. This deformity may be prevented by second ray amputation or first metatarsal phalangeal fusion. In the shorter metatarsal phalangeal joint level toe amputations, transferring the extensor tendon to the capsule may help elevate the metatarsal head, maintaining an even weight bearing distribution.[30]

Ray

A ray amputation removes the toe and all or some of the corresponding metatarsal. Isolated ray amputations can be durable; however, multiple ray amputations, especially in dysvascular patients, can narrow the foot excessively. This results in reduction of the weight bearing area with potential for pressure concentration, callus formation, and ulceration. Surgically, it is often difficult to close these wounds primarily because more skin is usually required than is readily available. Instead of closing these wounds under tension, it is usually advisable to leave the wound open and allow secondary healing.

The fifth ray amputation has been the most useful of all the ray amputations. A fifth ray amputation allows the entire ulcer to be excised and the wound primarily closed, removing exposed bone and infected areas.[30]

Midfoot

The transmetatarsal and Lisfranc's (tarsometatarsal) amputations are reliable and durable. Functionally, a healthy, durable soft tissue envelope is more important than a specific anatomic level, so bone should be shortened to allow soft tissue closure without tension, rather than to a specific anatomic level. A long plantar flap is preferable, but equal dorsal and plantar flaps work well, especially for metatarsal head ulcers.[25]

Muscle balance around the foot should be carefully evaluated preoperatively with specific attention to heel cord tightness, anterior tibialis, posterior tibialis, and peroneal muscle strength. Midfoot amputations significantly shorten the lever arm of the foot, so tendon Achilles lengthening is frequently needed to maintain a balanced foot. Tibial or peroneal muscle insertions should be reattached if they are released during bone resection. Postoperative casting reduces deformities, controls edema, stabilizes the soft tissues, and can speed rehabilitation.[24]

Hind Foot

Chopart's (tarsotarsal) amputation removes the forefoot and midfoot saving only the talus and calcaneus. Tendon transfers for rebalancing are required to prevent varus and equinus deformities. Achilles tendon lengthening, transfer of the anterior tibialis or extensor digitorum tendons to the talus, and postoperative casting are all usually necessary.

The Boyd or hind foot amputation is a talectomy with calcaneal-tibial arthrodesis after forward translation of the calcaneus. The Pirigoff hind foot amputation (talectomy with calcaneal-tibial arthrodesis) is performed after vertical transection of the calcaneus through the mid-body, and a forward rotation of the posterior process of the calcaneus under the tibia.[30] The Boyd and Pirigoff amputations are performed most commonly in children in an attempt to preserve length and the growth plates and prevent heel pad migration. Studies of children have shown improved function of hind foot amputations compared with the Syme amputation provided that the hind foot is balanced and not in equinus posture.[11]

Partial Calcanectomy

Partial calcanectomy (excision of the posterior process of the calcaneus) should be considered an amputation of the hind foot. In select patients with large heel ulceration or calcaneal osteomyelitis, this can be a functional alternative to a below-knee amputation.[31]

Syme's Amputation

The Syme level of amputation was described in 1842 as a disarticulation of the ankle affording ease of execution, less risk to life, and a comfortable residual limb resulting in some distinct advantages when it comes to mobility and prosthetic fitting.[33] The calcaneus and talus are removed while carefully dissecting bone to preserve the heel skin and fat pad to cover the distal tibia. The malleolus must be removed and contoured. Controversy exists on whether to remove the malleolus initially or as a second stage operation 6–8 weeks later. A late complication of Syme's amputation is the medial and posterior migration of the fat pad. Options to stabilize the fat pad span a variety of procedures, including tenodesis of the Achilles tendon to the posterior margin of the tibia through drill holes, and transferring anterior tibialis and extensor digitorum tendons to the anterior aspect of the fat pad. Postoperatively, casting can also help keep the fat pad centered under the tibia during healing.[13–15]

Syme's amputation produces an end bearing residual limb. Retaining the smooth, broad surface of the distal tibia and the heel pad allows direct transfer of weight from the end of the residual limb to the prosthesis with improved propioception. Because of its end bearing capacity, the amputee with a Syme amputation can occasionally ambulate without prosthesis. The bulbous distal end may allow the use of a prosthetic socket that is anatomically suspended, eliminating the need for any form of straps or sleeves proximally as auxiliary suspension. These two advantages are also the two main relative problems for prosthetic fitting. The long length of the residual limb places some limitation on the options for prosthetic foot/ankle systems that can be used and may cause a leg length discrepancy (long amputated leg). The bulbous nature of the distal residual limb that permits self-suspension of the prosthetic socket can result in prosthesis that may be cosmetically unacceptable.[8]

ACUTE POST AMPUTATION REHABILITATION

Pain control, maintenance of range of motion and strength, and promotion of wound healing are the goals of this stage in rehabilitation that begins with the surgical closure of the wound and culminates with healing after the sutures are removed.[9] Pain control and residual limb maturation should be aggressively pursued. Immediate postoperative plaster of Paris rigid dressing (for the Syme level) or soft elastic bandage and pneumatic compression are indicated for edema control. IPORD for the Syme may be complicated because of the tendency for the patient to attempt weight bearing.[4,24] IPORD techniques do offer the advantages of early rehabilitation, control of edema and pain, and soft tissue stabilization. This technique is preferred if the patient has no history of chronic arterial compromise and the expertise to apply it is available; otherwise, it is easily learned and well within the scope of interested physicians.[4] Soft compressive dressings alone are used in many centers; the dressing should be extended proximal to the mid tibia to improve suspension.[24]

Proper postoperative positioning and rehabilitation are essential to prevent ankle and knee contractures. This is also a time for patients to initiate emotional adaptation to their new body image and learn to function with crutches. A skin desensitization program that includes gentle tapping, massage, soft tissue and scar mobilization and lubrication is recommended for the patient who is managed with a removable, soft or elastic dressing.[8]

Acute Pain Management and Rehabilitation

Pain control should be the desired objective; initially a PCA system (patient controlled analgesia) followed by the use of scheduled oral analgesia is indicated. Local anesthetic mini-pumps can also be used to reduce postoperative pain.[10,21]

Whenever possible, patients should be placed on a high protein diet and in a cardiovascular conditioning program before the amputation.[5,8] Post amputation when the patient is medically stable, early mobilization, general endurance and strengthening exercise with emphasis on the avoidance of joint contractures, and improvement on sitting and standing balance are initiated. It is important to physically emphasize the remaining limbs, their strength and function with specificity of training as a preferred type of training. Strengthening of upper limb musculature is essential for wheelchair propulsion, transfers, walker, and crutch ambulation and should be aggressively pursued.[7–9]

POSTOPERATIVE CARE

Phantom Limb

Phantom limb sensation is the feeling that all or a part of the amputated limb is still present. This sensation is felt by nearly all acquired amputees, but is not always bothersome. Phantom sensation usually diminishes over time, and telescoping, the sensation that the phantom foot has moved proximal toward the stump, commonly occurs. As many as 70% of amputees perceive phantom pain in the first few months after amputation. However, such pain will usually disappear or decrease sufficiently so as not to interfere with prosthetic fitting and day to day activities.[23] A smaller percentage of patients will experience pain long term; others will have recurrence later in life. When it persists for more than 6 months, the pain usually becomes chronic and is extremely difficult to treat successfully. Perceived pain intensity is closely related to anxiety level, depression, prosthetic fitting problems, and other personal factors. The traditional explanation for phantom limbs and their associated pain is that the remaining nerves in the amputated limb continue to generate impulses that flow through the spinal cord and the thalamus to the somatosensory areas of the cerebral cortex. Another theory suggests that the phantom arises from excessive, spontaneous firing of spinal cord neurons that have lost their normal sensory input from the missing body part, while a third suggests that the phantom is caused by changes in the flow of signals through the somatosensory circuit in the brain.[21] The management of phantom limbs should include prosthetic socket revisions, desensitization techniques, transcutaneous nerve stimulation, neuro-pharmacologic intervention, and the voluntary control of the phantom limb. For severe cases, nerve blocks, steroid injections, and epidural blocks may be useful. Non-surgical interventions are far more successful than surgical ones.[1] Clearly, the source of phantom limbs is more complex than any of the theories here presented would suggest and treatment may be complex. An important issue to discuss with the patient is normal phantom sensation, phantom pain, and the relationship between tension, anxiety, stress, and pain perception.[1,10]

Joint Contractures

Joint contractures usually occur between the time medical treatment is sought and amputation is performed. In the Syme and partial foot amputation, the deforming forces may produce knee flexion and ankle plantar flexion and inversion. Tibialis anterior and extensor hallucis reattachment during surgery can prevent the post-amputation deforming forces. Efforts should be directed at prevention with aggressive rehabilitation, beginning before and soon after surgery.[4,7]

PRE-PROSTHETIC REHABILITATION

Not long ago, patients with partial foot amputations were provided at best with a modified shoe, and not much attention was paid to training or other special needs. In the last two decades, the advent of specialized treatment teams and new prosthetic devices has improved the outlook for the amputee. A pre-prosthetic rehabilitation program must be initiated as soon as possible, during which pain control and residual limb maturation should be continued. Soft elastic bandage and subsequent pneumatic compression are indicated for edema control. A skin desensitization program that includes gentle tapping, massage, soft tissue and scar mobilization, and lubrication should be continued.[7,8]

At times, delayed wound healing or other soft tissue or bone injuries will prevent weight bearing on the residual limb complicating the rehabilitation process. Because of architectural limitations, ambulation may be a requirement for a patient to return home, or because many patients view this function as the primary goal in their rehabilitation, it may be necessary to allow upright ambulation with a modified shoe (Darco) heel walker or a patellar tendon bearing orthosis, a walker, or crutches, which admittedly makes for gait deviations, but this is preferable to not being able to ambulate. The provision of front wheels to the walker or a reciprocating walker can improve gait when the device is necessary.[7]

Pneumatic compression can be used to further promote residual limb maturation, decrease swelling, desensitize the tissues, and increase tolerance to pressure. Serial circumferential measurements of the limb at pre-established locations and the patient's body weight are simple techniques to determine residual limb size stability prior to permanent prosthesis fabrication.

PROSTHETIC FITTING AND TRAINING

Prosthetic prescription options for the amputee have changed dramatically over the past 10 years. Selecting the most appropriate componentry for prosthetic restoration of foot amputation is a very challenging task in view of the variety and complexity of new components, socket fabrication techniques, suspension systems, and available materials. Ideally, a transdisciplinary expert team of professionals and the patient in close communication should accomplish this task.

Socket Characteristics

Following a lower limb amputation, the residual limb, instead of the foot, must bear the weight of the body when standing on the prosthesis. The socket provides the surface for contact and transfer of body weight from the residual limb to the prosthesis. It is this interface between residual limb and socket that is probably the most critical factor determining successful fit and function of a lower limb prosthesis. Varying type forces (e.g., weight bearing, shear, traction, hemodynamic) and magnitude occur at this interface. The socket must be designed in such a way as to limit the forces to not exceed residual limb tissues' tolerances in order to avoid skin breakdown and provide adequate comfort.

The amount of force the residual limb can tolerate varies with the amputation level and the status of the tissues. Disarticulations (e.g., Syme) with broad intact distal joint/bone surfaces are theoretically able to tolerate high forces concentrated on a small surface area. The end bearing capability of disarticulation amputations can minimize many of the socket interface problems seen with other levels of amputation.[12,17,19,27]

Levels of Amputation

TOE AND RAY AMPUTATION

Loss of one or more toes with preservation of the metatarsals will have minimal impact on level walking; the effect will be evident on more demanding activities such as running or jumping. A toe filler can be used in an orthopedic leather sole shoe to prevent collapse of the toe box preventing irritation of the residual foot skin and improving the shoe's appearance and support to the foot. A modified soft shoe with a carbon graphite insert may be used instead of an orthopedic shoe.[16] The loss of two or more rays will result in a narrower forefoot. Loss of the first or fifth toes will shift the normal weight bearing pattern to the adjacent metatarsal head, which may result in excessive pressure with potential callusing or skin breakdown, particularly in patients with impaired sensation secondary to diabetes or severe neuropathy. A shoe insert with modifications to redistribute weight bearing on the remaining metatarsal heads and supporting them in combination with a toe filler for the absent toe(s) may be necessary. Life-like silicone prosthetic replacements, which are intrinsically colored and mold shaped to match the opposite foot, are available for these levels of amputation.[20] The major drawback of this form of prosthetic replacement is their high cost and limited durability. In very active individuals, the silicone prosthesis may not provide sufficient resistance to ankle dorsiflexion in the stance phase, resulting in a drop off gait. This problem can be corrected by reinforcing the shoe with a metal or carbon graphite shank.

TRANSMETATARSAL AMPUTATION

With this amputation, the anatomic toe lever of the foot is shortened, reducing the ability to control ankle dorsiflexion in mid-stance and push off, which normally elevate the body's center of mass with a resulting drop off gait. The traditional prosthetic restoration includes a transmetatarsal silicone or soft plastic resin "slipper" or a custom shoe insert with arch support attached to a toe filler.[16,20] The slipper can be used in conjunction with a modified shoe with a steel or carbon graphite shank extended distally to the point of the former metatarsal heads to restore as normal toe lever length as is possible. The addition of a rocker sole to the shoe can also help to restore a more normal gait pattern. With the development of very thin, light weight carbon fiber inserts, such as those made by Springlite or Comcore, it is possible to incorporate the shank directly into the insert itself. Amputations through the more proximal portion of the metatarsals may be more amenable to a partial foot type of prosthesis similar to that used for the tarsometatarsal amputation.

TARSOMETATARSAL–TRANS TARSAL AMPUTATIONS

Tarsometatarsal (Lisfranc's) and mid tarsal (Chopart's) amputations are not amputation levels of choice, in part because of the difficulty that arises with prosthetic restoration and in part because of the resultant ankle deformity. Unless the extensor muscles of the ankle are reattached proximally, the residual foot assumes a plantar flexed position. Prosthetic options in the past have utilized a high top shoe, a boot, or AFO type of design to extend the prosthetic replacement above the ankle, attempting to better restore the biomechanics of walking and providing adequate suspension. Self-suspending sockets made of flexible resins or silicones with laminated forefoot and shank have resulted in often highly cosmetic and functionally acceptable prosthetic options for these previously difficult to manage amputation levels.[16,27,32] These latter designs often make it possible for the amputee to wear low quarter shoes instead of boots. Even with the best of these prostheses, it is often necessary to add a rocker sole to the shoe to simulate the action of normal push off.

Prosthetic requirements can vary widely over time. During the first year following amputation, many patients benefit from an ankle-foot orthosis with a long foot plate and a toe filler. This orthosis should be worn at all times except to bathe in order to prevent the development of an equinus deformity. Later on, a simpler design toe filler combined with a stiff sole high top shoe can be adequate.

SYME'S AMPUTATION

The distal half of the socket must either have an opening or have a circumference slightly larger than that of the distal residual limb to allow the residual limb to fit into the socket. The posterior or medial opening Syme prostheses permit opening or removal of part of the distal portion of the socket to allow passage of the bulbous residual limb end into the distal socket. Once in the prosthesis, the wall section door is replaced and held in place with a strap providing excellent suspension of the prosthesis.[8,19] These socket designs provide an outer socket contour that is closer to that of the anatomic leg, but still result in a limb that is larger in circumference than the non-amputated limb. The difficulty with these designs is the potential failure (fracture) of the socket anteriorly as a result of the stresses concentrated here during walking, especially at push off. Reinforcing this area of the socket with carbon fibers can reduce the frequency of this problem, but this may increase the overall weight of the device. The closed socket design is inherently stronger than those with posterior or medial windows. Thus a thinner lamination is possible resulting in a lighter prosthesis.[6] To permit entry of the residual limb into the socket, the distal diameter must be sufficient to allow passage of the bulbous residual limb. This means that the outer shape of the distal third to one half of the prosthetic socket will appear cylindrical and much larger than the non-amputated leg. The normal anatomic contours will not be present, resulting in poor cosmesis. With this type of design, either a removable expandable liner or a fixed Silastic flexible inner liner may be used. In the former the friction between the removable liner and the socket lamination provides the suspension, and in the latter the compression of the expandable inner wall of the socket as well as increased pressure of the enclosed chamber provides for suspension of the prosthesis.[34] If the chamber has an air leak, suspension may be compromised. This closed chamber prosthetic system will not permit transpiration, trapping heat in the air chamber and making this design less desirable for patients who have poor hygienic habits or reside in warm weather locations.

There are three choices for weight bearing in the Syme amputation. In distal end bearing, a distal end pad is used to optimize the weight bearing comfort. If the amputee is unable to tolerate distal end bearing, it is possible to add a patellar tendon bearing proximal brim trim line to the prosthesis and unload the distal end. Thirdly, it is possible to manufacture a prosthesis that will share the load between proximal and distal as tolerated by the patient. If necessary, it is possible to add any of the common transtibial prosthetic suspension systems such as a sleeve or supracondylar cuff.

Modifications to Syme sockets include a hybrid carbon graphite reinforced socket with a posterior opening with a flexible inner socket without the use of a door to close the opening.[17] This is usually done to provide relief for tender bony prominences. The open socket designs permit the prosthetist greater access to the distal socket should any modification or adjustment of the socket is necessary. The silicone sleeve design can also be implemented and allows for improved comfort and friction suspension but may affect cosmesis.

Traditionally, a modified SACH (solid ankle cushion heel) foot that has a lower profile has been used in the Syme prosthesis. Recently, several of the low profile energy storing feet have become available (i.e., Seattle Lite, Carbon Copy II) for the Syme level amputation. Of more recent introduction are the Flex Symes, the Allurion, and the low profile Spring Lite, which take advantage of carbon graphite construction and longer lever arms to improve on their dynamic response. Maintaining leg length equality can be problematic for the unilateral Syme's amputee.[26]

Training

Gait training is integral in the rehabilitation process. A new amputee or an experienced one who receives a prosthetic device that has different components should participate in such training. This program should be a coordinated effort between the physical, occupational, recreational therapists and the prosthetist with frequent physiatric input. Each one of the team members will use different techniques to teach and review all of the important topics that need to be learned by the amputee. The patient should work on how to put on and take off the prosthesis and how to determine the appropriate fit and prosthetic maintenance and care. Skin care and inspection techniques are also reviewed.[7,8]

Weight shifting techniques including the use of stepping and a balance board should be encouraged. Gait training initially for technique and then for velocity on flat surfaces is essential, as tolerated progressing to uneven surfaces and elevations as part of the training.

LONG-TERM FOLLOW-UP

The patient who has successfully completed a rehabilitation program should be seen for follow-up by a minimum of one of the team members at least every 3 months for the first 18 months. These visits may need to be more frequent and include other members of the team if the patient is having difficulties with prosthetic fitting, the residual limb, specific activities, or psychosocial adjustment. After this critical period, the patient should be seen at least every 6 months to ensure adequate prosthetic fit and function, determine the need for maintenance, and to assess the overall condition of the patient. It may be necessary to replace a Syme prosthesis or parts of it every 12–24 months; for the partial foot, more frequent replacements or adjustments may be necessary.

SUMMARY

The team should be able and ready to assist the patient throughout the rehabilitation program. This chapter reviews the surgical techniques, postoperative management, acute pain control, and phantom limb and pain. A detailed description of the different prosthetic options in the management of the different levels of partial foot and Syme's amputation is included. The long-term effects of amputation are also discussed. Patients with this type of amputation can be expected to return to independent functional level if a pain and scar free residual limb was created and no other significant co-morbidity exists.

REFERENCES

1. Bach S, Noreng MF, Tjelden NU: Phantom limb pain in amputees during the first 12 months following limb amputation, after preoperative lumbar epidural blockade. Pain 33:297–301, 1988.
2. Bone GE, Pomajzl MJ: Toe blood pressure by photoplethysmography: An index of healing in forefoot amputation. Surgery 89(5):569–574, 1981.
3. Burgess EM, Matsen FA, Wyss CR, Simmons CW: Segmental transcutaneous measurements of PO_2 in patients requiring below-knee amputations for peripheral vascular insufficiency. J Bone Joint Surg 64A:378–382, 1982.
4. Burgess EM, Romano RL, Zettl JH: The Management of Lower-Extremity Amputations. TR10-6, US Government Printing Office, 1969.
5. Dickhaut SC, DeLee JC, Page CP: Nutritional status: Importance in predicting wound-healing after amputation. J Bone Joint Surg 66A:71–75, 1984.
6. Doyle W, Goldstone J, Kramer D: The Syme prosthesis revisited. JPO 5(3):95–99, 1993.
7. Esquenazi A: Geriatric amputation rehabilitation. Clin Geriatr Med 9(4):731–743, 1993.
8. Esquenazi A: Rehabilitation of the lower limb amputee. In Rehabilitation of the injured soldier. Textbook of Military Medicine. Office of the Surgeon General, The Borden Institute, Washington, DC, 1999.
9. Esquenazi A, Meier R: Rehabilitation in limb deficiency. 4. Limb amputation. Arch Phys Med Rehab 77:S18–S28, 1996.
10. Fisher A, Meller Y: Continuous postoperative regional analgesia by nerve sheath block for amputation surgery: A pilot study. Anesth Analg 72:300–303, 1991.
11. Greene WG, Cary JM: Partial foot amputation in children: A comparison of the several types with the Syme's amputation. J Bone Joint Surg 64A(3):438–443, 1982.
12. Haberman LJ: The Garden State tri-wall expansion socket system (TESS). J Prosthet Orthot 1:213–219, 1989.
13. Harris RI: Syme's amputation, the technique essential to secure a satisfactory end-bearing stump. Part I. Can J Surg 6:456–469, 1963.
14. Harris RI: Syme's amputation, the technique essential to secure a satisfactory end-bearing stump. Part II. Can J Surg 7:53–63, 1964.
15. Harris RI: The history and development of Syme's amputation. Artif Limbs 6(4):4–43, 1961.

16. Hayhurst DJ: Prosthetic management of a partial-foot amputee. Inter-Clinic Information Bull 17:11–15, 1978.

17. Jendrzejczyk DJ: Flexible socket systems. Clin Prosthet Orthot 9:27–31, 1985.

18. Johansen K, Daines M, Howey T, et al: Objective criteria accurately predict amputation following lower extremity trauma. J Trauma 30(5):568–573, 1990.

19. Klasson B: Computer aided design, computer aided manufacture and other computer aids in prosthetics and orthotics. Prosthet Orthot Int 9:3–11, 1985.

20. Lange LR: The Lange silicone partial foot prosthesis. J Prosthetic Orthot 4:56–61, 1991.

21. Malawer MM, Buch R, Khurana JS, et al: Postoperative infusional continuous regional analgesia: A technique for relief of postoperative pain following major extremity surgery. Clin Orthop Rel Res 266:227–237, 1991.

22. Malone JM, et al: Prospective comparison of non-invasive techniques for amputation level selection. Am J Surg Vol 154, August 1987.

23. Melzack R: Phantom limbs. Scientific American, pp 120–126, April 1992.

24. Mooney V, Harvey JP, McBride E, Snelson R: Comparison of postoperative stump management: Plaster vs. soft dressings. J Bone Joint Surg 53A;241–249, 1971.

25. Pinzur MS, Kaminsky M, Sage R, et al; Amputation at the middle level of the foot. J Bone Joint Surg 68A:1061–1064, 1986.

26. Pinzur MS: New concepts in lower-limb amputation and prosthetic management. Instruct Course Lect 39:361–366, 1990.

27. Pritham CH, Filauer C, Filauer K: Experience with the Scandinavian flexible socket. Orthot Prosthet 39:17–32, 1985.

28. Ramsey DE, Manke DA, Sumner DS: Toe blood pressure: A valuable adjunct to ankle pressure measurement for assessing peripheral arterial disease. J Cardiovasc Surg 24:43–48, 1983.

29. Robertson PA: Prediction of amputation after severe lower limb trauma. J Bone Joint Surg 73B(5): 816–818, 1991.

30. Smith DG: Lower limb amputation surgery. In Physical Medicine and Rehabilitation: State of the Art Reviews, Vol 8, No 1, February 1994, pp 201–220. Philadelphia, Hanley & Belfus.

31. Smith DG, Stuck RM, Ketner L, et al: Partial calcanectomy for the treatment of large ulcerations of the heel, and calcaneal osteomyelitis: An amputation of the back of the foot. J Bone Joint Surg 74A(4):571–576, 1992.

32. Such CM: Thermoplastic application in lower extremity prosthetics. J Prosthet Orthot 3:1–8, 1990.

33. Syme J: On amputation at the ankle joint. London and Edinburgh, Monthly Journal of Medical Science, February 1843,3:XXVI:93.

34. Volkert R: Frame type socket for lower limb prostheses. Prosthet Orthot Int 6:88–92, 1982.

35. Waters RL, Perry J, Antonelli D, et al: The energy cost of walking of amputees: Influence of level of amputation. J Bone Joint Surg 58A:42–46, 1976.

SIKHA GUHA, MD

PHYSIATRIC MANAGEMENT OF VENOUS ULCERS

Assistant Professor
Department of Rehabilitation
  Medicine
Montefiore Medical Center
Albert Einstein College of Medicine
Bronx, New York

Reprint requests to:
Department of Rehabilitation
  Medicine
Montefiore Medical Center/Moses
  Division
111 East 210th Street
Bronx, NY 10467

Approximately 6.5 million people in the US have chronic skin ulcers. Venous leg ulcers account for up to 80–90% of all leg ulcers.[1] The morbidity of this condition is ubiquitous, and can affect any age group, unlike peripheral arterial disease. It can impose profound functional limitations on otherwise active individuals. In addition, wound healing becomes a long, tedious process with a disappointingly high recurrence rate. A practicing physiatrist will, undoubtedly, encounter many patients suffering from these lesions, and should, therefore, become adept in the management of these wounds.

A variety of terms are used to describe leg ulcers resulting from chronic venous insufficiency, including venous, venous stasis, varicose and gravitational ulcers. The most commonly used term, "stasis ulcer," may actually be a misnomer. Homans introduced the term in 1917 to describe venous ulcer formation, resulting from hypoxia induced by the stasis of blood within dilated subcutaneous veins. Since then, however, the stasis theory has been challenged by the findings of increased blood flow in the area of venous ulcers and not stasis.[59]

The precise etiology of venous ulcers is still unclear. Nevertheless, up to 76% of venous insufficiency can be diagnosed by clinical evidence alone.[32] In addition to the obvious ulcer, the patient will show other signs of the condition, such as varicose veins, which is a common initial sign; reddish-brown hyperpigmentation and purpura, which develop as a result of red blood cells collecting in the dermal layer of the skin; melanin deposition; and macrophages with hemosiderin gathering in the area of the wound.

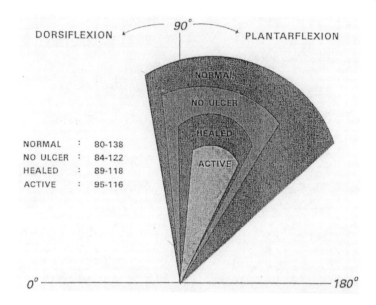

NORMAL   :   80-138
NO ULCER :   84-122
HEALED   :   89-118
ACTIVE   :   95-116

TABLE 1. Average range of ankle motion for four grups of limbs. Numbers associated with each group indicate mean angles reached on 180-degree scale with maximal dorsiflexion and plantar flexion. (From Back TL, Padberg FT, Araki CT, et al: Limited range of motion is a significant factor in venous ulceration. J Vasc Surg 22:519–523, 1995.)

Eczema, pruritus, erythema, and scaling are not uncommon. Some patients develop atrophie blanche, defined as smooth, ivory-white atrophic plaques of sclerosis, speckled with telangiectases.[33] Lipodermatosclerosis, an induration/fibrosis, is seen in long-standing disease.[39] Abnormal ankle range of motion and calf muscle dysfunction are correlated with the clinical severity of CVI and the development of venous ulceration[5] (Table 1). When ulcers develop near the Achilles tendon and are left untreated for a long period of time, the tendon may undergo fibrosis and shortening, a phenomenon that can exacerbate calf muscle dysfunction. The physician should anticipate a slower healing process when these signs are present.

Some clinicians arbitrarily use the criteria of an ABI (ankle-brachial index) > 0.8 and venous reflux > 0.5 s as a measurable way of diagnosing chronic venous insufficiency. We should emphasize that ABI by Doppler ultrasonography is useful only to exclude concomitant arterial disease and that it is unreliable in assessing arterial insufficiency in patients with diabetes mellitus, the elderly, and other conditions with calcified arteries.[35]

This chapter is intended to be a practical guide for clinicians in the management of venous ulcers in the office or out-patient clinic.

PATHOPHYSIOLOGY OF VENOUS CIRCULATION

Abnormalities of the Macrocirculation

VENOUS REFLUX AND INCOMPETENT VALVES

Macrocirculation of the lower extremity venous system consists of the deep, superficial, and communicating veins. The signs and symptoms of chronic venous

TABLE 2.   Incidence of Ulceration in Limbs with Chronic Venous Insufficiency;
Relationship to Ambulatory Venous Pressure

Pressure (mmHg)	Limbs with Ulcer (%)
< 30	0
31–40	11
41–50	22
51–60	38
61–70	59
71–80	68
> 80	73

Adapted from Nicolaides AN, Hussein MK, Szendro G, et al: The relation of venous ulceration with ambulatory venous pressure measurements. J Vasc Surg 17:414–419, 1973.

insufficiency (CVI) result from venous obstruction, venous reflux, calf muscle dysfunction, or a combination of these factors. Venous reflux is the principal cause of CVI and is the result of primary valvular incompetence or secondary failure due to post-thrombotic syndrome or venous obstruction. Venous ulceration is predominantly a manifestation of reflux, even in the presence of coincident obstruction.[47]

Ambulatory venous pressure (AVP) and venous recovery time (VRT) are only two of the many methods available to assess the macrocirculation of patients with CVI. AVP is simply the direct measurement of venous pressure during ambulation, and is used to detect venous hypertension. It has been reported that patients with AVP of less than 40 mmHg have a minimal incidence of venous ulceration as compared with 80% of patients with an AVP greater than 80 mmHg (Table 2). The AVP, however, is a measurement of the overall function of the venous system and does not differentiate between reflux, obstruction, or a combination of both.[51]

Air plethysmography permits the evaluation of venous reflux (venous filling index: VFI), calf muscle pump function (ejection fraction: EF), and overall lower extremity venous function (residual volume fraction: RVF). An abnormality in RVF, which correlates with ambulatory venous pressure, reflects inadequate calf muscle

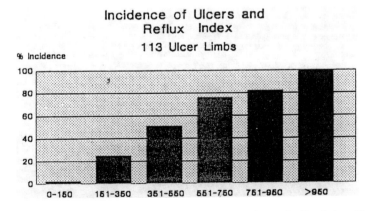

TABLE 3.   Relationship between incidence of stasis ulceration and reflux index. (From Raju S, Fredericks R: Hemodynamic basis of stasis ulceration: An hypothesis. J Vasc Surg 13:491–495, 1996.)

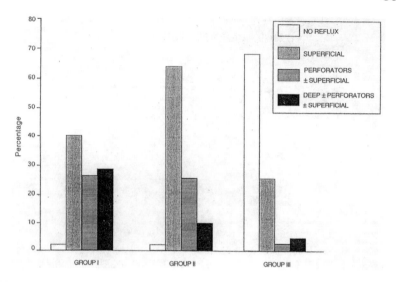

TABLE 4. Histogram shows percentage distribution of reflux in groups I (ulcerated), II (varicose veins), and III (contralateral "normals"). (From Van Rij AM, et al: Anatomic and physiologic characteristics of venous ulceration. J Vasc Surg 20:759–764, 1994.)

action (decreased EF), valvular reflux (increased VFI), or a combination of both. Ulcerated limbs tend to have lower EFs and higher RVFs than non-ulcerated or healed limbs[3] (Table 3).

Duplex scanning is employed for noninvasive detection and quantification of venous reflux. Reflux in the popliteal and infrapopliteal veins appears to have a more significant relationship to the skin changes and ulcer formation associated with advanced CVI than more proximal reflux[21,38,50] (Table 4). This may be because of peripheral venous refilling times and postexercise pressures being more abnormal when popliteal or calf veins are incompetent than when incompetence is confined to the above-knee veins.

Though these tests are available, in practice, it is not essential or practical for the physiatrist to use these methods to assess the functioning of the macrocirculatory system in the office. If these studies are required, such as prior to surgical interventions, the patients should be referred to vascular clinics/laboratories.

PERFORATOR VEIN INCOMPETENCE

Incompetent communicating veins were seen in the region of venous ulcers in up to 86% of ulcers by duplex exam.[26] Communicating vein incompetence may also contribute to recurrence of ulcers after vein stripping. The treatment is an interruption of the incompetent communicating veins.[29,52,66]

Abnormalities of Microcirculation

VENOUS HYPERTENSION (TABLE 5)

Ambulatory venous hypertension arises from valvular failure due to primary or secondary valvular damage. During exercise, pressure in the superficial veins does not fall and, as a result, damage may occur to the skin microcirculation.[15] The consequences of long-standing ambulatory venous hypertension include hemosiderosis

MICROVASCULAR DYSFUNCTION IN CHRONIC VENOUS INSUFFICIENCY

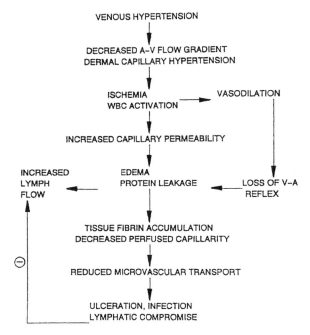

TABLE 5. Microvascular pathophysiology of chronic venous insufficiency: Calf pump failure leads to microvascular hypertension, edema, and a perfusion defect. Chronic vasodilation may contribute to failure of the V-A reflex. Lymphatic failure aggravates edema. (From McDonagh PF: The microvascular pathophysiology of chronic venous insufficiency. Yale J Biol Med 66:27–36, 1993.)

and lipodermatosclerosis, which often progress to venous ulceration with skin loss in the region proximal to the medial or lateral malleolus.

The higher the venous pressure during walking, the higher the incidence of ulceration.[40] Coleridge Smith demonstrated that skin capillaries of the lower limb dilated during venous hypertension, and that there was a reduction in flow velocity and shear rate. This favored leukocyte adhesion and trapping which over time led to damage of the microcirculation. Although ulcers may occur in limbs with little or no elevation of the ambulatory venous pressure, in general, there is a fairly close correlation between the incidence of ulcers and postexercise venous hypertension.[41]

ALTERED FUNCTION OF THE VENOUS ENDOTHELIUM

Microcirculatory capillary endothelial cells are morphologically and functionally altered in CVI. Examples of morphologic changes include an increased number of pinocytic vesicles within endothelial cells, a more irregular endothelial surface, and a widening of the interendothelial space. These changes suggest low-grade endothelial injury. Mononuclear cells, needed for wound healing, have diminished functional ability as well.[45] Even though lymphocytes and monocytes appear to infiltrate the skin more abundantly in patients with CVI, their functional impairment may contribute to the difficulty with healing venous ulcers. In addition, there are some biomechanical alterations seen in patients with CVI, such as an increased production of intracellular adhesion molecules (ICAM) and interleukin-1.[14,63]

ARTERIOVENOUS SHUNTING

It was postulated that microarteriovenous fistulae transmitted arterial pressure to the venous system, which lead to increased vascular permeability and deleterious effects on tissue metabolism. This theory, however, is no longer accepted since the presence of such fistulae has never been established.[28]

CAPILLARY CIRCULATION

In vivo microscopic studies have shown capillary microthrombosis within lipodermatosclerotic skin and a reduction in the number of capillaries in areas of prior ulceration (atrophie blanche). This suggests that the actual destruction of the cutaneous circulation may contribute to venous ulceration and perhaps to recurrent ulcer formation.[7,27]

LYMPHATIC CIRCULATION

The numbers of visible collecting channels are decreased, and the lymphatic network is disrupted in areas of damaged skin.[7]

Theories on the Mechanism of Tissue Damage and Ulceration

There are a number of theories regarding the etiologic factors for venous ulceration. The most prevalent theories are the fibrin cuff and white blood cell trapping theories (Table 6).

FIBRIN CUFF THEORY

In 1982, Browse postulated that semi-occlusive pericapillary fibrin cuffs resulted from leakage of fibrinogen into the interstitial tissues.[9,10] These cuffs then acted as a barrier to oxygen and nutrient diffusion into the interstitial tissues and cutaneous cells. These cuffs are more complex than originally thought. They appear to be composed not solely of fibrin but of a number of extracellular matrix proteins that can serve as potent chemoattractants and leukocyte and platelet activators and conceivably may serve as the basis for the chronic inflammatory response. There is also reduced fibrinolytic activity in patients with venous disease, which may explain why fibrin cuffs persist.[10,24,61,64]

A theoretical study to assess the physiologic effect of the fibrin cuff showed that there was no impairment in oxygen delivery to tissues. Even a cuff consisting of 100 times more fibrin would result in only a 50% reduction of oxygen delivery.[36] Furthermore, no difference in xenon clearance or time for reoxygenation was found between venous disease and control subjects.[12,56,58] These results suggest that it is unlikely there is an abnormality in oxygen delivery to the tissues of patients with CVI. Investigators thus far have been unable to conclusively demonstrate hypoxia of the perimalleolar tissues in patients with CVI, although the presence of fibrin cuffs in CVI is well documented.

WHITE CELL TRAPPING THEORY

The proposed mechanism is that WBCs become trapped in the microcirculation of patients with CVI, leading to microvascular congestion and thrombosis. The

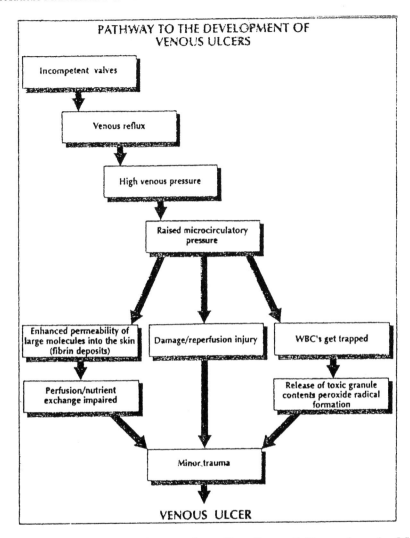

TABLE 6.   The pathogenesis of venous ulcers. (From Burton C: Venous ulcers. Am J Surg 167(A)(suppl), January 1994.)

trapped cells migrate into the interstitium and release lysosomal enzymes, resulting in tissue destruction.

In 1988, Coleridge Smith suggested that white cell sequestration (trapping) in the legs of patients with venous disease might be the main cause of tissue damage. Trapping occurred within 30 minutes of raising the venous pressure in control subjects, but was greater in patients with venous disease. Patients with venous disease were trapping 30% of the white cells, while normal subjects were trapping only 7%. In addition, venous hypertension lasting more than 30 minutes produced neutrophil degranulation and adhesion molecule expression.[54]

It was found that the number of functioning capillary loops was decreased after the legs were dependent for 30 minutes[14] and the ratio of WBC to RBC was decreased in the venous return from dependent limbs of CVI patients as opposed to venous blood from the same limbs in the supine position. These observations suggested that the WBCs plugged some of the dermal capillaries when the legs were in a dependent position. This, in turn, reduced perfusion of the capillaries, and thus, limited nutrient exchange.[60]

The second part of this theory is the activation of white cells. White cell activation results in the release of proteolytic enzymes, superoxide radicals, and chemotactic substances.[6] The majority of these cells are macrophages with a T-lymphocyte component. Tissue destruction may occur when an inflammatory response is produced in the skin, followed by an additional stimulus that activates the cells present in the tissues producing rapid skin necrosis. This is known as the Schwartzmann reaction and may explain why patients with lipodermatosclerosis have a higher risk of ulceration in response to minor leg trauma.[6]

LOCAL NEURAL CONTROL THEORY

A local sympathetic axonal reflex, the venoartriolar reflex, results in microvascular vasoconstriction in response to venous pressure above 25 mmHg. Normally, this reflex is abolished by activation of the calf muscle pump and reduction in venous pressure. In addition, axonal nociceptive C-fibers appear to be abnormal in CVI. These fibers are responsible both for transmitting pain sensation to the CNS, thereby preventing repetitive trauma to areas of injury, and for stimulating the release of vasodilator neuropeptides that act as growth factors for epidermal cells and fibroblasts.

There is evidence that the components of the cutaneous vasodilatory response, mediated by nociceptive C-fiber input, are dysfunctional in patients with severe CVI. This may contribute to venous ulceration by making the patient less sensitive to local trauma and by diminishing vasodilator neuropeptides, which could act as growth factors to stimulate healing after injury.[2,17,23]

In summary, no single theory completely explains the changes within the macrocirculation and microcirculation. It is clear, however, that venous hypertension transmitted to the cutaneous microcirculation results in cellular, microangiopathic, and functional abnormalities that result in lipodermatosclerosis and ulceration.

TREATMENT OF VENOUS ULCERS

As in all treatment strategies, it is important to first take a detailed history and perform a proper physical examination:

History

1. First, other causes of ulceration, in particular arterial, neoplastic, infectious, hematologic, or neurologic diseases should be excluded. Approximately 20% of patients with venous ulcers may have coexisting arterial disease.[11]

2. Prior deep vein thrombosis (DVT)—only 48% give a positive history.[49]

3. Use of immunosuppressants.

4. History of smoking.

5. Previous ulcer treatment or therapy and the individual's compliance.

6. Allergies: Estane, nylon and Lycra are used in compression hosiery. To limit the exposure to these potential allergens, these fibers are coated with cotton. Patients may be advised to apply a thin lining of cotton tubular bandage or stockinette under the stocking to prevent skin irritation.

Physical examination (Tables 7 and 8)

1. Pedal pulse palpation can be difficult in the presence of dependent edema. Doppler pedal pulse may not rule out a leg ulcer of mixed arterial and venous etiology.[22]

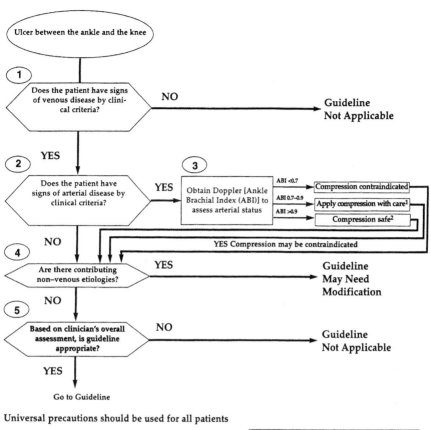

Universal precautions should be used for all patients

Footnote:

[1]Consider other findings, referral, or both for patients with significant arterial occlusive disease.

[2]See conditions that can falsely elevate ABI.

Codes	
Oval	= Presenting problem
Hexagon	= Diagnostic question
Rectangle	= Clinical action

TABLE 7. Venous leg ulcer diagnostic algorithm. (From McGuckin M: Venous leg ulcer guidelines. Ostomy/Wound Management, 1977.)

Ankle pressures are unreliable in both diabetic and artherosclerotic individuals. High levels of compression are contraindicated when an ABI is less than 0.8–0.9.

    2. Auscultation or the use of a Doppler probe over the varicosities to detect possible AV malformations.

    3. If there is edema, a duplex scan of the leg is necessary to exclude DVT.

    4. Evaluate the client's dexterity and other disabilities. Older people with degenerative arthritis of hand may not have the strength and dexterity to manipulate stiff stockings. Obese individuals may have difficulty with bending.

    5. Skin integrity: Look for newly healed ulcers where the skin and tissues remain friable, or areas that show signs of drainage and may breakdown imminently.

    6. Ankle range of motion (important for reasons described earlier).

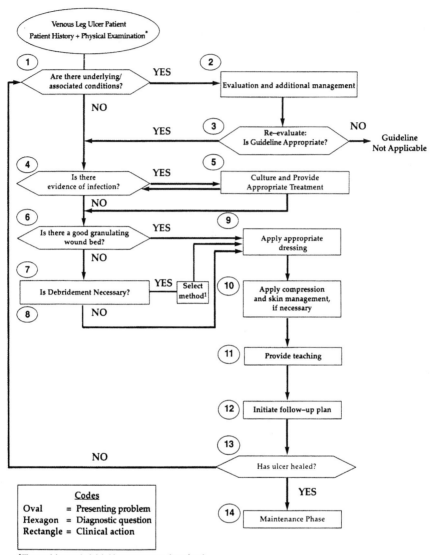

TABLE 8. Venous leg ulcer treatment algorithm. (From McGuckin M: Venous leg ulcer guideline. Ostomy/Wound Management, 1997.)

Pharmacotherapy

The following are some of the recommendations of the International Task Force on the management of active venous ulcers of leg.[13]

SYSTEMIC DRUGS

Diuretics have little role in the treatment of CVI. They can be used occasionally for short periods in patients with severe edema, but they must be used cautiously.

There are multiple other drug therapies to treat lipodermatosclerosis and venous ulceration.

Several systemic drugs, naftidrofuryl, flunarizine, oxypentifylline (fibrinolytic agent), oxerutins (phlebotrophic agent), micronized diosmin, and hemodialysate (fibrinolytic agent) have been tested in clinical trials with various results. Systemic antibiotics could not improve the overall healing rate or ulcer size. Healing was not influenced by positive or negative post-treatment cultures.[1]

Currently, there is no evidence to support the practice of routinely culturing leg ulcers or administering systemic drugs, since they have not been found to influence the outcome of wound healing. It is the recommendation of the International Task Force that further studies are required to better assess the efficacy of medications in the treatment of venous ulcers.

LOCAL AND TOPICAL THERAPIES

Studies demonstrate the efficacy of several types of local therapy. Cadexomer iodine (Iodosorb) is an iodine-containing hydrophilic starch powder used as a topical dressing for venous ulcers. It absorbs wound exudate and releases iodine as a bactericidal agent. This type of dressing has been shown to be effective in promoting ulcer healing by removing pus, debris, and exudate.[46,58] Human growth hormone (topical synthetic) demonstrates some effectiveness,[48] but further confirmation is required. Hydrocolloid dressing (Duoderm) and Dextranomer beads were found to be ineffective.[1]

Topical defibrotide was tested in conjunction with compression therapy in a crossover trial lasting two 3-month periods. The combined treatment (defibrotide + compression) showed a greater reduction in the ulcer area and a higher ulcer-healing rate as compared to compression alone.[44]

The V.A.C. (Vacuum Assisted Closure) Wound Closure System (VAC. KCL USA, Inc. P.O. Box 659505, San Antonio, TX) is being used for the treatment of venous ulcers. It is a negative pressure device. However, this author has little experience with the system in the treatment of venous ulcers.

The consensus of the International Task Force is that local therapies have not yet been proven to have an adjunctive role in the treatment of venous ulcers. Their continued use should be subject to further studies. Nevertheless, if venous hypertension (> 90 mmHg) is appropriately managed, approximately 86% of all venous ulcers will heal with little or no topical treatment.[16]

Compression Therapy

This mode of therapy is currently the mainstay of treatment of venous ulcers used by most practicing physiatrists. Thus, an in-depth review of compression therapy is warranted.

Compression therapy has been widely used in the treatment of venous leg ulcers for over 300 years. The mode of action is not clearly understood. It is postulated that the application of external pressure to the calf muscles raises interstitial pressure, decreases superficial venous pressure, and improves venous return. All these factors lead to a reduction in superficial venous hypertension and edema, which allows healing of the ulcer to occur. Compression can also lower venous pressures by improving the closure of the semi-lunar valves in the superficial veins and decreasing vein diameter. In addition, compression hosiery has been shown to improve the velocity of blood flow within the deep system. Others, however, believe that compression improves venous flow, venous refilling time and microcirculation, and the Starling equilibrium but not venous hypertension.

There are three modes of compression therapies: **compression bandaging, compression hosiery**, and **intermittent compression devices**.

Compression Bandaging

The Unna (Unna's) Boot

In 1883, Paul Gerson Unna, a German dermatologist, developed the Unna boot. It was the first widely published supportive leg wrap dressing for the treatment of venous ulcers. The Unna boot consists of a gauze bandage roll impregnated with zinc oxide, calamine, gelatin, and glycerine. Zinc oxide and calamine protect the skin and are astringents. Gelatin is a mechanical protective agent, and glycerine is a humectant that keeps the mixture moist.

The Unna boot is considered a semi-rigid dressing (SRD). The bandage adheres to the skin and forms a semirigid, inextensible dressing 24 hours after application. Various manufacturers produce Unna boots; Medicopaste bandage (Graham-Field), Gelocast (Beiersdorf), Unna-Flex (Convatec), and Domepaste.

Method of Application. There are different techniques for applying the Unna boot, but certain rules must be followed. For instance, the Unna boot must extend from the base of the toes to the lower border of the popliteal fossa, the heel must be covered by at least three layers of bandage, the ankle must be held in a neutral position while wrapping, and the wrap must be cut and restarted in a figure-8 fashion to avoid bunching. In addition, the wrap is rolled over the contours of the leg without tension. Localized supplemental pressure may be necessary. The finished product is covered with cotton tubular stockinet or an elastic bandage. The elastic support bandage protects clothing and also provides some compression. It must be changed after 1–4 weeks depending on the quantity of the drainage. Ideally, the pressure is 20–30 mmHg at the ankle, and 10 mmHg at the infra-patellar notch.

The dressing is removed by carefully cutting up the side of the Unna boot with bandage scissors so as not to injure the leg. The ulcer and leg are cleaned, and, if necessary, the wound is debrided. The leg must be dry and free of sediment from the previous Unna boot before reapplication.

Mechanism of Action of Unna Boot. Normally, leg edema is prevented by the calf muscle pump, which generates forces when the muscle contracts against the rigid fascia. It causes compression because the non-elastic bandage does not yield circumferentially whereas the contour of leg keeps adjusting segmentally while the ankle joint is in motion. In addition, the Unna boot, unlike any other bandage, adheres to the skin and exerts a shear force during ankle motion thus bringing the edges of the ulcer together.

Compression of the plantar veins discharges blood into the deep veins of the calf and may initiate the pumping process. During normal walking, the events are synchronized in the following order: first, dorsiflexion of the foot empties the distal calf veins; then weight bearing empties the foot; and finally, plantar flexion empties the proximal calf veins.[19] With each step, four pressure peaks, followed by valleys, can be traced, while the moving foot crosses the zero pressure point, at which the boot was applied. Therefore, the effect of the Unna boot seems to rest in the pressure changes that result in control of edema. The full effect of the Unna boot is reached after a few hours of walking or ankle motion (see Fig. 1). The main benefit of the Unna boot is from its compressive and moist-wound-healing effect rather than the chemical components of the dressing itself.

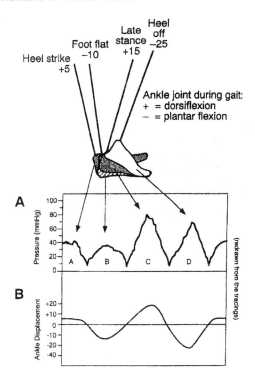

FIGURE 1. Pressure/displacement of ankle under Unna's boot during one step: A: active dorsiflexion; B: passive plantar flexion; C: Passive dorsiflexion; D: active plantar flexion. When ankle displacement is zero (position at which the boot was applied), pressures under boot reach minimum value = 4 times with each step. Composite redrawn from the tracings. (From Lippmann HI, Fishman L, Farrar RH, et al: Edema control in the management of disabling chronic venous insufficiency. Arch Phys Med Rehabil 75, April 1994.)

Indications. The Unna boot is used for ambulatory as well as non-ambulatory patients, if the ankle joint has at least 5 degrees of dorsiflexion and plantarflexion. Lippmann and Briere studied six healthy subjects lying supine on a tilt table at 10 degrees' inclination. Ankle movements were followed and segmental pressure changes were traced with the subjects **at rest.** They performed passive and active range of motion against manual resistance and isometric ankle motion in the resting ankle position. They compared the effects of a cotton wrap (control), two layers of supportive nylon hose, Ace bandages, and Unna boot. The Unna boot was found to be most effective with maximum compression values distally and lowest proximally. The two-way stretch transmitted negligible forces, the Ace bandage set up a hindrance from center to proximal, and the cotton wrap had no effect. Thus, Unna boots can be used at rest as long as ankle ROM is performed be it passive, active or isometric.[31]

The Unna boot is ideal for patients who cannot perform dressing changes because of physical limitations, including arthritis, hemiparesis, and obesity, and non-compliance with other venous ulcer treatments.

Contraindications. Contraindications of Unna boot are acute pulmonary edema, cellulitis, deep venous thrombosis, arterial insufficiency, weeping dermatitis, and wound infection.

Ankle circumferences of less than 18 cm and edema extending above the knee may make the patient ineligible for compression therapy. Compression at the ankle can cause pressure necrosis over the anterior tendons because they are at bony high points on the leg, resulting in high levels of pressure over a small circumference (Laplace's law). It is often difficult to maintain adequate compression over fleshy, poorly defined limbs, and thus the Unna boot tends to roll down the leg and may be ineffective in controlling edema above the knee.

Advantages and Disadvantages. One of the advantages of Unna boot treatment is its relatively low cost ($10–15 per application). In addition, it usually does not interfere with the patient's work schedule and regular activities. It is well suited to the moist wound-healing environment. It requires minimal patient compliance because the dressing is usually applied and removed by a health care professional.

In certain instances, the Unna boot is applied in an open heel method to take advantage of the following:

1. It is easier to apply and better tolerated by patients.

2. It can be used with regular shoes.

3. The condition of the heel can be monitored in the ambulatory as well as bedridden patients.

4. This can be used in patients with concomitant venous and arterial insufficiency (eliminating pressure on the heel).

5. Ambulatory patients can maintain greater ankle mobility and, as a result, it can activate the muscle pump under compression.

6. It prevents frozen ankles and tight heel cords.

The disadvantages of the Unna boot include inability to monitor the ulcer between dressing changes, the need for health care personnel to apply the dressing, and relative discomfort of the bulky dressing. In addition, the accumulation of ulcer drainage under the dressing can become malodorous and cause maceration of the adjacent tissue, and may encourage fungal overgrowth and, consequently, extension of the wound.

Personal hygiene is an important issue. In order to keep the Unna's boot dry, patients often resort to sponge bathing, instead of taking showers.

The Unna boot paste with its antiseptic and anti-pruritic properties can cause skin sensitization, particularly contact dermatitis secondary to the paraben preservative. Poorly applied, excessively constrictive Unna boots can result in localized purpura, cyanosis, and tissue necrosis.

Ulcer care system (Jobst) is a double hosiery system that can be used as an alternative to the Unna boot for individuals who can change their own dressings. It consists of a hydrophilic polyurethane sponge, covered with a hydrophobic membrane, which is applied to the venous ulcer under a two-layer surgical elastic stocking. This dressing is usually changed daily, thus offering a level of personal hygiene not available with the Unna boot.[53]

OTHER COMPRESSION BANDAGES

Compression bandages are typically used for CVI with ulceration. Interface pressure depends on the tension of the bandage and on the radius of the limb as stated in Laplace's law (pressure = tension/radius). According to Laplace's law, the interface pressure under a compression bandage diminishes gradually with the increasing radius, from the distal to the proximal leg.[20]

In order to reach the same tension, an elastic bandage has to be stretched more than an inelastic bandage. Bandages need to be applied with a greater tension on large or edematous legs than on thinner legs. Conversely, thin legs need careful protection over bony prominences and tendons where interface pressures can be as high as 100 mmHg. In graduated or graded compression, the interface pressure below the knee should be approximately 70% of that at the ankle.

Classification of Bandages by Applied Pressure. No universally agreed classification system exists for bandages. The British National Formulary uses a descriptive classification system. The classification used in the NHS (National Health Service) Drug Tariff divides bandages into three types depending on the elasticity: Class 1, 2, and 3. Class 1 and 2 apply low and moderate pressure, respectively.

Class 3 reduces venous hypertension and is further subdivided into types 3a, 3b, 3c, and 3d. They represent the degree of compression that can be applied (20, 30, 40, and 50 mm Hg, respectively) to an average sized ankle.

Bandages can be further described as retention and support bandages. Retention bandages are lightweight, and conforming, and are used primarily, to keep dressings in place. Support bandages, have more elasticity and can be used for sprains and strains.

Compression bandages can be further categorized as long, medium, and short stretch bandages, based on their extensibility.

Short, Medium, and Long Stretch Bandages. Short stretch bandages provide low resting pressures, which increase with activity (walking), as the calf muscle pump works against a semi-rigid bandage. Therefore, this may be unsuitable for applying sustained compression to the leg of an inactive individual. For this reason, they are referred to as providing "inelastic" compression. Comprilan dressing (Beiersdorf-Jobst, Inc., Toledo, OH) is an example of this type of bandage. Unlike the Unna boot and four-layer bandages, they can be washed and reused. The four-layer and short stretch bandages reduce edema and improve ulcer healing better than the Unna boot.[18]

It is important to note that, with short stretch bandages, the interface pressure decreases significantly in the supine position, while long stretch bandages maintain their interface pressure regardless of body position. Therefore, short stretch bandages can be used safely in PVD and diabetic patients, who must be protected from sustained interface pressures. In addition, short stretch bandages lose more than half of their pressure over a wear time of several days, whereas long stretch bandages sustain their interface pressure over a more prolonged period of wear time.[20] The short stretch bandages, therefore, may require more frequent replacement.

Long stretch bandages provide sustained compression therapy, constantly compressing the leg throughout the duration of the treatment, regardless of the patient's activity. However, long stretch bandages require a higher compression to achieve the same pressure as short stretch bandages. Such high pressures can be tolerated while walking, but not when lying down or sitting. The tolerance for the same amount of initial pressure is much better for short stretch bandages. Moreover, there is an immediate decrease of edema after some minutes of walking, leading to a pressure decrease and to a loosening of the short stretch bandage.

Cohesive bandages are considered **medium stretch bandages**. Since these bandages adhere to themselves, they are used as the outermost layer in layered bandaging to prevent slippage. Manufacturers claim pressures of 14–25 mmHg at the ankle.

Combination/Multilayer Bandages. Lower compression bandages are used in a multilayer arrangement, with each layer having an additive compressive effect, thus providing at least 40 mmHg pressure at the ankle. Examples of the multilayer system include the Profore four-layer High Compression Bandage (Smith and Nephew, Largo, FL) System and the Charing Cross four-layer bandage (widely used in the UK and developed in Charing Cross Hospital, London, UK).

Each layer has a function. The innermost layer acts as padding, which absorbs exudates and redistributes pressure around the bony prominences of the ankle and tibial crest. It also allows evaporation of moisture. The second layer is a standard crepe bandage and preserves the elastic energy of the compression bandage. The third layer is a lightweight elasticated (type 3a) compression bandage applied in a figure-8 configuration and provides a compression pressure of 18–20 mmHg. The fourth or outermost layer is a cohesive bandage. It maintains all layers firmly in place for at least a week. This elastic bandage applies a compression pressure of 22–25 mmHg. The third and fourth layers must be applied with a 50% stretch or mid-stretch and 50% overlap between turns. The combination of these two layers provides approximately 40 mmHg at the ankle.

The advantage of a multilayer system is that mistakes in applying tension tend to average out. In one study, the four-layer system achieved higher initial compression pressures and sustained those pressures over 1 week, whereas the initial pressure recorded in the Unna's boot was not maintained throughout the 7 days of therapy. In addition, the application technique does not require a great deal of skill.

Profore-Lite is a three-layer system; thus lower compressive pressures of 25–30 mmHg are present at the ankle. It is indicated for an individual with an ABI of 0.6–0.7.

Ankle Compression Elastic Bandages (ACE). ACE bandages do not provide adequate compression for patients with venous hypertension and CVI. The actual amount of pressure can exceed the recommended pressure and may unintentionally become a tourniquet.

PROPER APPLICATION OF BANDAGE

The application of bandages and maintenance of appropriate pressure gradients are highly operator-dependent and technique-dependent. The bandages should be applied with uniform tension thereby providing gradual compression from the ankle to the knee in accordance with Laplace's law. The pressure actually applied depends on the skill of the individual applying the bandage and the size, girth, and shape of the leg. Some bandages have extension indicators (rectangles that become stretched into squares when the correct extension is reached). Incorrect application can produce a tourniquet effect or even a reverse-pressure gradient. An interface pressure of approximately 40 mmHg, measured at the gaiter area (4–5 cm above the medial malleolus) is generally agreed to be a safe effective target level in compression therapy. Pressures above 50 mmHg in healthy volunteers showed a marked reduction in subcutaneous tissue and muscular blood flow.[42]

COMPRESSION HOSIERY

Compression hosiery is used more frequently in the prevention of recurrent ulceration rather than for the treatment of active ulcers.

MEASUREMENTS FOR THE COMPRESSION GARMENTS

Ideally, the leg should be measured early in the day, after removal of the compression bandage or as soon as the ulcer has healed. The patient's feet should be flat on the floor. Both legs are measured because of variation in leg size and girth. Three measurements are usually needed for below-knee stockings: the circumference of the narrowest part of the ankle above the malleoli, the length of the leg from the base of the heel to just below the knee, and the circumference of the widest part of the calf. If the measurements do not fall within the parameters set forth by the manufacturer, custom-made stockings may be required.[4]

PRESCRIPTION OF THE COMPRESSION HOSIERY

When a prescription is written for a compression hosiery, the following should be specified:
- Type: Below-knee stockings are prescribed for patients with venous insufficiency. Thigh length with a suspender is usually prescribed for lymphedema. In general, above-knee hosiery have several disadvantages over the shorter below-knee hosiery. For example: (1) They may create a garter effect at the knee or groin during knee flexion. (2) Edema of the thigh cannot be adequately controlled. (3) They are expensive. (4) They are poorly tolerated by the patients. (5) They are difficult to don and doff.
- Open-toe is easier to apply, and patients find them more comfortable than the closed-toe. When there are overlapping toes or painful bunions, the closed-toe is preferred.
- Class of stocking: Class I, II, or III. Class II and III are most commonly prescribed.

Compression stockings should be removed at bedtime and reapplied on waking. They should be washed regularly in cold water and dried away from direct heat so that they will last longer. It is recommended that stockings are replaced at 6-month intervals and both extremities measured each time.

CLASSIFICATION OF THE COMPRESSION HOSIERY

Stockings are categorized according to the pressure exerted at the beta-area, the narrowest part of the ankle just proximal to the malleoli.[62] LaPlace's law ($P = T/r$) states: "The pressure in a cylinder exerted by uniform tension in the wall is inversely proportional to the radius of the cylinder." Thus, gradient compression therapy delivers a higher pressure at the ankle (small radius), with a decline in pressure at the knee (larger radius). There are many classifications for compression hosiery, which may confuse the clinician.

According to the British standard (Dale and Keachie 1995), there are three classes of hosiery (see Table A below).[4]

TABLE A. The British Standard

Class	Support at Ankle	Indications
Class I	Light at the ankle 14–17 mmHg	Mild varicose veins, venous hypertension in pregnancy
Class II	Medium at the ankle 18–24 mmHg	Mild edema, moderate to severe varicose veins, recent recurrence of ulcer, small people
Class III	Strong support 25–35 mmHg	Severe varicose veins Prevent venous ulcers Large heavy leg

The European standard has four different classes (see Table B below).

TABLE B. Classes of Compression According to the European Standard[4]

Class	Support at the Ankle
Class I	18.4–21.1 mmHg
Class II	25.2–32.3 mmHg
Class III	36.5–46.6 mmHg
Class IV	Over 59 mmHg

The Comite European de Normalization (CEN) classification (see Table C below).

TABLE C. CEN (Comite European de Normalization) Classification[62]

Class	Pressure	Absolute Pressure (mmHg)	Absolute Pressure (hPa)	Simplification
Class I	Mild	15–21	20–28	25
Class II	Moderate	23–32	31–43	25–35
Class III	Strong	34–46	45–61	35–45
Class IV	Very strong	> 49	> 65	> 45

In general, external pressures provided by compression therapy range from 20–50 mmHg.[25] This classification is the simplest and used by most physiatrists.

20–30 mmHg	Mild compression
30–40 mmHg	Moderate compression
40–50 mmHg	High compression

The human leg has an irregular shape, and the actual pressure is lowest in the beta-area (posterior and/or inferior to the malleolus) and highest in the pre-tibial area. The pressure over the beta-area is significantly reduced because of the elliptical shape of the human leg and expansion of the stocking over the malleoli. A built-in foam pad may be required to provide adequate pressure in the desired area. The medial side of the leg at the beta level is the most important area because 80% of all venous ulcerations of the leg occur in this area. It is also the lowest point of the muscle pump. Therefore, patients should start with a Class II and quickly change to a Class III stocking. If the patient is unable to tolerate a Class III, a kidney bean shaped foam pad may be inserted under a Class II stocking, particularly, over previously ulcerated areas.

T.E.D. (thrombo embolic disease) anti-embolic stocking (Kendall) provides approximately 18 mmHg and is used for DVT prophylaxis. However, its clinical value for this purpose has not been documented.

Potential hazards of compression hosiery are pressure necrosis, friction damage from poorly fitted hosiery, tourniquet effect, and skin allergies. In patients with fibrous and bony ankylosis of the ankle joint or shortened Achilles tendon, the effectiveness of the compression hosiery is significantly reduced.

MECHANISM OF ACTION OF COMPRESSION STOCKINGS AND BANDAGES

Investigators have used *static* (parameters at rest) and *dynamic* (assess the pumping efficiency of the calf muscle pump) tests to evaluate the efficacy of the graded compression stockings.

Static Tests. Siegel, using Doppler ultrasound, demonstrated a large increase in the femoral vein velocity with compression stockings.[55] Compression stockings increased the rate of clearance of radioisotope markers and radiologic contrast media from recumbent patients. This may explain their efficacy in preventing DVT. In other studies, however, the standing venous pressure was not influenced by the application of stockings.[43]

Dynamic Tests. Venous ulceration results from a failure of exercise to reduce the venous pressure in the veins of the lower limbs due to disease of the deep, superficial, or communicating veins. Although some controversies remain regarding the mechanisms that are responsible for calf muscle pump failure, the resulting pressure abnormalities can be observed and measured easily.

Normally, during ambulation, the dorsal foot vein pressure falls to 0–20 mmHg from a resting level of 80–100 mmHg. Upon standing, the foot vein pressure usually takes > 20 seconds to return to the resting level. In patients with CVI, the foot vein pressure remains high or may show a rapid return to the resting level after exercise. The ambulatory foot vein pressure is generally accepted as reflecting pressure abnormalities in the supramalleolar region, where ulcers commonly occur. It is, therefore, one of the predictors of ulcer formation in patients with CVI. There is controversy as to whether the use of compression stockings will restore the raised ambulatory venous pressure to normal. According to plethysmographic measurements of venous reflux (time to return to resting level after exercise), the efficacy of stockings is **not** by restoring competence of the deep or superficial veins.[57] Other studies suggest the following mechanisms of action:

1. Reduce edema and enhance blood flow.
2. Enhance fibrinolysis by the local release of plasminogen, which stimulates the breakdown of pericapillary fibrin deposits.
3. Alter the venoarterial reflex or TcO2, although, Leu found no evidence of change in these parameters.
4. Preventing the WBC trapping phenomenon.[60]

INFLUENCE OF THE ELASTIC COMPRESSION STOCKINGS ON DEEP VENOUS HEMODYNAMICS

Elastic compression stockings do not exert a significant compressive effect on the deep venous compartment of the leg, nor do they have a clear benefit on their hemodynamic parameters. Stockings may aid in the healing of venous ulcers by favorably altering microvascular dynamics and regional Starling forces leading to relief of edema and improvements in skin nutrition and oxygen delivery.[34]

COMPRESSION DEVICES

INTERMITTENT PNEUMATIC COMPRESSION

Intermittent pneumatic compression devices have been used both for the treatment of venous leg ulcers and the prevention of deep vein thrombosis. Compression is achieved by using inflatable below-knee boots, which produce a pressure gradient of between 30 and 70 mmHg. Intermittent pneumatic compression is often used as an adjunct to compression hosiery or bandages, but have been used alone. This technique is utilized in patients with venous ulceration who cannot tolerate bandages/hosiery, have fixed ankle joints, or who need particularly high pressures.

RECURRENT ULCERS

Recurrent ulcers are an important and complex problem. Some of the factors responsible for recurrence are as follows:

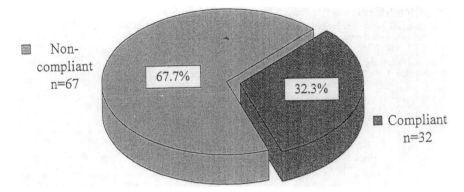

□ Non-
compliant
n=67

67.7%

32.3%

■ Compliant
n=32

FIGURE 2. Distribution of compliance for 99 patients enrolled in ambulatory care program for treating venous ulcers. Compliant patients adhered strictly to protocol. (From Erickson CA, Lanza DJ, Karp DL, et al: Healing of venous ulcers in an ambulatory care program: The role of chronic venous insufficiency and patient compliance. J Vasc Surg 22:629–636, 1995.)

1. Noncompliance with wearing compression hosiery. In a randomized controlled trial undertaken in Riverside Health Authority, the recurrence rate in patients who were compliant was 28% at 18 months, as opposed to 57% in patients who did not wear stockings[37] (Fig. 2).
2. Severity of the underlying disease and the previous size of the ulcer.
3. Poor skin quality.
4. Difficulty with donning and doffing stockings.
5. The presence of (deep) venous incompetence. Ulcer recurrence was 90% in patients with persistent short-saphenous vein incompetence.[8]

Nonhealing Ulcers

When an ulcer does not respond to the usual methods of treatment and becomes a chronic nonhealing ulcer, one should look for other causes of ulceration, such as arterial disease, malignancy (Marjolin's ulcer), factitious ulcer, heterotopic ossification,[30] and fungal infection.

CONCLUSION

- Compression therapy has been shown to be superior to non-compression therapy for ulcer healing.
- Multi-layer systems are more effective than single-layer systems.
- High compression is more effective than low compression, but should be avoided if the ABI is less than 0.8–0.9.
- Unfortunately, many patients tolerate high compression rather poorly. Although, the higher compression is theoretically optimal, the practitioner may have to settle for a lower compression for comfort and ease of application, and to ensure better patient compliance. Studies have shown that as little as 24 mmHg pressure at the ankle can be therapeutic.[65]
- Rather than advocate one particular system, the practitioner should utilize any correctly applied high compression method in patients with uncomplicated venous disease.

REFERENCES

1. Alinovi A, Bassissi P, Pini M: Systemic administration of antibiotics in the management of venous ulcers: A randomized clinical trial. J Am Acad Dermatol 15:186-191, 1986.
2. Andron ME, Helme RD, McKernan S: Microvascular skin responses in elderly people with varicose leg ulcers. Age Ageing 20:124, 1991.
3. Araki CT, Back TL, Padberg FT, et al: The significance of calf muscle pump function in venous ulceration. J Vasc Surg 20:872, 1994.
4. Armstrong S: Compression hosiery product review. Professional Nurse, October 1998, Vol. 14 No. 1, pp 49–56.
5. Back TL, Padberg FT, Araki CT, et al: The significance of calf muscle pump function in venous ulceration. Vasc Surg 22:519, 1995.
6. Bergan JJ, Yao JST: Venous Disorders. Philadelphia, WB Saunders, 1991, pp 47–48.
7. Bollinger A, Leu AJ: Evidence for microvascular thrombosis obtained by intravital fluorescence videomicroscopy. VASA 20:252, 1991.
8. Bradbury AW, Ruckley CV: Foot volumetry can predict recurrent ulceration after subfascial ligation of perforators and saphenous ligation. J Vasc Surg 18:789–795, 1993.
9. Browse NL, Gray L, Jarrett PEM, et al: Blood and vein-wall fibrinolytic activity in health and vascular disease. Br Med J 1:478–481, 1977.
10. Burnand KG, Whimster I, Naidoo A, et al: Pericapillary fibrin in the ulcer-bearing skin of the leg: The cause of lipodermatosclerosis and venous ulceration. Br Med J 285:1071, 1982.
11. Capeheart JK: CVI: A focus on prevention of venous ulceration. Wound Ostomy Continence Nursing 23: 227–234, 1996.
12. Cheatle TR, McMullin GM, Farrah J, et al: Three tests of microcirculatory function in the evaluation of treatment for CVI. Phlebology 5:165–172, 1990.
13. Clement DL: Venous ulcer reappraisal: Insights from an International Task Force. J Vasc Res 36(suppl 1):42–47, 1999.
14. Coleridge Smith PD: The role of white cell trapping in the pathogenesis of venous ulceration. Phlebol Dig 4:4, 1992.
15. Coleridge Smith PD: The microcirculation in venous hypertension. Cardiovasc Res 32:789–795, 1996.
16. Cordts PR, Hanrahan LM, Rodriguez AA et al: A prospective randomized trial of Unna's boot vs Duoderm CGF hydroactive dressing plus compression in the management of venous leg ulcers. J Vasc Surg 15:480–486, 1992.
17. Dulsgaard CJ, Haltgardh-Nilsson A, et al: Neuropeptides as growth factors: Possible role in human diseases. Regul Pept 25:1, 1989.
18. Fletcher A, Cullum N, Sheldon, Trevor A: A systematic review of compression treatment for venous leg ulcers. BMJ 315:576–580, 1997
19. Gardner AMN, Fox RH: The Return of Blood to the Heart: Venous Pumps in Health and Disease. London, John Liberty Eurotext Ltd., 1989.
20. Hafner J, Luthi W, et al: Instruction of compression therapy by means of interface pressure measurement. Dermatol Surg 26:481–487, 2000.
21. Hanraham LM, Araki CT, Rodriguez AA, et al: Distribution of valvular incompetence in patients with venous stasis ulceration. Vasc Surg 13:805, 1991.
22. Harding KG: Wound care: Putting theory into clinical practice. In Krasner D (ed): Chronic Wound Care: A Clinical Source Book for Health Care Professionals. King of Prussia, PA, Health Management, 1990, pp 19–30.
23. Henriksen O: Local sympathetic reflex mechanism in regulation of blood flow in human subcutaneous adipose tissue. Acta Physiol Scand Suppl 450:7, 1977.
24. Herrick SE, Sloan P, McGurk M, et al: Sequential changes in histologic pattern and extracellular matrix deposition during the healing of chronic venous ulcers. Am J Pathol 141:1085, 1992.
25. Ibrahim S, MacPherson DR, Goldhaber SZ: Venous insufficiency: Mechanisms and management. Am Heart J 132:856–860, 1996.
26. Labropoulos N, Giannoukas AD, Nicolaides AN, et al: New insights into the pathophysiologic condition of venous ulceration with color-flow duplex imaging: Implications for treatment? J Vasc Surg 22:45, 1995.
27. Leu AJ, Leu H-J, Frazeck UK, et al: Microvascular changes in chronic venous insufficiency: A review. Cardiovasc Surg 3:237, 1995.
28. Lindemayer W, Lofferer O, Mostbeck A, et al: Arteriovenous shunts in primary varicosis? A critical essay. Vasc Surg 6:9, 1972.
29. Linton RR, Hardy CB: Postthrombotic syndrome of the lower extremity: Treatment by interruption of the superficial femoral vein and ligation and stripping of the long and short saphenous veins. Surgery 24:452, 1948.

30. Lippmann HI, Goldin RR: Subcutaneous ossification of legs in chronic venous insufficiency. Radiology 74:279–288, 1960.
31. Lippmann HI, Briere J-P: Physical basis of external supports in chronic venous insufficiency. Arch Phys Med Rehabil1 52(12):555–559, 1971.
32. Lopez A, Phillips TJ: Venous ulcers. Wounds 10:149–157, 1998.
33. Maessen-Visch MB, Koedam MI, Hamulyak K, Neumann HAM: Atrophie blanche. Int J Dermatol 38:161–172, 1999.
34. Mayberry JC, Moneta GL, De Frang RD, et al: The influence of elastic compression stockings on deep venous hemodynamics. J Vasc Surg 13:91, 1991.
35. McGuckin M, Stineman M, Goin J, Williams S: Draft guideline: Diagnosis and treatment of venous leg ulcers. Ostomy Wound Management 42:48–78, 1996.
36. Michel CC: Oxygen diffusion in oedematous tissue and through pericapillary cuffs. Phlebology 5:223–230, 1990.
37. Moffat CJ: A pioneering service to the community: The Riverside Community Leg Ulcer Project. Professional Nurse April:486–497, 1994.
38. Moore DJ, Himmel PD, Sumner DS: Distribution of venous valvular incompetence in patients with the postphlebitic syndrome. Vasc Surg 3:49, 1986.
39. Nemeth AJ, Eaglstein WH, Falanga V: Clinical parameters and transcutaneous oxygen measurements for the prognosis of Venous ulcers. J Am Acad Dermatol 20:186–189, 1989.
40. Nicolaides AN, Zukowski A, Lewis R, et al: Venous pressure measurements in venous problems. In Bergan JJ, Yao JST (eds): Surgery of the Veins. Orlando, FL, Grune & Stratton, 1985, pp 111–118.
41. Nicolaides A, Christopoulos D, Vasdekis S, et al: Progress in the investigation of chronic venous insufficiency. Ann Vasc Surg 3:278–292, 1989.
42. Nielsen HV: External pressure-blood flow relations during limb compression in man. Acta Physiol Scand 119:253–260, 1983.
43. O'Donnell TF, et al: Effect of elastic compression on venous hemodynamics in postphlebitic limbs. JAMA 242:2766–2768, 1979.
44. Ormiston MC, Seymour MTJ, Venn GE, et al: Controlled trial of iodosorb in chronic venous ulcers. Br Med J 291:308–310, 1985.
45. Pappas PJ, Teehan EP, Fallek SR, et al: Diminished mononuclear cell function is associated with chronic venous insufficiency. Vasc Surg 22:580, 1995.
46. Parvulesco J: Micro-coagulo-chirurgie-nouvelle therapie esthetique des varicosities telangiectasiques. Phlebologie 44:193–200, 1991.
47. Raju S, Fredericks R: Venous obstruction: An analysis of 137 cases with haemodynamic, venographic, and clinical correlations. J Vasc Surg 14:305–311, 1991.
48. Rasmussen LH: Evaluation of recombinant human growth hormone for wound management. Dan Med Bull 43:358–370, 1995.
49. Reinhardt LE: Venous Ulceration: Compression as the mainstay of therapy. J WOCN 26:39–44, 1999.
50. Rosfors S, Lamke LO, Nordstrom E, et al: Severity and location of venous valvular insufficiency: The importance of distal valve function. Acta Chir Scand 156:689, 1990.
51. Rutherford, RB (ed): Vascular Surgery, 5th ed. Philadelphia, WB Saunders, 2000, p 1983.
52. Rutherford R B (ed): Vascular Surgery, 5th ed. Philadelphia, WB Saunders, 2000, p 1916.
53. Samson RH: Compression stockings and non-continuous use of polyurethane foam dressings for the treatment of venous ulceration: A pilot study. Phlebology 19(1):68–72, 1995.
54. Shields DA, Andaz S, Timothy-Antoine CA, et al: CD11b/CD18 and neutrophil activation in venous hypertension. J Dermatol Surg Oncol 20:72, 1994.
55. Sigel B, Edelstein A, Felix WR, et al: Compression of the deep venous system of the lower leg during inactive recumbency. Arch Surg 106:38–43, 1973
56. Sjerson P: Blood flow in cutaneous tissue in man studied by washout of radioactive xenon. Circ Res 25:215–229, 1969.
57. Somerville JJJF, et al: The effect of elastic stockings on superficial venous pressures with venous insufficiency. Br J Surg 61:979–981, 1974.
58. Stilbe E, Cheatle TR, Coleridge Smith PD, et al: Liposclerotic skin: A diffusion block or a perfusion problem? Phlebology 5:231–236, 1990.
59. Schwartzberg JB, Kirsner RB: Stasis in venous ulcers: A misnomer that should be abandoned. Dermatol Surg 26:683–684, 2000.
60. Thomas PRS, Nash GB, Dormandy JA: White cell accumulation in dependent legs of patients with venous hypertension: A possible mechanism for trophic changes in the skin. Br Med J 296:1693–1695, 1988.
61. Vanscheidt W, Laff H, Wokalck H, et al: Pericapillary fibrin cuff: A histologic sign of venous ulceration. Cutan Pathol 17:266, 1990.

62. Veraart Joep CJM, Pronk G, Martino Neumann AA: Pressure differences of eElastic compression stockings at the ankle region: American Society for Dermatologic Surgery, Inc. Dermatol Surg 23:935–939, 1997.
63. Veraart JCJM, Verhaegh MEJM, Neumann HAM, et al: Adhesion molecule expression in venous ulcers. VASA 2:243, 1993.
64. Wolf JH, Morland M, Browse NL: The fibrinolytic activity of varicose veins. Br J Surg 66:185, 1979.
65. Zink M, Rousseau P, Holloway AG: Lower extremity ulcers. In Bryant RA (ed): Acute and Chronic Wounds: Nursing Management. St.Louis, Mosby, 1992, pp 164–212.
66. Zukovsxky AJ, Nicolaides AN, Szendro G, et al: Haemodynamic significance of incompetent calf perforating vein. Br J Surg 78:625–629, 1991.

MOOYEON OH-PARK, MD

USE OF ATHLETIC FOOTWEAR, THERAPEUTIC SHOES, AND FOOT ORTHOSES IN PHYSIATRIC PRACTICE

Assistant Professor
Department of Rehabilitation
  Medicine
Montefiore Medical Center/
  Weiler Division
Bronx, New York

Reprint requests to:
Department of Rehabilitation
  Medicine
Montefiore Medical Center/
  Weiler Division
Eastchester Road
Bronx, NY 10461

Physiatrists frequently encounter patients who need therapeutic footwear and foot orthoses (FOs) for the conservative management of foot disorders. although selection of appropriate footwear is usually the most crucial part of successful management of foot problems, physicians often perceive footwear as outside their domain, and overlook its significance. Prescribing FOs requires focused history taking and biomechanical evaluation of the patient from the foot to the trunk.

Most of the medical literature on the subject of footwear is written by non-physiatrists and is often sports-oriented. This chapter emphasizes the thought process from the diagnosis and identification of possible underlying biomechanical abnormalities to the prescription of footwear and FOs.

ASSESSMENT OF THE PATIENT

Detailed history taking and physical examination are discussed in the chapter Problem-Oriented History Taking and Physical Examination of Patients with Foot Pain. The choice of materials and design of footwear and FOs depends on the age and lifestyle of the patient. For relatively sedentary patients, the same footwear can be worn for different activities, whereas athletes may need special shoes for specific sports activities.

Body habitus is another important consideration. For example, FOs are known to be much less effective for obese people with tibialis posterior insufficiency, who will often require a more aggressive approach such as an AFO (ankle foot orthosis).[3] Obese patients may actually experience less shock absorption from shoes with a soft midsole than from those with firmer ones due to "bottoming-out" of the materials.

The pronation-supination response is a closed chain of movements encompassing the entire lower extremity and trunk in which proximal pathology may lead to compensatory motion of distal joints and vice versa. Clinicians should therefore be cautious in prescribing corrective FOs for patients with primary pathology in proximal structures. Patients with femoral anteversion, for example, may have limited external rotation of the hip resulting in compensatory pronation of the subtalar complex. In this instance, an FO designed for pronation control may actually interfere with the patient's gait. Valgus or varus deformities of the knee may also result in compensatory pronation. Unless the proximal deformities are addressed, attempts to correct the pronation will not be successful.

Similarly, proximal symptoms often originate from abnormal biomechanics of the distal segment. For example, pes anserine bursitis, patellofemoral syndrome, or iliotibial band syndrome all may result from excessive pronation of the subtalar complex.

The degree of flexibility of the heel cord and subtalar complex dictates further management of subtalar control. When possible, ankle dorsiflexion (DF) ROM should be evaluated in the subtalar neutral position. A tight heel cord (< 10 degrees of ankle dorsiflexion in subtalar neutral) inevitably forces the subtalar complex toward excessive pronation during stance phase to achieve dorsiflexion of the foot. If the patient has a tight heel cord with a correctable pronation deformity, restoration of ankle DF ROM should be attempted by stretching the gastrocsoleus muscle while maintaining the subtalar joint in a neutral or slightly inverted position.[31] This can be done by wearing an FO with pronation control or placing a medial wedge under the midfoot and hindfoot, while stretching. For patients with tight heel cords in spite of stretching exercises, the only alternative is to provide mild heel elevation. Ideally, the lift should be placed on the footwear rather than on the FO to improve control of the subtalar complex.[17]

The more the axis of the subtalar complex is deviated medially, the less effective an FO can be due to decreased leverage for controlling pronation. In such cases, patients often require more extensive bracing to provide direct subtalar and midtarsal control, such as UCBL or supramalleolar orthoses (SMO). Rigid deformities must be managed with **accommodative** footwear, FOs, or AFOs. For partially correctable pronation deformities, physical therapy to restore flexibility of the subtalar midtarsal articulations is recommended prior to prescribing orthoses.

In addition to evaluation for structural forefoot (FF) deformities such as FF varus or valgus, assessment for a hypermobile first ray is important for proper posting because it can present with similar abnormal biomechanics.

The patient's old footwear and FOs, especially unsuccessful ones, provide valuable information for diagnosis and successful treatment. While a pattern of excessive medial outsole wear and a stretched medial counter indicate excessive pronation, a stretched posterior counter, bulge of uppers at the metatarsals, or outsole wear on the middle portion of the metatarsal area can be seen when the shoe is too tight. An oblique toe break line on the vamp is common in patients with hallux limitus or rigidus. Outsole wear under the 2nd metatarsal area may indicate a hypermobile 1st ray, while wear under the great toe may represent forefoot valgus with a plantarflexed 1st ray. Wear on the distal tip of the outsole, especially in children, suggests tight heel cords with or without spasticity, or dorsiflexion weakness.

ATHLETIC FOOTWEAR

Athletic footwear has been gaining popularity with the increasing health consciousness among the general population including the elderly. As a result, it has become an acceptable alternative for a therapeutic footwear. Many patients with foot problems can be managed with walking sneakers and an FO, if needed.

Advantages of athletic footwear

Relatively inexpensive and diverse choices available

Good suspension (high vamp)

1/8"–3/16" removable sock liner (useful for temporary modifications)

Lightweight

Stretchable soft upper

Relatively good plantar pressure relief[30]

Washable

Limitations of athletic footwear

Limited depth (forefoot: 1/2", hindfoot: 1 1/4"–1 1/2", not enough for severe deformities)

Relatively weak medial counter

Flexible sole may need reinforcement (i.e., for placement of a rocker sole)

Low heel height (flattening the arch of the foot in patients with heel cord tightness)

Technically more demanding to modify than therapeutic shoes

Difficult to provide in-shoe relief (i.e., on the midsole material)

Socially unacceptable in some patients

Not reimbursable

The "**last**" of the athletic footwear affects its function. The term last is used in four different ways[13,18,24]:

1. Shape of the footwear (straight, semicurved, curved).
2. Construction.
    Board last: The upper is sewn to an innersole board, providing stability and rigidity.
    Slip last: The upper is stitched together on the underside, for flexibility and light weight.
    Combination last: board last for hindfoot (HF) and slip last for forefoot (FF)
3. Foot mold itself from which the shoe is made.
4. Relative width of FF to HF, shoes with a "combination last" may refer to a wider FF relatively to HF.

In general, sneakers with a straight last and board construction are recommended for pronated feet and those with a curved last and slip construction are recommended for supinated feet. The features of running and walking sneakers are compared in Table 1. Often there are hybrids of the two, and the features described are not strictly applied to all athletic footwear. Figure 1 shows typical walking sneakers with the explanation of their features.

Patients should be taught how to choose the right type and size of athletic footwear. Although the size and the width marked on the sneakers can be used as a guideline, there is a great variability among different brands and styles. In our practice, patients are instructed as follows. If the insoles are removable, the patient should place them on the floor and stand on them. There should be enough space for the width of a thumb (1/2–3/4") between the longest toe and the tip of the insole. The widest part of the foot should coincide with the widest part of the insole, and the feet should not spread beyond the border of the insole. Women may buy women's (not men's) sneakers, as they have an appropriately narrower heel.

TABLE 1. Comparison of Running and Walking Sneakers

	Running Sneakers	Walking Sneakers
Last (shape)	Semicurved or curved	Semicurved or straight
Last (construction)	Slip last or combination last	Board last or combination last
Upper material	Combination of leather and fabric	Mostly leather
Height of toe box	Relatively low	Relatively high
Midsole	Firm	Firm
Outsole	Rough grain for better grip	Finer grain
Medial counter	Strong	Strong
Weight	Light weight	Slightly heavier
Toe spring	Higher	High
Color	Various colors	Conservative and simple colors
Designed for	Sprinting and running	Stability and control on walking

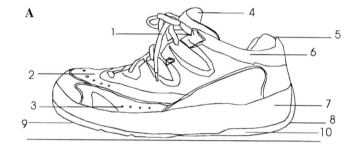

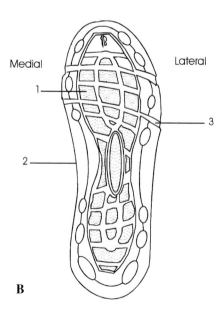

FIGURE 1. Walking sneakers.
(a) Lateral view
1. Laces with four eyelets for proper suspension.
2. Simple soft leather upper, without seams for easy stretching.
3. Breathing holes in the upper as well as medial and lateral counters.
4. Tongue reduces shear. Tongue pad can be applied to make the sneakers snug.
5. Achilles notch for relief of Achilles tendon, heel grip can be applied.
6. Pillow top for comfort.
7. Midsole for structural stability of the sneakers.
8. Beveled heel dampens plantarflexion momentum by shortening leverage arm.
9. Toe-spring to improve roll over. Lighter alternative to rocker sole.
10. Outersole made of strong carbon rubber.
(b) Plantar view
1. Fine, multidirectional tread pattern for walking and turning.
2. Last (shape) straight or semicurved shape. Last (construction)-board last or combination last.
3. Transverse groove along the toebreak line to reduce friction.

Often, sneakers will have stretched after several weeks of use, and become too loose. To restore a good fit, the patient can insert a 3-mm thickness of Poron or firm Plastazote under the sock liner or add tongue pads. In athletes, wearing additional socks is a good option because it can reduce shear. Correspondingly, if sneakers need to be made roomier, the sock liner can be removed. This, however, may not provide enough cushioning, in which case the best solution is often purchasing a new pair of sneakers. Local deformities such as bunions or claw toes can be accommodated by stretching with a ball and ring shoe stretcher (shoemaker's swan) after moistening the area.

The midsole provides the structural integrity of athletic footwear and may deteriorate after several months, even if not used. In running sneakers, the shock-absorbing capability of the midsole is estimated to deteriorate to 70% after 500 miles. The wrinkles on the midsole are often signs of midsole aging and packing of the material as a result of repetitive impact.

The midsole is often made of EVA (ethyl vinyl acetate), polyurethane, or a combination with air cells. Although the air-midsole provides excellent shock absorption and durability, it is difficult to modify and does not provide a great deal of subtalar control.

The physician may try temporary modifications in sneakers before a definitive FO is prescribed. Temporary modifications include placement of various pads, wedges, carbon plates, and local relief using an extra layer of insole. Padding or wedging should be minimal at first, and progressively built up as the patient's tolerance improves. When focal pressure relief is necessary, an extra layer of insole ($\frac{1}{8}$" firm Plastazote) with a hole (relief) corresponding to the painful point can be inserted under the original insole. The location of the hole can be determined by the lipstick technique (similar to the technique described in the appendix), and the size usually depends on the structure to be relieved. For conditions such as painful callus, metatarsalgia, or sesamoiditis, when additional relief is needed, this method may be combined with padding. Table 2 includes the equipment and materials used for trial modifications in the office. The locations of various pads and wedges are illustrated in Figure 2. Temporary office application of metatarsal pads and wedges in athletic footwear is described in the appendix at the end of the chapter.

Technically demanding modifications such as widening the shank or a "buttress flare" (extension of the sole to reinforce the medial or lateral counter) can be provided

TABLE 2. Materials for Temporary Trials

Metatarsal and neuroma pads of various sizes and heights (felt or rubber)
HF & FF wedges
Barton wedges
Cuboid pads
Heel lifts ($\frac{1}{4}$", $\frac{3}{8}$")
Silicone heel cups (small, medium, and large sizes)
Springlite carbon plates covered with $\frac{1}{8}$" PPT (flexible type preferred)
Fabric tape (1", 2")
Other equipment
Skeletal model of the foot for patient education
Walking sneaker with removable insole for patient education
$\frac{1}{8}$" firm black Plastazote sheet
Lipstick, transparent tape
Ball and ring stretcher (shoemaker's swan)

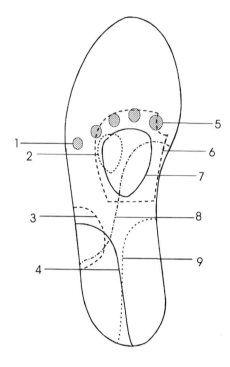

FIGURE 2. Placement of various pads and wedges on the ⅛" Plastazote.
1. 5th metatarsal head (localized by lipstick technique)
2. Neuroma pad
3. Cuboid pad
4. Lateral heel wedge
5. 1st metatarsal head (localized by lipstick technique)
6. Sesamoid relief
7. Metatarsal pad
8. Barton wedge
9. Medial heel wedge

by the pedorthotist.[38] Inserting a steel shank between the midsole and outersole converts sneakers to sturdy footwear suitable for a double upright AFO.

THERAPEUTIC SHOES (ORTHOPEDIC SHOES)

Traditionally, the term "orthopedic shoes" implies sturdy shoes with a steel shank, a long, strong medial counter, and a Thomas heel for medial support. The advantages of such shoes include the stronger medial counter and roominess, and for some patients, they are more socially acceptable than athletic footwear. The limitations, however, are higher cost and weight, and for some patients they are less cosmetically appealing.

The outersole is made of leather, crepe (blown rubber), or carbon rubber. Crepe soles are widely used because they are lightweight and easily modifiable. Another advantage of crepe soles is they can be easily modified from within the shoe ("in-shoe relief") when relieving the insole alone is not enough to accommodate a plantar prominence.

Modifications of Outersoles

A beveled heel shortens the leverage of plantar flexion at the ankle, reducing the stress on ankle dorsiflexors during the loading response. Similarly, a solid ankle cushion heel (SACH) acts as an extrinsic shock absorber simulating plantar flexion of the ankle and reduces stress on the ankle dorsiflexors.

A rocker sole with a steel shank reduces pressure over the great toe and metatarsal heads, and minimizes the need for dorsiflexion at the metatarsophalangeal (MTP) joints. The location, axis, and height of rockers vary with the patient's needs. In general, the more distal the rocker is placed, the more distal the location of effective pressure relief. For example, according to one study,[10] the

TABLE 3. Biomechanical Effects of Modified Outersoles

	Biomechanical Effect	Clinical Use
Soft heel/SACH	Simulates ankle PF, reduces stress on ankle dorsiflexors, decreases flexion momentum at the knee	Anterior shin splints, patellofemoral syndrome, ankle fusion, prosthetic feet, solid AFO, ankle pain aggravated by movement such as arthritis
Beveled heel	Delays heel strike, decreases lever arm of ankle PF reducing the stress on ankle dorsiflexors, similar to being barefoot	Similar to soft heel/SACH, no need for additional materials for the heel modification, simpler than SACH
Rocker sole	Simulates dorsiflexion effect of FF, helping toe clearance, relieves stress on forefoot, reduces the "nutcracker" effect	Hallux rigidus, metatarsalgia, FF plantar ulceration, frequently used with SACH, requires caution for patients with impaired balance (e.g., diabetic neuropathy or elderly)

axis of the rocker may be placed at 65% of shoe length from the heel for relief at the toes and at 55–60% for relief at the metatarsal heads. The higher the rocker, the greater the effect, but this is limited by what is practical and safe.[35] Patients should be trained to take shorter strides in rocker shoes for optimal pressure relief. Since a rocker sole alone may increase plantar pressure in both the heel and the midfoot, it should be used with caution in cases of midfoot-collapse secondary to Charcot neuroarthropathy.[35]

Placing a rocker on sneakers is technically demanding and thus done infrequently. Biomechanical effects of modified outersoles are summarized in Table 3.

Footwear Consideration in Diabetes or Peripheral Vascular Disease

The role of therapeutic footwear in diabetic patients is mainly prevention of initial or recurrent ulceration rather than actual healing of ulcers. For therapeutic shoes to be successful, underlying abnormal biomechanics should be addressed in conjunction with effective patient education. Heel cord tightness is often an underlying culprit for increased plantar FF pressure and for midfoot Charcot neuroarthropathy. Tight heel cords prevent the tibia from rolling over the foot during stance phase and place stress on the midfoot ("nutcracker effect") contributing to midfoot collapse. Once the midfoot Charcot neuroarthopathic process has occurred, stretching of the gastrocsoleus may actually worsen the problem by causing further stress, and surgical correction of equinus is often required for proper treatment in addition to immobilization and nonweight bearing. A solid ankle AFO with a rocker sole (Charcot restraint orthotic walker, or "CROW") is often utilized because it reduces stress to the midfoot avoiding the nutcracker effect.[25]

Patients with diabetic neuropathy or other sensory impairment often choose shoes that are too tight, requiring vigilance on the part of the clinician. Overly large shoes, on the other hand, can also be problematic because they allow excessive mediolateral slippage and shear, leading to callus or ulcer formation.[4] Shear can be reduced by using a tongue pad, rocker sole, beveled heel or SACH, high top shoes, double socks, or shear-absorbing insole materials (e.g., Poron or PPT).

In the patient with a partial foot amputation, a full-length shoe with rocker sole tends to be heavy, and often provides an unstable base owing to the requisite height of the rocker. A short ("stubby") shoe is an alternative that may be better at preventing ulcer recurrence. Another inexpensive option is a sneaker with a soft sole or a transverse slit on the outsole along the distal margin of the stump. This minimizes shear between the distal margin of the stump and the sole of the sneaker.[11]

Plastazote shoes allow room for a simple dressing and accommodate deformities although they are not very durable. Since Plastazote has closed cells, patients may feel hot and sweaty unless ventilation holes are provided.

Temporary footwear such as IPOS or Darco shoes with a "negative" heel (anterior heel height higher than posterior) are used in the DM patient with FF ulcers. Precautions are necessary for patients with impaired balance such as those with neuropathy or elderly patients. Patients with equinus deformities should not wear these shoes because they may develop new plantar ulcers where the FF makes contact with the distal edge of the negative-heeled footwear.

Triple depth shoes are now commercially available to provide more room for accommodation. Custom-made shoes, however, are sometimes necessary for patients with severe deformities from arthritis, Charcot foot, or partial foot amputation. These shoes are expensive and may not provide room for a wound dressing owing to their precise fit. Once they are fabricated, major modifications may not be possible, so the clinician should take this into consideration to avoid ordering them prematurely when there is a wound or surgical procedure is anticipated.

Limb Length Discrepancy (LLD)

Assessment of limb length while weight bearing is more practical than tape measurement or radiologic methods because compensatory mechanisms may take place at multiple levels during walking. The examiner may notice compensatory responses such as excessive pronation or flexion of the knee in the longer limb.

The practitioner should keep a set of heel lifts of various thickness—⅛ inch (3 mm), ³⁄₁₆ inch, ¼ inch (6 mm) and ½ inch (12 mm)—in the office. Commercially available heel lifts are made of felt or synthetic cork. Generally, ¼ inch (6 mm) is the maximum thickness for in-shoe lifts, although some high top shoes might accommodate up to ⅜" without causing heel slippage.

There is also an upper limit to the amount of outsole lift that can be added to the heel without an accompanying sole lift. Generally, any heel lift greater than a ½ inch should be accompanied by a sole lift. The sole lift tapers up to the toe (toe crest), which assists rollover similarly to a rocker sole.

Footwear Recommendations for the Elderly

Physiologic changes of the foot in the elderly include decreased flexibility (especially tight heel cords), soft tissue atrophy, and a widened forefoot. Footwear should be designed for safety and balance with financial considerations, as necessary. Most foot problems in the elderly can be addressed conservatively with proper shoes and orthoses. Although the elderly often do not tolerate rigid insoles or shoes, excessively thick or soft soles can be also be problematic as a result of poor sensory feedback when standing or walking.[32–34]

Sneakers can be a satisfactory alternative to formal orthopedic therapeutic shoes, particularly if financial resources are limited. Sneakers with a fine tread pattern (to prevent catching), proper suspension with laces, and a broad heel base are a good choice.[14] Since sneakers have a relatively low heel compared with regular shoes, patients with tight heel cords may have difficulty maintaining heel-to-toe balance or complain of calf discomfort. Gastrocsoleus lengthening is a slow, tedious process that takes at least several months, and is often difficult for the elderly. Heel lifts are particularly useful for these patients and can gradually be lowered over several months to allow for slow stretching.

For fashion reasons, women's shoes are often narrow around the ball area, and many elderly women have great difficulty finding proper fitting shoes because of a deformed and widened forefoot.[7] Thus, in order to obtain footwear with sufficient room for the forefoot, they may buy shoes that are otherwise too large.

Shoes with poor suspension such as pumps will tend to slip off from the feet during swing phase, even if they're the correct size. To avoid the slippage of the feet, patients tend to choose tight pumps of a smaller size. These patients should be encouraged to find proper fitting shoes with a good suspension, even if they must sacrifice style. Shoes with a stiff outsole (insufficient toebreak), or a posteriorly flared heel can also make the shoes feel too large. This can be remedied by manually breaking the sole at the toebreak line, beveling the heel, using a tongue pad, as needed.

Some patients also have difficulty with fit as a result of fluctuating edema from various causes including medications (e.g., nonsteroidal antiinflammatory drugs, calcium channel blockers, or ACE inhibitors). Shoes that fit when the feet are swollen become too loose after the swelling has subsided and may increase the risk of falls in the elderly. Thus, edema control and medication adjustment are priorities before prescribing shoes for swollen feet. Also, shoes with multiple separate insoles that can accommodate the range of edema should be sought.

FOOT ORTHOSES

As a general principle, external shoe modifications are more for sagittal plane control while internal modifications including FOs are for frontal or transverse plane control. The effectiveness of the FO may vary depending on the activities of the patients. An FO that is effective during walking, for example, may not be very effect during running. According to Stacoff, FOs appear to dampen muscular activity, rather than realign skeletal structures, during running.[37]

The range of motion and the suppleness of the ankle, subtalar, and midtarsal joints should be examined prior to prescribing an FO. Examination of an old FO, whether failed or successful, can provide valuable clues for designing a new one. In the case of a failed FO, clinicians should look for the possible reasons for failure such as inappropriate choice of material, excessively high arch, lack of lateral balance (a vertical "ledge" to prevent lateral slippage of the foot), overly high heel lift, or excessive padding for comfort inside the UCBL or SMO. Common reasons an initially effective FO becomes less effective later on include deterioration of the materials, development of new biomechanical deficits, and changing of footwear.

Functional (corrective) FOs are designed to maintain normal subtalar and midtarsal biomechanics, thereby allowing improved functioning of the more distal and proximal parts of the kinetic chain. **Accommodative** FOs are used when deviation of the subtalar and midtarsal joints is rigid or when a local relief is required for a painful area. The practitioner may prescribe an FO that combines these functions for partially correctable problems.

Many minor foot problems can be remedied with ready-made FOs with minimal adjustments. Custom-made orthoses, however, often provide a better fit, superior shock absorption, and better control of excess mobility. The practitioner should check the FO after fabrication to ensure that it meets the needs of the patient rather than allowing direct delivery to the patient. Subsequently, the patient should be evaluated periodically, perhaps every 3–6 months.

Materials

In contrast to children, the adult foot is less flexible and often cannot tolerate rigid materials such as laminated plastics. The practitioner and pedorthist should

TABLE 4.   Summary of Materials for Foot Orthosis

	Materials	Features
Plastics for rigid FO or AFO, splint	Laminated plastic	Most rigid, heavy duty AFO for obese or spastic patients
	Polypropylene	Tg* of –20 degrees, more rigid than polyethylene, widely used for AFO, UCBL
	Polyethylene	Tg* of –25 degrees, mostly for splinting
Plastics for insole materials	Polyethylene (Plastazote, Alliplast, Pelite)	Polyethylene with closed cells, different durometer grades available
Synthetic rubber	Spenco (Spenco Medical Corp., Waco, TX)	Neoprene closed cell foam enclosing nitrogen bubbles with nylon top cover
		Absorbs shock, retains heat, used as a cover material of FO
	Lynco (Apex, NJ)	Open cell Neoprene with nylon top cover, dissipates heat, less shock absorption
Polyurethane	Poron (Poron division of Rogers Corp., Woodstock, CT) PPT (Professional Protective Tech., Langer Laboratories, NY)	Open cell polyurethane Not heat moldable, excellent shock absorption, dissipates heat, durable, easy to modify on a grinding wheel
Viscoelastic	Sorbothane Viscolas Viscolite	Excellent shock absorption, but heavy
EVA (ethyl vinyl acetate)		Heat moldable, different durometer grades available. Most commonly used in the midsole of running shoes
Carbon graphite (Springlite)		Laminated sheets of carbon graphite fiber cloth with a rigid shell; thinner than other thermoplastic materials
Leather		Good thermal conductivity, absorbs and redistributes moisture from the foot

*Tg (glass transition temperature): the temperature above which deformation of material occurs.

discuss the choice of materials based on age, body weight, and the goals of the FO. The pedorthist may provide information about the materials such as resistance to deformation, durability, and cost. Materials frequently used for FOs are summarized in Table 4.[19] Accommodative FOs are usually made of softer materials, while functional orthoses require relatively rigid materials for control and support.

Materials with closed cells, such as **Spenco** (rubber), absorb shear and vertical load but tend to retain heat and moisture. Most materials with open cells dissipate heat and moisture but provide less shock absorption with the exception of **Poron** (open cell polyurethane), which provides excellent shock absorption as well. When the insoles are made of multiple layers, materials that resist "bottoming-out" such as Poron or PPT are used as a top layer for comfort and shear reduction. **Leather** is not a good cover material because it allows excessive sliding. Medium density materials are used as a middle layer for durability, and rigid materials as a bottom layer to provide structural stability. Footwear functionally acts as the base of the FO and therefore should be considered thoroughly as an integral part of the FO. Footwear with a firm midsole and counter is recommended to provide a stable structural base. Athletic footwear with the above features may be an alternative, although many popular sneakers such as those with an air cushion may not be the ideal choice because of a less stable midsole. High top shoes are often recommended for children to add ankle stability and improve suspension.[15]

Patients are advised not to use the same FO in different footwear without checking with the physician or orthotist, since the length, width, shape, and heel height of the footwear may differ. Shoes with different heel heights can result in dramatic difference in function of subtalar and midtarsal joints. If the patient transfers an FO fabricated for a higher-heeled shoe to a lower-heeled shoe, the medial arch of the foot tends to collapse further and press down on the top of the orthosis, leading to medial arch irritation. If the shoe insole is too narrow or too wide, the FO may tilt or shift medially inside the shoe becoming less effective or causing irritation from its lateral edge. Ideally, patients should purchase the footwear prior to fabrication of the FO, so that it can be fitted accordingly.

Key Points in FOs Designed for Pronation Control

1. The goal of an FO is dampening rather than completely blocking pronation. Completely blocking pronation may lead to other symptoms such as knee or back pain.

2. Clinicians should check for underlying biomechanical abnormalities including those of proximal joints.

3. General guidelines for trial of posting (wedge) are as follows: hindfoot (HF) varus with medial heel wedge, HF and forefoot (FF) varus with medial HF and FF wedge, FF valgus with lateral FF wedge. Posting materials for trials are commercially available (Apex, Inc.).

4. The foot with a rigid pronation deformity can not pronate any more, and therefore, like the cavus foot, provides poor shock absorption. FO design should take this into account, and the materials and design should emphasize superior shock absorption rather than pronation control.

5. For the pronated foot with excessive medial deviation of the subtalar axis, an ordinary FO with posting alone cannot provide sufficient leverage to control the pronation. Direct control of the calcaneus with a UCBL or AFO is often required.[16]

6. FOs are less effective in patients with tight heel cords. If necessary, adding a heel lift on the outsole of shoe is preferable to adding it on the FO itself to accommodate the tight heel cord.

7. In order to avoid irritation of the plantar fascia, the medial arch of the FO or UCBL should not be too prominent. Grinding a shallow furrow on the dorsal aspect of the orthosis provides accommodation for the flexor hallucis longus tendon and plantar fascia.[16]

8. Combining footwear with a weak lateral counter and an FO with a prominent medial arch support may result in peroneal muscle overuse syndrome. Footwear with a strong lateral counter may reduce the lateral sliding of the foot in this situation.

9. Footwear with a straight last and a strong medial counter is recommended for control of flexible pronation. For the fixed pronation deformity, footwear with an accommodative medial counter is necessary to avoid irritation of talo-navicular area.

Key Points in FOs Designed for Supination Control

FOs or footwear for the supinated foot are designed mainly to accommodate rather than correct the deformities since they are frequently not flexible. Another goal in the design of FOs or footwear for these patients is prevention of secondary injuries such as lateral ankle sprains.

USE OF FOOTWEAR AND FOS IN SPECIFIC CONDITIONS

Tight Shoe Syndrome

In ancient China, beginning in early childhood, a young woman's feet were tightly bound and squeezed into tiny shoes for beauty. The consequences were severe foot deformities, intractable pain, and subsequent difficulty in walking. While not as extreme, an analogy can be made to the behavior of modern women who squeeze their feet into tight "pumps."

Tight shoes often aggravate multiple foot problems, including interdigital neuroma, metatarsalgia, hallux valgus, hallux rigidus, plantar fasciitis, and poorly defined foot pain.[8] Relief often occurs simply from wearing roomier shoes. Fortunately, with increasing health consciousness, the design of women's shoes is slowly adopting the concept of "health" over "beauty."

Morton's Interdigital Neuritis

Since tight shoes are the main culprits of interdigital neuritis, wearing roomy footwear is a mandatory first step for successful treatment. A metatarsal pad can be placed proximal to the metatarsal heads with the apex of the pad (thickest part) under the midshaft of the metatarsals. Another option is a neuroma pad, which is smaller than a metatarsal pad and is placed between the two metatarsal shafts to widen the inter-metatarsal space.

Metatarsalgia

Contributing factors include obesity, tight heel cords, fat pad atrophy, and tight shoes. Orthotic intervention includes metatarsal pads, metatarsal relief in the insole, a rigid shank shoe with a rocker sole, and a Springlite carbon plate in roomy footwear. Synovitis with subluxation of the 2nd MTP joint should be differentiated, as it is often resistant to the above-mentioned modifications. Patients show overriding or splitting of the 2nd toe from the other toes. A drawer sign is an important clinical test of subluxation in which the pain is reproduced by applying vertical stress at the MTP joint.[21]

A metatarsal pad with a corrective strap (commercially available as a Budin splint) placed in roomy footwear is a good option for conservative treatment.

Sesamoiditis

Sesamoiditis is often confused with other painful conditions of the 1st MTP joint such as synovitis or arthritis. The tenderness typically shifts anteriorly with dorsiflexion of the 1st MTP joint because the sesamoids are in the tendon of flexor hallucis brevis muscle. In order to relieve the symptoms effectively, sesamoid relief should be small and specifically located for the involved sesamoid (usually tibial sesamoid). Generous relief around the entire 1st MTP joint may not be effective because it allows the involved sesamoid to bear excessive weight.

Hallux Limitus (HL) and Rigidus (HR)

The practitioner needs to evaluate whether HL and HR is primary or secondary. Secondary HL may be related to excessive pronation with tight heel cords, a collapsed medial longitudinal arch from Charcot neuroarthropathy, tethering of the flexor hallucis longus tendon, or a deep posterior compartment syndrome of the leg.

A foot orthosis with an excessively high medial arch support induces functional HL and results in an iatrogenic "hallux limitus gait." The patient may present with a flat foot gait or walking on the lateral side of the foot to avoid discomfort on the medial arch. Frequently there is medial fascial pain as well as lateral foot pain. The footwear may show signs of lateral weight bearing such as an over-stretched lateral counter or an excessive wear pattern on the lateral outsole. Lowering the medial arch of the FO often relieves the symptoms.

Orthotic management of HL and HR consists of footwear with a high toe box and rocker sole, or for use with sneakers a Morton's extension or Springlite carbon plate under the innersole; both minimize the need for dorsiflexion of the MTP joint.

Plantar Fasciitis

Plantar fasciitis is usually a self-limiting condition and responds to conservative treatment. It is often aggravated by wearing footwear with low-heels or hard soles. Tight shoes seem to be another contributing factor because they do not allow the feet to spread and provide shock absorption.

Conservative treatment includes avoiding prolonged standing, night splinting, fascial taping,[9] mobilization of the plantar fascia, and stretching of the gastrocsoleus and plantar fascia (see the chapter Hindfoot Pain and Plantar Fasciitis for details). Roomy footwear with firm heel counters combined with heel elevation using soft heel cups dampens the stress on the plantar fascia. There is no universal FO for the treatment of plantar fasciitis because it can occur in either the pronated or supinated foot. Thus, the design of the FO should be individualized to address the underlying abnormal biomechanics. A night splint keeps the fascia in the elongated position and is quite effective, particularly in relieving morning pain.[6,12]

Clinical presentation of nerve entrapment in the foot may mimic plantar fasciitis. The FO for **Baxter's nerve entrapment** is designed to control excessive pronation with local relief under the point of maximum tenderness.[2] **Tarsal tunnel syndrome** and **jogger's foot** are treated with similarly.

Peri-Cuboidal Pain

Patients may have lingering pain around the lateral midfoot after ankle or foot trauma. Causes of chronic peri-cuboidal pain include peroneal tendinitis, calcaneal-cuboid synovitis, injury of the metatarso-cuboidal articulations, and lateral plantar fasciitis.

Acute or recurrent subluxation of the metatarso-cuboidal articulations occurs in sports injuries, especially with concurrent ankle inversion. The likely mechanism is a strong rotational force on the cuboid by the peroneus longus tendon when the patient attempts to evert the foot against the inversion force.[22,23] A pronated foot is prone to develop this condition as a result of the laxity of the midfoot.

Management of peri-cuboidal pain includes mobilization of the midfoot, cuboid padding, and taping.[27] Pronation control with simultaneous midfoot stabilization is difficult to achieve by ordinary FOs. An orthosis with mediolateral support such as UCBL or SMO is a better option. A cuboid pad can be incorporated into these orthoses to support the peri-cuboidal articulations. The size and accurate placement of the cuboid pad (posterior to 5th metatarsal base) are essential for its effectiveness.[17] A functional metatarsal brace originally designed for fracture of 5th metatarsal can be another viable alternative.[5]

Sinus Tarsi Pain

Sinus tarsi pain is a frequent complaint in patients with a history of recurrent inversion injuries as well as in some rheumatologic conditions. Often local steroid injection provides temporary relief. Clinicians may try to attain symptomatic relief by using wedges (mostly medial) during evaluation in the office. If effective, a UCBL or SMO can be prescribed for long-term use.

Heel Pad Atrophy

Heel pad atrophy is not an uncommon condition especially in the elderly or obese. The typical presentation is diffuse pain on the plantar aspect of the heel after prolonged weight bearing. In our experience, a soft heel cup alone is frequently not effective because it is unable to keep the heel pad from spreading. Shoes with a strong heel counter and heel elevation in conjunction with a soft heel cup keep the fat pad under the calcaneus and provide symptomatic relief. The commercially available plastic heel cups with heel fat pad-containing features can be used as well. Low-dye taping (described in Hindfoot Pain and Plantar Fasciitis) can also be used as an adjunctive therapy.

Fat pad atrophy in the elderly is one aspect of generalized soft tissue atrophy throughout the plantar aspect of the foot. Placing 3–5 mm thick soft insoles made of Spenco, Poron, or PPT in roomy footwear provides symptomatic relief. Incorporating a metatarsal pad may additionally improve the metatarsal pain. The initial metatarsal pad should be soft and of low height. As the patient becomes tolerant of the pad, the height and firmness of the pad can be increased gradually.

Haglund Deformity (Prominent Superior Calcaneal Protuberance)

A Haglund deformity (see the chapter Hindfoot Pain and Plantar Fasciitis) is treated with a heel lift and a horseshoe pad inside the heel counter. The heel lift increases the space between the Achilles tendon and the bony protuberance and reduces irritation by positioning the tubercle above the heel counter. Management of insertional Achilles tendinitis includes a heel lift, gastrocsoleus stretching, and dampening of excessive pronation, although the mechanism of pronation control is not clearly defined.[26,29]

Posterior Tibialis Tendon (PTT) Insufficiency

Nonoperative treatment of PTT insufficiency used to be considered ineffective, and therefore surgical intervention had been widely advocated in the past. More recently, early aggressive conservative treatment using a UCBL, SMO, or short rearentry AFO has become widely accepted based on successful outcome studies.[3,36,40] These orthoses are designed to align the subtalar complex by directly controlling calcaneal eversion and forefoot abduction allowing healing of the PTT. The lateral border of the UCBL or SMO is formed up to the fifth metatarsal shaft for proper control of forefoot abduction.[28] Failure to adhere to these principles makes the UCBL less effective in controlling pronation, as does excessive padding for comfort inside the UCBL. The short rear-entry AFO is designed to control internal rotation of the tibia additionally, which is often difficult to achieve. There are not many options of conservative treatment other than an AFO in patients with excessive obesity, fixed deformity of the subtalar joint, or tight heel cords.[3]

Lateral Ankle Sprain/ Peroneal Tendinitis

A lateral hindfoot wedge may be taped under the sock liner of the sneakers as a temporary modification. Sneakers with a wide-based heel (basketball sneakers) are preferable. In most instances, expensive custom made FOs are not necessary. A short Unna boot with a lateral wedge can control the pain and swelling while allowing ambulation. A pneumatic ankle brace (Air-Stirrup; Aircast, Inc.), frequently prescribed for ankle sprains, may not provide sufficient control of the subtalar complex, although it may offer some edema control and sensory feedback.

Cavus Feet

Patients with cavus feet often present with excessive callus formation, metatarsalgia, and recurrent ankle inversion injuries. A relatively soft FO is usually prescribed to compensate for the inherent rigidity of cavus foot. Often custom FOs are required because the pre-fabricated FO cannot sufficiently redistribute pressure over the entire foot and support the high arch. A soft FO with a high arch support, however, tends to increase the tendency of inversion. A lateral heel flair and/or wedge placed on the footwear may counteract this varus tendency if the subtalar complex remains somewhat flexible. In such cases, purchasing sneakers with these features is a less expensive option than adding modifications. Since the arch of the cavus foot is located at the thickest and most rigid part of the FO, a groove for relief of the plantar fascia can be provided for comfort.[17] The traditional approach utilizing rocker soles, SACH, lateral flairs, and posting in orthopedic shoes may result in poor patient compliance due to weight, bulkiness, and poor cosmesis.

In Charcot-Marie-Tooth disease (CMT), the cavus foot is characterized by HF varus and FF valgus with a plantar flexed first ray (medial cuneiform and first metatarsal).[1,39] These deformities may be flexible initially but become rigid later on. The FO for patients with CMT requires frequent reassessment as the disease progresses. Surgical consultation is often advisable because these patients may benefit from various soft tissue or skeletal procedures.[20]

Forefoot Equinus

FF equinus refers to a plantar flexed FF and should be differentiated from ankle equinus. In order to advance the tibia over the foot during the stance phase, the patient compensates with maximum ankle DF or knee extension. These abnormal biomechanics result in anterior ankle or posterior knee pain over a period of time. Since the gastrocsoleus muscle is often maximally stretched already in some patients, further stretching exercises may actually aggravate the ankle and knee pain. Accommodating the FF equinus with a heel lift should be the mainstay of orthotic management.

CONCLUSION

The majority of painful foot conditions can be managed in the physiatrist's office using biomechanical principles for diagnosis and treatment. Examination of footwear and FOs provides valuable clues for diagnosis and insight for further management. The physiatrist should develop a keen eye in evaluating footwear and FOs and hands-on skills for temporary modifications. The information obtained from these temporary modifications will guide further orthotic management, and also improve the treatment outcome and coordination between the physician and orthotist or pedorthist.

APPENDIX. TEMPORARY OFFICE APPLICATION OF METATARSAL PADS IN SNEAKERS

1. Advise the patient to purchase walking sneakers with removable sock liners. Remove the insole from the sneaker and place it on the $\frac{1}{8}$" firm Plastazote sheet. Trace the outline of the sock liner on the Plastazote and cut the Plastazote along the tracing. Choose the type of relief or support to be provided (i.e., neuroma pad, metatarsal pad or wedge).

2. Mark the area to be relieved (i.e., metatarsal head), with lipstick, on the plantar aspect of the patient's foot. Place the Plastazote innersole inside the sneaker and have the patient insert his foot carefully. Ask the patient to take a few steps to imprint the markings into the Plastazote insole sheet.

3. Remove the Plastazote from the sneaker and re-examine it by placing it against the plantar surface of the foot to ensure the accuracy of the imprint.

4. Place the pad on the Plastazote proximal to the marked location and secure it with transparent tape. Transparent tape shows the exact location of the pad and allows for easy repositioning.

5. Put the Plastazote (with pad) into the sneaker and cover it with the original sock liner.

6. Ask the patient to walk for several minutes. A therapeutic response is usually seen immediately. If the patient complains of a "lump on the bone," the pad should be repositioned.

7. The patient should use the temporary innersoles for a 10–14 day trial. At the follow-up visit, a permanent insole can be ordered based on the result and information obtained.

8. A neuroma pad or medial or lateral wedge can be applied similarly.

REFERENCES
1. Alexander IJ, Fleissner PR Jr: Pes cavus. Foot Ankle Clin 3(4):723–735, 1998.
2. Baxter DE, Pfeffer GB, Thigpen M: Chronic heel pain. Orthop Clin North Am 20(4):563–569, 1989.
3. Chao W, Wapner KL, Lee TH, et al: Nonoperative management of posterior tibial tendon dysfunction. Foot Ankle Internat 17(12):736–741, 1996.
4. Curtis LA, Prichard K, Redford JB: Prescription shoes and foot orthoses. PM&R STARS 14(3):455–469, 2000.
5. Dameron TB Jr: Fractures of the proximal fifth metatarsal: Selecting the best treatment option. J Am Acad Orthop Surg 3:110–114, 1995.
6. Davis PF, Severud E, Baxter DE: Painful heel syndrome: Result of non-operative treatment. Foot Ankle Internat 15(10):531–535, 1994.
7. Frey C, Thompson F, Smith J: Update on women's footwear. Foot Ankle Internat 16(6):328–331, 1995.
8. Frey C, Thompson F, Smith J, et al: American orthopedic foot and ankle society women's shoe survey. Foot Ankle 14(2):78–81, 1993.
9. Goslin R, Tollanfield DR, Rome K: Mechanical therapeutic in the clinic. In Tollafield DR (ed): Clinical Skills in Treating the Foot. New York, Churchill Livingstone, 1997, pp 187–216.
10. Grifka JK: Shoes and insoles for patients with rheumatoid foot disease. Clin Orthop Rel Res 340:18–25, 1997.
11. Habershaw G, Dovan JC: Biomechanical considerations of the diabetic foot. In Kozak GP (ed): Management of Diabetic Foot Problems. Philadelphia, WB Saunders, 1984, pp 27–44.
12. Hermann TJ: The foot and ankle in football. In Samara GJ (ed): Rehabilitation of the Foot and Ankle. St. Louis, Mosby, 1995, pp 259–268.
13. Johnson JA: Running shoes and orthoses: A practical approach. J Back Musculoskeletal Rehab 6:71–80, 1996.
14. Kim DJ, Oh-Park M: Foot problems related to functional impairment in the elderly. J Musculoskeletal Rehab 12:7–24, 1999.
15. Kirby KA: Trouble shooting functional foot orthoses. In Valmassy RL (ed): Clinical Biomechanics of the Lower Extremities. St. Louis, Mosby, 1996, pp 327–348.
16. Kirby KA, Green DR: Evaluation and nonoperative management of pes valgus. In DeValentine SJ (ed): Foot and Ankle Disorders in Children. New York, Churchill Livingstone, 1992, pp 295–326.
17. Lester JJ: Prescription writing for functional and accommodative foot orthoses. In Valmassy RL (ed): Clinical Biomechanics of the Lower Extremities. St. Louis, Mosby, 1996, pp 195–306.
18. Levitz S, DeFrancisco JA, Guberman R, et al: Current footwear technology. Clin Podiatr Med Surg 5(3):737–751, 1988.
19. Levitz S, Whiteside LS, Fitzgerald TA: Biomechanical foot therapy. Clin Podiatr Med Surg 5(3):721–736, 1988.

20. Mann RA: Pes cavus. In Coughlin MJ (ed): Surgery of Foot and Ankle. St. Louis, Mosby, 1999, pp 768–783.
21. Marder R, George JL: Sports Injuries of the Ankle and Foot. New York, Springer, 1996, pp 71–122.
22. Marshall P: The rehabilitation of overuse foot injuries in athletes and dancers. Clin Sports Med 7:175–191, 1988.
23. Marshall P, Hamilton WG: Cuboid subluxation in ballet dancers. Am J Sports Med 20:169–175, 1992.
24. Martin DR: How to steer patients toward the right sport shoe. Physician Sports Med 25(9):138–144, 1997.
25. Mehta JA, Brown C, Sargeant N: Charcot restraint orthotic walker. Foot Ankle Int 19(9):619–623, 1998.
26. Mohr RN: Achilles tendinitis. Rationale for use and application of orthotics. Foot Ankle Clin 2(3):439–456, 1997.
27. Mooney M, Maffey-Ward L: Cuboid plantar and dorsal subluxations: Assessment and treatment. J Orthop Sports Phys Ther 20:220–226, 1994.
28. Noll KH: The use of orthotic devices in adult acquired flatfoot deformity. Foot Ankle Clin 6(1):25–36, 2001.
29. Novacheck TF: Running injuries: A biomechanical approach. J Bone Joint Surg 80A:1220–1233, 1998.
30. Perry JE, Ulbrecht JS, Derr JA, et al: The use of running shoes to reduce plantar pressures in patients who have diabetes. J Bone Joint Surg 77(12):1819–1828, 1995.
31. Reily MA: Guidelines for Prescribing Foot Orthotics. Thorofare, Slack, 1995, pp 26–27.
32. Robbins S, Waked E: Balance and vertical impact in sports: Role of shoe sole materials. Arch Phys Med Rehabil 78:463–487, 1997.
33. Robbins S, Waked E, Allard P, et al: Foot position awareness in younger and older men: The influence of footwear sole properties. J Am Geriatr Soc 45(1):61–66, 1997.
34. Robbins S, Gouw GJ, McClaran J: Shoe sole thickness and hardness influence balance in older men. J Am Geriatr Soc 40(11):1089–1094, 1992.
35. Schie CV, Ulbrecht JS, Becker MB, et al: Design criteria for rigid rocker shoes. Foot Ankle Internat 21(10):833–844, 2000.
36. Sferra JJ, Rosenberg GA: Nonoperative treatment of posterior tibial tendon pathology. Foot Ankle Clin 2(2):261–273, 1997.
37. Stacoff A, Reinschmidt C, Nigg BM, et al: Effects of shoe sole construction on skeletal motion during running. Med Sci Sports Exerc 33(2):311–319, 2001.
38. Steb HS, Marzano R: Conservative management of posterior tibial tendon dysfunction, subtalar joint complex, and pes planus deformity. Clin Podiatr Med Surg 3:439–451, 1999.
39. Wapner KL: Pes cavus. In Myerson MS (ed): Foot and Ankle Disorders. Philadelphia, WB Saunders, 2000, pp 919–941.
40. Wapner KL, Chao W: Nonoperative treatment of posterior tibial tendon dysfunction. Clin Orthop 365:39–45, 1999.

LEW C. SCHON, MD
KENNETH J. MROCZEK, MD
C. CHRISTOPHER STROUD, MD

PHYSIATRIC MANAGEMENT OF SPORTS-RELATED FOOT AND ANKLE INJURY

From the Department of
  Orthopaedic Surgery
Union Memorial Hospital
Baltimore, Maryland

Reprint requests to:
Lew C. Schon, MD
c/o Lyn Camire, Editor
Department of Orthopaedics
Johnston Professional Building
  #400
3333 North Calvert Street
Baltimore, MD 21218

Athletic injuries to the foot and ankle may result from a single traumatic event or from repetitive, overuse stresses. The diagnoses of some injuries, such as a displaced ankle fracture, may be obvious on clinical and radiographic examination. Other injuries, such as peroneal tendon dislocations or navicular stress fractures, may require a more discerning clinical eye. Furthermore, some diagnoses may require that the examiner be familiar with the activities of the specific sport; this is most evident in dance-related sports such as ballet. Once the condition is correctly diagnosed, a treatment plan is formulated, taking the sport-related goals of the athlete into account if possible. For example, surgical intervention in a ballerina with posterior ankle impingement may be either accelerated or delayed depending on professional goals or schedules. In all cases, the clinician's primary goal is to return an athlete to sport as quickly as possible; however, further injury or permanent sequelae should not be risked. This article focuses on ligamentous, tendinous, and bony injuries about the foot and ankle. Common injuries such as ankle sprains were included owing to their prevalence; however, less common injuries with more serious implications such as Lisfranc fracture-dislocations are also discussed.

LIGAMENTOUS INJURIES

Ligamentous injuries, commonly known as sprains, occur most often at the ankle, the first metatarsophalangeal, and the tarsometatarsal joints. The vast majority of ankle sprains are lateral, but medial and syndesmotic injuries can occur either in isolation or in combination. The lateral ligament complex of the ankle is composed of the anterior talofibular ligament, calcaneofibular ligament, and posterior talofibular ligament. The usual mechanism of injury for these ligaments is inversion, with the anterior talofibular ligament most commonly involved. Medial sided or deltoid ligament injury usually occurs secondary to an eversion or abduction force, and syndesmotic sprain typically results from external rotation. With any of these sprains, the patient will often describe a twisting or rolling injury occasionally associated with a tearing or popping sensation. Difficulty with weight bearing may be encountered depending on the severity of injury.

Physical examination will reveal localized edema, ecchymosis, and tenderness over the affected ligaments. Stability testing with anterior draw or varus stress may demonstrate laxity, but in the acute setting, these maneuvers are misleading and difficult to perform owing to pain and swelling. A complete examination should always be performed to search for associated neurovascular, muscular, tendinous, and osseous pathology. Special attention should be paid to assessing syndesmotic injury by direct palpation and provocative testing because athletes with syndesmotic involvement take longer to return to sport than those with isolated lateral ligamentous injury.[1,19] Syndesmotic damage may be indicated by pain anteriorly in the region of the syndesmosis with external rotation or as noted with the squeeze test, compression in the coronal plane of the fibula to the tibia proximal to the syndesmosis.[1,19,55] Proximal fibular tenderness suggests a possible high fibula or Maisonneuve fracture. These fractures are associated with syndesmotic and deltoid injuries.

In general, when evaluating a ligamentous injury, standard ankle radiographs are indicated in the presence of bony tenderness, significant ecchymosis and swelling, marked instability, or deformity. Suspicion of a proximal fibula fracture warrants full-length anteroposterior and lateral tibia radiographs in addition to standard ankle views.

Although an anatomic classification for lateral ankle sprains exists, the authors prefer the grading system based on the severity of damage to the ligament. A grade 1, or mild sprain, represents microscopic damage to the ligament; there is no laxity present upon examination. Mild laxity and instability is present after the ligament sustains macroscopic injury or a partial tear in a grade 2 or moderate sprain. In a grade 3 or severe sprain, the ligament ruptures with gross laxity and instability upon examination.

A consensus exists for functional treatment of acute grade 1 and 2 sprains, but treatment for acute grade 3 sprains remains controversial.[22,28,59,64,68,69,77] Based on their meta-analysis of randomized, controlled studies from 1966 to 1998, Pijnenburg and associates[59] concluded that operative treatment led to fewer episodes of giving way than did functional treatment, and functional treatment was more effective in terms of residual pain and giving way than was minimal to no treatment. Kannus and Renstrom[22] recommend initial functional treatment even for elite athletes, arguing that it provides the quickest return to activity while avoiding the risks of surgery. The authors further stress that while 10–20% of ankles in acute grade 3 sprains may require future reconstruction, multiple studies have shown that delayed repair or reconstruction provides comparable results to primary repair.

Initial treatment begins with rest, ice, compression, and elevation. For comfort, the patient may be immobilized in a neutral position for a short period, but should be quickly graduated to a protected range of motion with a stirrup brace. In two military groups treated by functional bracing, Eiff and colleagues[11] documented a quicker return to full duty with no significant difference in residual symptoms for the group that was quickly mobilized after 2 days as compared with those who underwent 10 days of immobilization. A physical therapy program should focus on range of motion exercises, peroneal strengthening, Achilles stretching, and proprioception. A clinically stable ankle should be protected for approximately 1 month, whereas an unstable ankle should be protected for 3–6 months.

Chronic lateral ankle instability may be divided into mechanical instability and functional instability. Mechanical instability, or joint subluxation, may be appreciated on physical examination. Functional instability refers to patients who experience symptoms of giving way regardless of a clinically stable ankle. In a recent review, Hertel[18] lists balance deficits, proprioception deficits, delayed peroneal muscle reaction time, altered common peroneal nerve function, and strength deficits as conditions that exist in patients with functional instability. In this chronic setting, the clinician should rule out additional causes of the symptoms and review previous treatment to ensure that it has been appropriate. If the patient has not had a complete course of treatment or continues to be deficient in peroneal strength, appropriate therapy should be instituted. Patients who continue to be symptomatic regardless of conservative measures may be considered candidates for surgical intervention. Preoperative stress radiographs (Fig. 1) and magnetic resonance imaging (MRI) are usually obtained to assess instability and rule out associated occult lesions such as osteochondral talus fractures or peroneal tendon tears.

Multiple surgical procedures have been described for lateral ankle instability using either local ligaments or tendons to gain varying degrees of stability. The more anatomic the reconstruction, the less the compromise of the range of motion. The

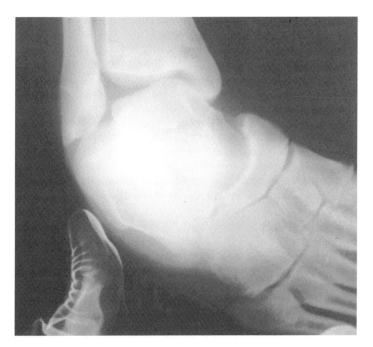

FIGURE 1. Anteroposterior radiograph of an unstable ankle being stressed. Note opening of lateral joint space when varus stress is applied.

current authors prefer an imbrication of the ligaments described by Karlsson and associates.[23] Patients with inadequate tissue for repair require reconstruction with a tendon graft such as a split peroneal brevis tendon graft. Postoperatively, a splint in mild dorsiflexion to neutral is worn for 10–14 days. Dorsiflexion and eversion exercises are begun at 2 weeks, while limiting plantarflexion and inversion to approximately 15° until 4 weeks. The patient then undergoes a progressive rehabilitation course beginning with in-line walking, jogging, and running, and then advancing to cutting activities usually by 10–14 weeks. A lace-up brace is generally worn for 6 months.

A sprain of the metatarsophalangeal joint has been termed a "turf toe." The classic injury occurs when the hallux of a football player is hyperextended while playing on artificial turf.[5,6,63] Other mechanisms of injury have been reported.[6] Since the usual mechanism is dorsiflexion, the plantar capsuloligamentous complex including the plantar plate and sesamoids is injured to various degrees. An impaction fracture of the dorsal articular surface of the metatarsal head may occur as the base of the proximal phalanx hyperextends. Any marked swelling warrants radiographic evaluation to rule out a fracture. Tenderness will be present on the plantar aspect of the joint, but may additionally be noted over fracture sites or ligament injuries. Initial treatment is conservative with rest, ice, compression, and elevation. Increasing the stiffness of the forefoot of the shoe may aid in recovery and may be a preventive measure.[5] Although this may seem like a minor injury, an athlete with a severe sprain may miss up to 6 weeks of participation.[6]

Injuries to the tarsometatarsal or Lisfranc joints are relatively less common, but it is critical to diagnose this disabling injury. A Lisfranc sprain, dislocation, or fracture-dislocation is thought to occur as a result of forced plantarflexion or abduction.[8,34] Localized swelling and tenderness should alert the clinician to perform maneuvers that stress these joints. Pain resulting from passive sagittal plane motion or abduction of a foot positioned in pronation with the heel stabilized is strongly suggestive of injury.[8] Diastasis between the first and second metatarsal bases, an avulsion fracture of the second metatarsal base, and failure of the medial aspects of the second metatarsal base and middle cuneiform to line up on anteroposterior and oblique radiographs indicate a Lisfranc rupture or fracture.[8,34] In unclear cases, stress or weight bearing radiographs or fluoroscopic examination are indicated.[8,34] Stable injuries require a nonweight bearing cast or boot brace for approximately 6 weeks. Complete ligament ruptures and fracture-dislocations are best treated by open reduction and internal fixation (Fig. 2). In a report on 19 athletes sustaining varying degrees of Lisfranc sprains or fracture-dislocations, the mean time for return to sport for those sustaining minor sprains was 3 months.[8]

TENDINOUS INJURIES

Achilles Tendon

Achilles tendon disorders occur frequently in athletes and may be divided into tendinitis and rupture. Achilles tendinitis may be further subdivided into noninsertional and insertional. Athletes subject to repetitive stresses classically suffer from noninsertional Achilles tendonitis, whereas older, sedentary individuals are typically afflicted with insertional tendinitis.[50] The distinction between the two is easily made by point of maximal tenderness. Puddu and colleagues[61] classified noninsertional Achilles tendinitis into paratendinitis, paratendinitis with tendinosis, and tendinosis. Although this classification seems logical, distinguishing between the various entities

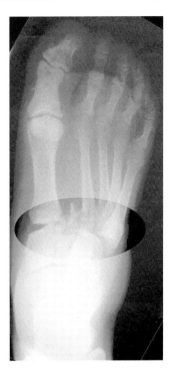

FIGURE 2. An anteroposterior radiograph of a Lisfranc
fracture-dislocation of the midfoot.

is often clinically difficult. Diffuse fusiform swelling with crepitus in the Achilles
tendon as it moves through its sheath usually represents paratendinitis, whereas
thickening with point tenderness suggests tendinosis.

Treatment of noninsertional Achilles tendinitis begins with activity modification
or restriction, stretching, nonsteroidal anti-inflammatory medications, and possibly
heel lifts or orthotic devices. The more severe cases may require immobilization in a
boot brace until the symptoms have improved. Orthotic management to control hindfoot motion in athletes who overpronate may be appropriate because the increase in
subtalar motion is thought to play a role in causing or aggravating Achilles tendon
problems.[21,50,51] A brisement, which is an injection of 2–6 mL of sterile saline, lido-
caine, and/or bupivicaine into the tendon sheath, can be beneficial for refractory cases
of chronic paratendinitis because it distends the abnormal sheath away from the
tendon.[20,50] Athletes who have exhausted a prolonged nonoperative course may require surgical tenolysis of the Achilles with tendon debridement and possible reconstruction if tendinosis is very severe.[20,31,50,56] Recovery will depend on the magnitude
of the problem and its treatment, but can range from 6 weeks to 1½ years.

Patients who suffer an acute Achilles tendon rupture usually give a history of a
sudden pain in the posterior distal calf. The pain is often described as being hit with
a bat or kicked, and patients may describe an associated audible snap. The diagnosis
may be missed since the patient may still be able to ambulate and have active dorsiflexion as a result of remaining plantar flexors such as the flexor hallucis longus
(FHL), flexor digitorum longus, posterior tibias, and the peroneals. However, patients will be unable to perform more strenuous tests such as single or repetitive heel
rises. A palpable defect is usually evident approximately 4 cm proximal to the insertion, but this defect may be masked by swelling. Various clinical tests have been described

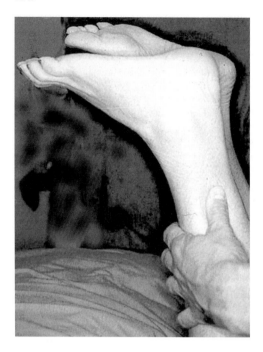

FIGURE 3. An Achilles tendon rupture in the near ankle demonstrating a lack of the normal plantar flexed position.

to assist in making the diagnosis of Achilles tendon rupture. In the Thompson calf squeeze test, the examiner squeezes the posterior calf of a prone patient with the knee flexed at 90°. Plantarflexion occurs on the side with an intact Achilles tendon, whereas no motion or minimal plantar flexion occurs after a rupture. An altered resting position of the ankle may be observed with the patient prone while the knee is flexed (Fig. 3). A rupture is diagnosed if the foot falls into neutral or dorsiflexion while the resting position on the intact side is approximately 15° of plantar flexion. In a prospective study, Maffulli[29] determined that the sensitivity and positive predictive value of the calf squeeze test, knee-flexion test, and the presence of a palpable gap to be 0.96, 0.88, and 0.73, respectively, in 133 Achilles tears confirmed during open surgical repair. The highest positive predictive value was 0.98 for the calf squeeze test.

While the recommended treatment for acute Achilles tendon ruptures has alternated between nonoperative and operative management over the years, the current trend is towards surgical repair, especially in athletes.[30,49,50] Cetti and colleagues' treatment[33] reported a higher percentage of patients returning to the prior sports activity level after operative treatment than after nonoperative treatment. Many authors now advise an aggressive postoperative course involving varying degrees of immediate or early protected motion and weight bearing.[32,46,47,71,78] The current authors' postoperative course includes nonweight bearing and splinting in 20° of plantarflexion for 10–14 days. The patient is then put in a removable brace and allowed to bear weight on the sole of the foot in the plantar flexed position. The brace is then removed for active range of motion from full plantar flexion to neutral with the knee flexed. Swimming is allowed at this point. At 6 weeks after repair, the ankle is placed in a neutral position and active range of motion is gradually increased. An exercise bike may be used without the brace at 6 weeks. By 10–12 weeks, the brace can be discontinued and activity can progress from walking to jogging and then running.

Peroneal Tendons

Injuries to the peroneal tendons may be divided into tendinitis, tears, and sub-luxation or dislocation. Tendinitis of the peroneals usually occurs secondary to overuse. The athlete will complain of pain and swelling over the peroneals. Localized tenderness will be present in the region, and resisted eversion will reproduce pain. The mainstay of treatment is nonoperative and includes rest, nonsteroidal antiinflammatory medications, bracing, and physical therapy. A stirrup brace or a lateral heel wedge to limit excursion may be beneficial, while a course of immobilization in a cast or boot may be necessary for more severe cases. Occasionally, surgical exploration with tenosynovectomy may be required.

Split tears of the peroneus brevis usually occur in the region of the fibular tip. Numerous authors have reported these tears in association with lateral ankle insta-bility.[4,66,70] Examination and treatment of split tears is similar to peroneal tendinitis. Patients who undergo conservative treatment unsuccessfully may require an operation to elliptically excise the tear and perform side-to-side repair. Various disorders of the peroneus longus tendon that occur in association with a painful os peroneum and cause plantar lateral foot pain have been described by Sobel and colleagues.[70] Rupture of the peroneus longus through a fracture of the os peroneum and treatment by surgical repair has been reported.[57,58] Cuboid subluxation has been described as a source of lateral foot pain; however, other, more common causes must be ruled out, such as peroneal tendinitis, calcaneal-cuboid synovitis, stress fractures, and lateral plantar fasciitis.[36,37,45,52] The current authors believe cuboid subluxation rarely occurs and is a diagnosis of exclusion.

Peroneal tendon dislocation is a result of injury to the superior peroneal reti-naculum (SPR). When it occurs, typically among skiers, two pops may be felt along the lateral ankle as the tendons dislocate and relocate.[12,48,54] Eckert and Davis[10] observed three patterns of injury while treating 73 skiers with peroneal dislocation and injury to the SPR. In type I injuries, the SPR is simply torn off the fibula, whereas a fibrocartilaginous rim is pulled off along with the SPR in type II injuries. Avulsion of the posterolateral fibula with the fibrocartilaginous rim and SPR occurs in type III injuries. Some authors have reported rare cases of subluxation of the peroneal ten-dons within the SPR.[16,40]

Because the tendons often relocate and may only spontaneously dislocate, the diagnoses may be missed. Swelling, ecchymosis, or tenderness may be present behind the lateral malleolus in the acute setting. Resisted eversion and dorsiflexion will often reproduce pain and possible dislocation. Active circumduction may also reproduce dislocation. Standard radiographs may diagnose the avulsion fracture that occurs with a type III injury.

Nonoperative treatment with a brief period of immobilization in a cast or boot may be tried, especially in the acute phase, but surgical intervention should be considered in athletic individuals. McLennan found conservative measures to fail in 44% of 19 individuals with acute or chronic peroneal dislocations, and Escalas and colleagues reported that 28 of 38 skiers were treated unsuccessfully by simple immobilization in a compressive bandage.[12,41] Patients with chronic dislocations usu-ally present with prolonged symptoms, and surgery is usually warranted. Possible procedures include addressing the SPR by direct repair or reconstruction with trans-ferred tissue.[10,12,41] Bone block, groove-deepening, and rerouting the tendons under the calcaneofibular ligament have similarly been proposed.[38,43,60,67,81]

For acute injuries, the current authors prefer reduction of the tendon with repair of the retinaculum, cartilaginous rim, and posterolateral fragment to the fibula. If a flat or convex peroneal tendon sulcus is encountered, a concomitant groove-deepening procedure is performed. Postoperatively, the patient is splinted in neutral and kept nonweight bearing for 10–14 days. A weight bearing cast or boot is used for the following 4 weeks. Once the athlete regains full range of motion and strength, he or she may return to full activity. This process usually takes 3–4 months.

In chronic situations, the current authors prefer groove-deepening because this near-anatomic, isometric reconstruction allows excellent range of motion without sacrificing any structures. After an initial 2-week period of splinting and nonweight bearing, the patient is allowed to progress to weight bearing and to graduate to a stirrup brace. At this time, a gentle strengthening program such as stationary bicycling or stair stepping is begun avoiding plantarflexion and inversion past 15°. At 6 weeks, the patient may begin full plantar flexion and dorsiflexion with a more aggressive strengthening program while weaning out of the brace for activities with low risk of inversion injury. The brace should be worn for riskier activities, and circumduction should be avoided for the first 3 months after surgery. Straightforward running may begin at 8 weeks, but cutting sports should be delayed until 12 weeks. For added protection, a brace should be worn during sport activities for 5 months.

FHL Tendinitis and Posterior Impingement Syndrome

FHL tendinitis typically occurs in dancers, but it may also occur in other athletes.[14,15,26,65,79] In the classic example, a dancer will experience pain in the posteromedial ankle or arch with a clicking sensation during pointing. Triggering or intermittent locking of the great toe may develop when there is a tear or thickened nodule in the tendon. Localized swelling and tenderness may be present in the posteromedial ankle between the retromalleolar region and the sustentaculum. Active motion of the great toe and ankle may reproduce triggering, crepitus, or symptoms along the FHL. Posterior impingement syndrome typically develops secondary to an os trigonum, trigonal process, or soft tissue impingement.[14] Full plantar flexion lateral radiographs will reveal the more common osseous forms (Fig. 4). A bone scan

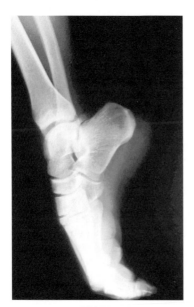

FIGURE 4. A lateral radiograph of an impinging trigonal process. The trigonal process is located on the posterior talus and impinges against the calcaneus in the plantar flexed position.

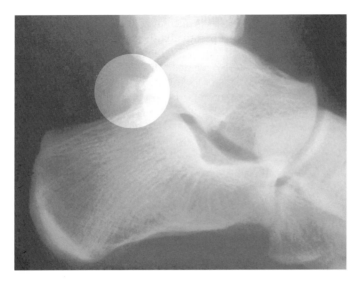

FIGURE 5. A lateral radiograph demonstrating an os trigonum. The os trigonum is also located posteriorly on the talus.

demonstrating focal uptake in the posterior talus may be helpful in questionable cases. Differentiating between FHL tendinitis and posterior impingement syndrome can be difficult because both are associated with pain in the posterior ankle and the conditions often coexist. In Hamilton and colleagues' retrospective review[15] of their operative treatment of 41 ankles in 37 dancers, the two conditions coexisted in 63% of the ankles. A careful history and physical examination should allow the clinician to distinguish the two entities. Posteromedial ankle tenderness is found in FHL tendinitis, whereas the tenderness in posterior impingement is posterolateral. In general, dorsiflexion of the great toe reproduces the symptoms of tendinitis, while plantar flexion of the ankle will induce posterior impingement symptoms. Furthermore, relief from an injection of local anesthetic (with or without steroid) placed posterolaterally near the posterior process should confirm posterior impingement syndrome.

The treatment for both conditions begins with nonoperative measures including avoidance of the offending activities, physical therapy, and a course of nonsteroidal antiinflammatory mediations. Injections may be used when these measures fail. Immobilization may be tried in resistant cases. If these nonoperative measures are unsuccessful, surgical intervention may be indicated. For cases of pure posterior impingement, the surgeon will excise the os trigonum or trigonal process through a posterolateral approach. In a subset of nine professional ballerinas who preoperatively had severe restriction, Marotta and Micheli reported that all returned to unrestricted dance activities by a mean of 3 months, although a fair number had occasional discomfort.[35] Arguing less surgical morbidity and a shorter recovery time, other authors have described arthroscopic techniques with good results.[39] Surgical release for FHL tendinitis, with possible debridement and repair of tears, is performed using a posteromedial approach. A coexisting os trigonum may also be excised through this same incision (Fig. 5). Using stringent criteria, good to excellent results have been reported in most dancers who had either posterior impingement syndrome or FHL pathology alone or in combination.[15]

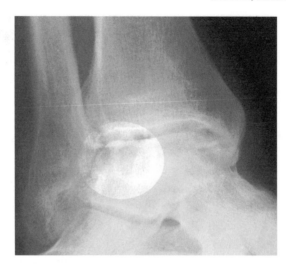

FIGURE 6.   An oblique radiograph demonstrating a lateral osteochondral lesion of the talus.

The current authors' postoperative regimen for posterior impingement or FHL tendinitis includes splint immobilization in dorsiflexion or neutral for 10 days. Active range of motion exercises for the toe and ankle start after discontinuing the splint. At 3–6 weeks, floor or pool barre work begins, with regular barre work commencing at 4–6 weeks. The dancer may begin center work and go en pointe at 8–14 weeks. Return to full dance will usually occur at 12–24 weeks.

OSTEOCHONDRAL LESIONS

Numerous terms have been used to describe defects in the articular cartilage and underlying cancellous bone of the talus. These osteochondral lesions may be discovered after acute trauma or while working up an athlete with chronic ankle pain. In the chronic setting, patients may report generalized ankle pain and swelling or, more specifically, may complain of mechanical symptoms such as clicking or the sensation of a loose body. Physical examination may confirm either diffuse tenderness or localized tenderness on the talus. Crepitation with ankle motion may indicate a loose body.

Diagnostic imaging should start with standard anteroposterior, lateral, and mortise weight bearing radiographs (Fig. 6). Since not all lesions will be discovered on plain radiographs, advanced imaging such as MRI or computerized tomogram (CT) may be indicated. MRI has the advantage of detecting lower grade lesions and the integrity of the overlying articular cartilage (Fig. 7). Compared with radiographs, both MRI and CT provide better detail on the location and size of the lesions.[72] Berndt and Hardy[3] described a classification system based on plain radiographs. Type 1 lesions show evidence of subchondral compression. In type II lesions, the osteochondral flap is partially detached, whereas in type III lesions, the flap is completely detached, but not displaced. A displaced osteochondral flap represents a type IV lesion. CT and MRI classifications have been developed.[2,13]

Nonoperative treatment strategies include restriction from sporting activities, rest, and cast immobilization ranging from 3 weeks to 4 months. Indications for nonoperative treatment vary, but usually include patients with minor symptoms and

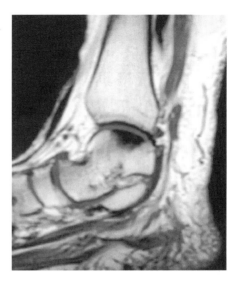

FIGURE 7. A sagittal MRI of a centrally located osteochondral lesion of the talus.

lower grade lesions. In a recent literature review, the overall success rate for nonoperative treatment was 45%.[73] Surgical intervention may be indicated when lesions are advanced and when conservative treatment fails. Most procedures may be performed arthroscopically, but larger lesions may require a formal arthrotomy. Excision with curettage and drilling resulted in an average 85% success rate, whereas simple excision alone had only an average 38% success rate.[73] Cancellous bone grafting, osteochondral transplantation, and internal fixation show promise, but further study is needed.[73,76]

FRACTURES

Fractures of the fifth metatarsal may be separated into tuberosity fractures, acute fractures of the metaphyseal-diaphyseal junction, chronic fractures of the metaphyseal-diaphyseal junction, and oblique or spiral fractures of the distal aspect.[68] Symptomatic treatment with limited activity and a postoperative shoe (with or without immobilization) is recommended for avulsion or tuberosity fractures.[7,80] Although the expected return to athletic activity has been reported to be approximately 4–6 weeks, the current authors have found the athlete may require up to 10 weeks for full recovery.[7,80] Nonunion is rare, and some cases of nonunion are not symptomatic. Where symptoms persist, excision or internal fixation may be performed.[68]

The acute fracture of the metaphyseal-diaphyseal region may be treated nonoperatively in a nonweight bearing cast for approximately 6–9 weeks.[27,74,82] Since nonoperative management requires prolonged immobilization and carries a significant chance of nonunion, many authors recommend percutaneous screw fixation for athletes.[44] Percutaneous screw fixation may return an athlete to full competition after an average of 8.5 weeks (range, 7–12 weeks).[44] Chronic or stress fractures of the metaphyseal-diaphyseal may present after an apparently acute episode; therefore, a careful history focusing on the presence of prodromal symptoms and a critical analysis of the radiographs are essential. Radiographic evidence for a stress fracture includes a widened radiolucent fracture line indicating bone resorption, periosteal reaction, lateral margin callus, and intramedullary sclerosis.[9,74] Percutaneous screw fixation is recommended for athletes with this type of stress fracture.[9,24,68] Acute oblique or

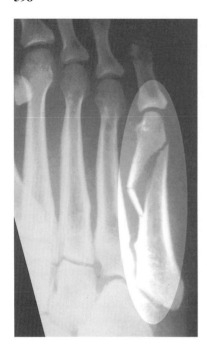

FIGURE 8. An oblique radiograph showing a distal fifth metatarsal fracture, a "dancer's fracture."

spiral fracture of the distal shaft of the fifth metatarsal may occur in athletes and dancers[53] (Fig. 8). This fracture, sometimes referred to as a "dancer's fracture," can heal with conservative treatment, but surgical intervention may be indicated for intraarticular involvement distally, more than 5 mm of displacement, metatarsal plantar keratosis from stress transfer, imbalance of the metatarsals, or hallux rigidus.[68]

Stress fractures in the other metatarsals may occur as well. Stress fractures of the second metatarsal base have been reported in ballerinas.[17,42] Diagnosis is based on clinical examination and a radiologic workup. If plain radiographs are negative, an MRI or bone scan is recommended when substantial clinical suspicion is present.[17,42,68] The patient usually responds to activity modification.[17,42,68] Distal metatarsal or isthmus fractures are typical in runners. Activity modification or rest is the recommended treatment. When stress fractures do not respond to relative rest, screw fixation with or without bone grafting may be warranted.

The diagnosis of a navicular stress fracture is often delayed.[25,75] The patient will give a vague history of insidious, poorly localized pain related to activity.[62] Tenderness over the dorsal proximal navicular, the "N" spot, suggests the diagnosis.[25] The radiologic evaluation includes standard radiographs, bone scans, and, most importantly, a CT scan.[25,62] Once the diagnosis is made, treatment should consist of 6–8 weeks of nonweight bearing casting or bracing.[25,62,75] In 86 athletes with navicular stress fractures confirmed by CT scan, Khan et al.[25] showed nonweight bearing casting for greater than 6 weeks to have an 86% success rate of returning to sport versus a 26% success rate of activity limitation. Fractures that do not respond to this treatment may be successfully treated by percutaneous screw fixation.

REFERENCES

1. Alonso A, Khoury L, Adams R: Clinical tests for ankle syndesmosis injury: reliability and prediction of return to function. J Orthop Sports Phys Ther 27:276–284, 1998.

2. Anderson IF, Crichton KJ, Grattan-Smith T, et al: Osteochondral fractures of the dome of the talus. J Bone Joint Surg Am 71:1143–1152, 1989.
3. Berndt AL, Harty M: Transchondral fractures (osteochondritis dissecans) of the talus. J Bone Joint Surg 41A:988–1020, 1959.
4. Bonnin M, Tavernier T, Bouysset M: Split lesions of the peroneus brevis tendon in chronic ankle laxity. Am J Sports Med 25:699–703, 1997.
5. Clanton TO, Butler JE, Eggert A: Injuries to the metatarsophalangeal joints in athletes. Foot Ankle 7:162–176, 1986.
6. Clanton TO, Ford JJ: Turf toe injury. Clin Sports Med 13:731–741, 1994.
7. Clapper MF, O'Brien TJ, Lyons PM: Fractures of the fifth metatarsal. Clin Orthop 315:238–241, 1995.
8. Curtis MJ, Myerson M, Szura B: Tarsometatarsal joint injuries in the athlete. Am J Sports Med 21:497–502, 1993.
9. DeLee JC, Evans JP, Julian J: Stress fracture of the fifth metatarsal. Am J Sports Med 11:349–353, 1983.
10. Eckert WR, Davis EA Jr.: Acute rupture of the peroneal retinaculum. J Bone Joint Surg 58A:670–672, 1976.
11. Eiff MP, Smith AT, Smith GE: Early mobilization versus immobilization in the treatment of lateral ankle sprains. Am J Sports Med 22:83–88, 1994.
12. Escalas F, Figueras JM, Merino JA: Dislocation of the peroneal tendons. Long-term results of surgical treatment. J Bone Joint Surg 62A:451–453, 1980.
13. Ferkel RD: Articular surface defects, loose bodies, and osteophytes. In Arthroscopic Surgery: The Foot and Ankle. Philadelphia, Lippincott-Raven, 1996, pp 145–170.
14. Hamilton WG: Conditions seen in classical ballet and modern dance. In Gould JS (ed): Operative Foot Surgery. Philadelphia, WB Saunders Co, 1994, pp 954–975.
15. Hamilton WG, Geppert MJ, Thompson FM: Pain in the posterior aspect of the ankle in dancers. Differential diagnosis and operative treatment. J Bone Joint Surg 78A:1491–1500, 1996.
16. Harper MC: Subluxation of the peroneal tendons within the peroneal groove: A report of two cases. Foot Ankle Int 18:369–370, 1997.
17. Harrington T, Crichton KJ, Anderson IF: Overuse ballet injury of the base of the second metatarsal. A diagnostic problem. Am J Sports Med 21:591–598, 1993.
18. Hertel J: Functional instability following lateral ankle sprain. Sports Med 29:361–371, 2000.
19. Hopkinson WJ, St.Pierre P, Ryan JB, Wheeler JH: Syndesmosis sprains of the ankle. Foot Ankle 10:325–330, 1990.
20. Johnston E, Scranton P, Pfeffer GB: Chronic disorders of the Achilles tendon: Results of conservative and surgical treatments. Foot Ankle Int 18:570–574, 1997.
21. Jones DC: Achilles tendon problems in runners. Instr Course Lect 419–427, 1998.
22. Kannus P, Renstrom P: Treatment for acute tears of the lateral ligaments of the ankle. Operation, cast, or early controlled mobilization. J Bone Joint Surg 73A:305–312, 1991.
23. Karlsson J, Bergsten T, Lansinger O, Peterson L: Reconstruction of the lateral ligaments of the ankle for chronic lateral instability. J Bone Joint Surg 70A:581–588, 1988.
24. Kavanaugh JH, Brower TD, Mann RV: The Jones fracture revisited. J Bone Joint Surg 60A:776–782, 1978.
25. Khan KM, Fuller PJ, Brukner PD, et al: Outcome of conservative and surgical management of navicular stress fracture in athletes. Eighty-six cases proven with computerized tomography. Am J Sports Med 20:657–666, 1992.
26. Kolettis GJ, Micheli LJ, Klein JD: Release of the flexor hallucis longus tendon in ballet dancers. J Bone Joint Surg Am 78:1386–1390, 1996.
27. Lehman RC, Torg JS, Pavlov H, DeLee JC: Fractures of the base of the fifth metatarsal distal to the tuberosity: A review. Foot Ankle 7:245–252, 1987.
28. Lynch SA, Renstrom P: Treatment of acute lateral ankle ligament rupture in the athlete. Sports Med 27:61–71, 1999.
29. Maffulli N: The clinical diagnosis of subcutaneous tear of the achilles tendon. A prospective study in 174 patients. Am J Sports Med 26:266–270, 1998.
30. Maffulli N: Rupture of the achilles tendon. J Bone Joint Surg Am 81:1019–1036, 1999.
31. Maffulli N, Binfield PM, Moore D, King JB: Surgical decompression of chronic central core lesions of the Achilles tendon. Am J Sports Med 27:747–752, 1999.
32. Mandelbaum BR, Myerson MS, Forster R: Achilles tendon ruptures: A new method of repair, early range of motion, and functional rehabilitation. Am J Sports Med 23:392–395, 1995.
33. Mann RA: Bunion surgery: Decision making. Orthopedics 13:951–957, 1990.
34. Mantas JP, Burks RT: Lisfranc injuries in the athlete. Clin Sports Med 13:719–730, 1994.

35. Marotta JJ, Micheli LJ: Os trigonum impingement in dancers. Am J Sports Med 20:533–536, 1992.
36. Marshall P: The rehabilitation of overuse foot injuries in athletes and dancers. Clin Sports Med 7:175–191, 1988.
37. Marshall P, Hamilton WG: Cuboid subluxation in ballet dancers. Am J Sports Med 20:169–175, 1992.
38. Martens MA, Noyez JF, Mulier JC: Recurrent dislocation of the peroneal tendons. Results of rerouting the tendons under the calcaneofibular ligament. Am J Sports Med 14:148–150, 1986.
39. Marumoto JM, Ferkel RD: Arthroscopic excision of the os trigonum: A new technique with preliminary clinical results. Foot Ankle Int 18:777–784, 1997.
40. McConkey JP, Favero KJ: Subluxation of the peroneal tendons within the peroneal tendon sheath. A case report. Am J Sports Med 15:511–513, 1987.
41. McLennan JG: Treatment of acute and chronic luxations of the peroneal tendons. Am J Sports Med 8:432–436, 1980.
42. Micheli LJ, Sohn RS, Solomon R: Stress fractures of the second metatarsal involving Lisfranc's joint in ballet dancers. A new overuse injury of the foot. J Bone Joint Surg 67A:1372–1375, 1985.
43. Micheli LJ, Waters PM, Sanders DP: Sliding fibular graft repair for chronic dislocation of the peroneal tendons. Am J Sports Med 17:68–71, 1989.
44. Mindrebo N, Shelbourne KD, Van Meter CD, Rettig AC: Outpatient percutaneous screw fixation of the acute Jones fracture. Am J Sports Med 21:720–723, 1993.
45. Mooney M, Maffey-Ward L: Cuboid plantar and dorsal subluxations: Assessment and treatment. J Orthop Sports Phys Ther 20:220–226, 1994.
46. Mortensen HM, Skov O, Jensen PE: Early motion of the ankle after operative treatment of a rupture of the achilles tendon. A prospective, randomized clinical and radiographic study. J Bone Joint Surg Am 81:983–990, 1999.
47. Motta P, Errichiello C, Pontini I: Achilles tendon rupture. A new technique for easy surgical repair and immediate movement of the ankle and foot. Am J Sports Med 25:172–176, 1997.
48. Murr S: Dislocation of the peroneal tendons with marginal fracture of the lateral malleolus. J Bone Joint Surg Br 43:563–565, 1961.
49. Myerson MS: Achilles tendon ruptures. Instr Course Lect 48:219–230, 1999.
50. Myerson MS, Mandelbaum B: Disorders of the Achilles tendon and the retrocalcaneal region. In Myerson MS (ed): Foot and Ankle Disorders, pp 1367–1398. Philadelphia, WB Saunders, 2000.
51. Myerson MS, McGarvey W: Disorders of the Achilles tendon insertion and Achilles tendinitis. Instr Course Lect 48:211–218, 1999.
52. Newell SG, Woodle A: Cuboid syndrome. Phys Sports Med 9:71–76, 1981.
53. O'Malley MJ, Hamilton WG, Munyak J: Fractures of the distal shaft of the fifth metatarsal: "Dancer's fracture." Presented at the 24th Annual Meeting of the American Orthopaedic Foot and Ankle Society, New Orleans, February 27, 1994.
54. Oden RR: Tendon injuries about the ankle resulting from skiing. Clin Orthop 216:63–69, 1987.
55. Ogilvie-Harris DJ, Reed SC: Disruption of the ankle syndesmosis: Diagnosis and treatment by arthroscopic surgery. Arthroscopy 10:561–568, 1994.
56. Paavola M, Kannus P, Paakkala T, et al: Long-term prognosis of patients with achilles tendinopathy. An observational 8-year follow-up study [in process citation]. Am J Sports Med 28:634–642, 2000.
57. Patterson MJ, Cox WK: Peroneus longus tendon ruptures as a cause of chronic lateral ankle pain. Clin Orthop 365:163–166, 1999.
58. Peacock KC, Resnick EJ, Thoder JJ: Fracture of the os peroneum with rupture of the peroneus longus tendon. A case report and review of the literature. Clin Orthop 202:223–226, 1986.
59. Pijnenburg AC, Van Dijk CN, Bossuyt PM, Marti RK: Treatment of ruptures of the lateral ankle ligaments: A meta-analysis. J Bone Joint Surg Am 82:761–763, 2000.
60. Poll RG, Duijfjes F: The treatment of recurrent dislocation of the peroneal tendons. J Bone Joint Surg Br 66:98–100, 1984.
61. Puddu G, Ippolito E, Postacchini F: A classification of Achilles tendon disease. Am J Sports Med 4:145–150, 1976.
62. Quirk R: Stress fractures of the navicular. Foot Ankle Int 19:494–496, 1998.
63. Rodeo SA, O'Brien S, Warren RF, et al: Turf-toe: an analysis of metatarsophalangeal joint sprains in professional football players. Am J Sports Med 18:280–285, 1990.
64. Safran MR, Zachazewski JE, Benedetti RS, Bartolozzi AR, Mandelbaum R: Lateral ankle sprains: A comprehensive review part 2: Treatment and rehabilitation with an emphasis on the athlete. Med Sci Sports Exerc 31:S438–S447, 1999.
65. Sammarco GJ, Cooper PS: Flexor hallucis longus tendon injury in dancers and nondancers. Foot Ankle Int 19:356–362, 1998.

66. Sammarco GJ, DiRaimondo CV: Chronic peroneus brevis tendon lesions. Foot Ankle 9:163–170, 1989.
67. Sarmiento A, Wolf M: Subluxation of peroneal tendons. Case treated by rerouting tendons under calcaneofibular ligament. J Bone Joint Surg 57A:115–116, 1975.
68. Schon LC: Decision-making for the athlete: The leg, ankle, and foot in sports. In Myerson MS (ed): Foot and Ankle Disorders. Philadelphia, WB Saunders, pp 1435–1476, 2000.
69. Scioli MW: Injuries about the ankle: instability of the ankle and subtalar joint. In Myerson MS (ed): Foot and Ankle Disorders. Philadelphia, WB Saunders, pp 1399–1419, 2000.
70. Sobel M, Geppert MJ, Olson EJ, et al: The dynamics of peroneus brevis tendon splits: A proposed mechanism, technique of diagnosis, and classification of injury. Foot Ankle 13:413–422, 1992.
71. Speck M, Klaue K: Early full weightbearing and functional treatment after surgical repair of acute achilles tendon rupture. Am J Sports Med 26:789–793, 1998.
72. Stroud CC, Marks RM: Imaging of osteochondral lesions of the talus. Foot Ankle Clin 5:119–133, 2000.
73. Tol JL, Struijs PA, Bossuyt PM, et al: Treatment strategies in osteochondral defects of the talar dome: A systematic review. Foot Ankle Int 21:119–126, 2000.
74. Torg JS, Balduini FC, Zelko RR, et al: Fractures of the base of the fifth metatarsal distal to the tuberosity. Classification and guidelines for non-surgical and surgical management. J Bone Joint Surg 66A:209–214, 1984.
75. Torg JS, Pavlov H, Cooley LH, et al: Stress fractures of the tarsal navicular. A retrospective review of twenty-one cases. J Bone Joint Surg 64A:700–712, 1982.
76. Toth AP, Easley ME: Ankle chondral injuries and repair. Foot Ankle Clin 5:799–840, 2000.
77. Trevino SG, Davis P, Hecht PJ: Management of acute and chronic lateral ligament injuries of the ankle. Orthop Clin North Am 25:1–16, 1994.
78. Troop RL, Losse GM, Lane JG, et al: Early motion after repair of Achilles tendon ruptures. Foot Ankle Int 16:705–709, 1995.
79. Tudisco C, Puddu G: Stenosing tenosynovitis of the flexor hallucis longus tendon in a classical ballet dancer. A case report. Am J Sports Med 12:403–404, 1984.
80. Wiener BD, Linder JF, Giattini JF: Treatment of fractures of the fifth metatarsal: A prospective study. Foot Ankle Int 18:267–269, 1997.
81. Zoellner G, Clancy W Jr: Recurrent dislocation of the peroneal tendon. J Bone Joint Surg 61A:292–294, 1979.
82. Zogby RG, Baker BE: A review of nonoperative treatment of Jones' fracture. Am J Sports Med 15:304–307, 1987.

JOHN A. DiPRETA, MD
WEN CHAO, MD
KEITH L. WAPNER, MD

CONSERVATIVE MANAGEMENT OF FOREFOOT AND MIDFOOT PAIN AND DYSFUNCTION

From Pennsylvania Orthopaedic
  Foot and Ankle Surgeons
Philadelphia, Pennsylvania

Reprint requests to:
Pennsylvania Orthopaedic Foot
  and Ankle Surgeons
230 West Washington Square
Fifth Floor
Philadelphia, PA 19106

Pain in the foot can be a debilitating problem. From an anatomic standpoint, it may be localized to the forefoot, midfoot, or hindfoot. It may be manifested or interpreted by the patient as localizing to the plantar and/or dorsal aspect of the foot. Because of the broad differential diagnosis, a precise history and careful physical examination are essential elements in determining the cause of pain.

In this chapter, we explore some of the common causes of forefoot and midfoot pain. We address them anatomically according to their distribution in the forefoot and midfoot.

FOREFOOT

First Metatarsophalangeal Joint

The two most common disorders causing pain or discomfort of the first metatarsophalangeal (MTP) joint are hallux valgus and hallux rigidus.[12]

HALLUX VALGUS

The hallux valgus deformity is a static subluxation of the first MTP joint. The great toe deviates laterally, while the first metatarsal migrates medially. With lateral movement of the hallux, deformity may develop in the second toe as well. The hallux may displace either dorsally or plantarly relative to the 2nd toe.[23]

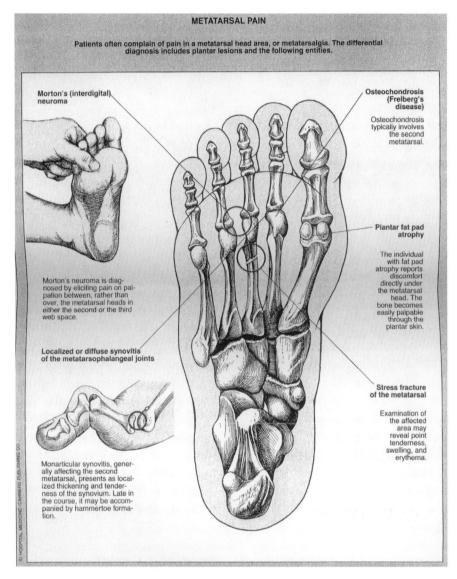

METATARSAL PAIN

Patients often complain of pain in a metatarsal head area, or metatarsalgia. The differential diagnosis includes plantar lesions and the following entities.

Morton's (interdigital) neuroma

Morton's neuroma is diagnosed by eliciting pain on palpation between, rather than over, the metatarsal heads in either the second or the third web space.

Localized or diffuse synovitis of the metatarsophalangeal joints

Monarticular synovitis, generally affecting the second metatarsal, presents as localized thickening and tenderness of the synovium. Late in the course, it may be accompanied by hammertoe formation.

Osteochondrosis (Freiberg's disease)

Osteochondrosis typically involves the second metatarsal.

Plantar fat pad atrophy

The individual with fat pad atrophy reports discomfort directly under the metatarsal head. The bone becomes easily palpable through the plantar skin.

Stress fracture of the metatarsal

Examination of the affected area may reveal point tenderness, swelling, and erythema.

© HOSPITAL MEDICINE / CAHNERS PUBLISHING CO.

FIGURE 1. Causes of first metatarsophalangeal joint pain. (From Wapner KL: Foot pain: Where and why? Hosp Med 28:105–121, 1992.)

ANATOMY

The 1st MTP joint is composed of the proximal phalanx and the 1st metatarsal. It is stabilized by collateral ligaments and the intrinsic muscles of the foot that insert onto the base of the proximal phalanx. This is augmented by the extrinsic musculature, specifically, the EHL and FHL. Because there are no muscular attachments to the metatarsal head, this articulation is particularly vulnerable to extrinsic forces. Once the joint destabilizes and the proximal phalanx begins to subluxate laterally,

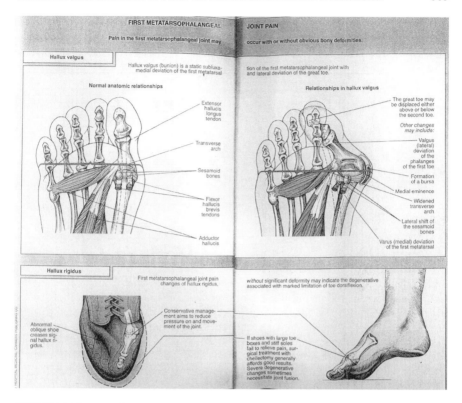

FIGURE 1 (Cont.). Causes of first metatarsophalangeal joint pain. (From Wapner KL: Foot pain: Where and why? Hosp Med 28:105–121, 1992.)

the muscles that normally act to stabilize the joint become a deforming force as their pull becomes lateral to the axis of the MTP joint[9] (Fig. 1).

ETIOLOGY

This deformity almost exclusively occurs in people who wear shoes (Fig. 2). Conversely, not all individuals who wear high-fashion footwear develop hallux valgus, and thus there may be some predisposing factors that make hallux valgus more likely in certain individuals. Intrinsic causes include hereditary factors, pes planus, metatarsus primus, varus, hypermobility of the first metatarsocuneiform joint, amputation of the 2nd toe, and joint hyperelasticity.[9]

PATHOPHYSIOLOGY

The hallux valgus deformity can be appreciated by examining the articulations of the metatarsophalangeal and metatarsocuneiform joints. The most stable MTP joint has a flat articular surface. A rounded head is more prone to develop an unstable articulation. A congruent joint likewise is more stable, whereas an incongruent joint is unstable and the deformity will persist. The position of the metatarsal head is also influenced by the position of the metatarsocuneiform (MTC) joint. A more horizontally oriented joint is more resistant to varus deviation of the first metatarsal than an obliquely oriented articulation.

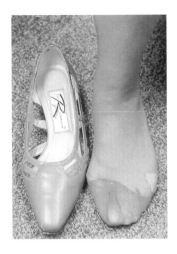

FIGURE 2.   Demonstration of disparity of shoe size and shape of foot.

The deformity of hallux valgus consists of an enlarged eminence on the dorso-medial aspect of the metatarsal head. This results in pressure against the enlarged area, which may cause a painful bursa or excessive pressure on the cutaneous nerve over the prominence. The medial capsular tissue of the MTP joint attenuates secondary to the medial displacement of the metatarsal head and the lateral translation of the proximal phalanx.

Other changes include contracture of the lateral capsular tissue. With progressive deformity, the adductor hallucis migrates beneath the metatarsal head creating varying degrees of pronation of the proximal phalanx. Because the normal anatomic relationships have been disturbed, the hallux bears less weight. This causes lateral transfer of the weight bearing surface, which can create painful calluses underneath the 2nd or 3rd metatarsal heads.

Symptoms related to the HV deformity most commonly are localized to the dorsomedial prominence. Symptoms typically are worsened by dress or high-heeled shoes. In addition, with progressive lateral drift of the hallux, deformities of the 2nd toe can develop. The hallux may either override or migrate under the 2nd toe with the 2nd toe relatively unaffected. On the other hand, the 2nd MTP joint may subluxate or dislocate and a hammer toe deformity may be created. In this situation, an individual may complain of pain about the proximal interphalangeal (PIP) joint of the toe or underneath the 2nd metatarsal head.

PATIENT EVALUATION

A careful history is an essential aspect of determining the cause and ultimately the treatment of a HV deformity. Complaints of pain in the region of the medial eminence are the predominant presentation. A symptomatic callus beneath the 2nd metatarsal head may also be present. Information should be obtained regarding the patients level of activity, occupation, athletic inclinations, preference in shoe wear, and reasons for electing surgery.

Physical examination includes evaluation of gait and palpation of affected areas in both the seated and standing positions. ROM of the MTP joint is assessed as well as the ability to correct the deformity. Diminished ROM may be reflective of a laterally inclined metatarsal head or cartilage degeneration. Mobility of the 1st MTC joint should also be noted. The plantar aspect of the foot is examined for symptomatic

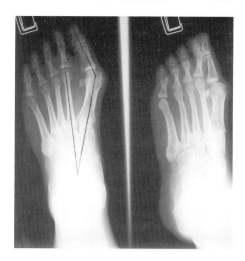

FIGURE 3. Radiograph depicting the hallux valgus (HV) angle and the intermetatarsal (IM) angle.

keratoses beneath the metatarsal heads. In addition, the intermetatarsal spaces are palpated for evidence of neuritic symptoms. Evaluation of vascular supply and neurologic function must also be completed.[12]

RADIOGRAPHS

Radiographs are done with the patient erect and are taken in the anteroposterior (AP), oblique, and lateral projections. From the radiographs, the following information is obtained.[9,12]

1. Hallux valgus angle—this angle is created by lines that bisect the longitudinal axis of the proximal phalanx and 1st metatarsal (normal value: 0–15 degrees).

2. Intermetatarsal angle—angle created by lines bisecting the 1st and 2nd metatarsal shafts (normal: 9 degrees) (Fig. 3).

3. Interphalangeal angle—created by lines bisecting longitudinal axes of the proximal and distal phalanges (normal: 10 degrees). (Fig. 4).

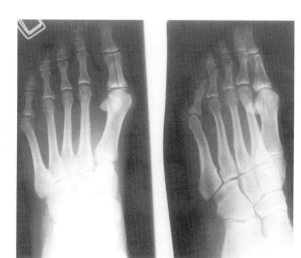

FIGURE 4. Radiograph depicts the interphalangeal angle, assessing for hallux interphalangeus.

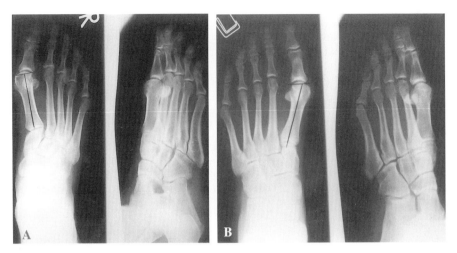

FIGURE 5.   Demonstration of the distal metatarsal articular angle. *A*, Normal. *B*, Abnormal.

4. Distal metatarsal articular angle—angle created by the articular surface of the metatarsal head and a line bisecting the longitudinal axis of the 1st metatarsal (normal: 10 degrees) (Fig. 5).

5. Determination of joint congruency.

6. MTC joint angle to assess for orientation. Normally less than 10 degrees of medial obliquity is seen. Greater than this is considered unstable. The base of the 1st metatarsal should be observed for the presence of a lateral facet, which may preclude reduction of the IM angle.

7. Arthrosis of the first MTP joint.

8. Size of the medial eminence. This is determined by drawing a line along the medial aspect of the metatarsal shaft.

CONSERVATIVE MANAGEMENT

Treatment for HV should start with a shoe that is of sufficient size to relieve pressure over the medial prominence. A soft leather shoe with a wide toe box and soft sole can give significant relief of symptoms. Likewise, modification of shoes by relieving pressure over the medial prominence through stretching the shoes may prove useful. For those reluctant to undergo surgical correction, custom-made footwear may be indicated. The use of over-the-counter appliances such as bunion pads, night splints, and bunion splints may also help.

The use of orthotics has not demonstrated the ability to prevent the progression of the HV deformity. In fact, it may place more pressure against the medial eminence because of the space that it occupies within the shoe.

SURGICAL TREATMENT

The decision to proceed with surgery depends upon several issues:

1. The patient's chief complaint, occupation, recreational activities
2. Physical examination
3. Radiographic findings
4. Age
5. Neurovascular status of the foot
6. Patient expectations

Patient expectations cannot be overemphasized. Expectations must be clearly stated, and the outcomes of surgery and its complications must be carefully discussed with the patient. The choice of the surgical procedure is determined by the magnitude of deformity, the congruency of the first MTP joint, presence of arthrosis at the first MTP joint, and hypermobility of the first MTC joint.

The procedures, techniques, and complications are beyond the scope of this chapter, and the reader is referred to standard textbooks on foot and ankle surgery.

HALLUX RIGIDUS

Hallux rigidus is a painful affliction of the 1st MTP joint characterized by restricted dorsiflexion and proliferation of periarticular bone.[12] Other terms used to describe this condition include hallux limitus, dorsal bunion, hallux dolorosus, hallux malleus, and metatarsus primus elevatus. It is thought that hallux rigidus may be more debilitating than hallux valgus because of its limitations on motion and its effects on ambulation.[1]

In the adult, hallux rigidus is considered a secondary deformity and is unilateral in the majority of cases. The basic pathologic entity is that of degenerative arthritis. The classic location of the cartilage loss is on the dorsal one half to two thirds of the metatarsal head.

ETIOLOGY

Trauma is thought to be the most common cause. It may result from a single episode or from repetitive microtrauma. Forced hyperextension or forced plantar flexion may create compressive forces, which in turn may create chondral or osteochondral injury. This acute injury may evolve into chronic discomfort. An osseous injury may be detected on radiographs, but cartilaginous injury may be diagnosed by clinical exam and clinical suspicion. Rodeo et al described limitation of motion of the 1st MTP joint after turf-toe injury in professional football players.[18]

PHYSICAL FINDINGS

Patients will usually present with complaints of pain and stiffness localized to the 1st MTP joint. Symptoms are typically aggravated by ambulation and relieved by rest.

The classic physical finding is limitation or absence of dorsiflexion at the first MTP joint. On forced dorsiflexion, pain is elicited with bony impingement between the base of the proximal phalanx and dorsal metatarsal osteophytes. Plantar flexion may be normal; however, pain may be elicited with impingement of synovial or capsular tissue or the EHL tendon as it passes over the dorsal osteophyte. Physical manifestations may vary from synovial hypertrophy early in the disease to significant proliferative osteophyte formation in later stages. Hyperextension may be noted at the interphalangeal joint as a compensatory mechanism.

A prominent ridge of bone may be palpable on the dorsal aspect of the 1st metatarsal head and base of the proximal phalanx. Skin irritation may develop with pressure from footwear over the dorsal exostosis.

Aberration in gait is noted with the patient bearing weight on the lateral aspect of the foot to minimize dorsiflexion of the 1st MTP joint. Paresthesias may also be noted in the 1st web space as a result of compression of the dorsal digital nerve against the dorsolateral osteophyte.[1]

RADIOGRAPHS

As with any foot deformity, radiographic views taken in the AP, oblique, and lateral projections are mandatory. The AP projection will demonstrate non-uniform joint space narrowing with associated flattening and widening of the metatarsal head.

In advanced stages, subchondral cysts and sclerosis of the 1st metatarsal head along with widening of the base of the proximal phalanx may be seen. Osteophyte formation is seen more prominently laterally than medially on AP radiographs. A central articular osteochondral defect may also be present. In the lateral projection, a prominent dorsal osteophyte is seen and may appear to course proximally along the dorsal 1st metatarsal shaft. Osteophyte formation may be noted on the proximal phalanx, and loose bodies may also be present.[6]

TREATMENT

Treatment is dependent upon the symptoms and severity of the degenerative process. In early stages where synovial irritation is the primary symptom, use of NSAIDs in conjunction with a stiff insole to minimize motion of the MTP joint is recommended. An insole with a Morton extension can reduce MTP motion and can be moved from shoe to shoe. An extended steel or fiberglass shank between the inner and outer sole may be used to reduce MTP motion. Orthoses to reduce midfoot pronation may be helpful; however, these diminish room available in the shoe and may lead to increased pressure along the dorsal exostosis. Shoes with low heels when the patient has no significant equinus deformity, and roomy toe-box may suffice to accommodate an enlarged MTP joint. Taping to decrease dorsiflexion of the hallux may also alleviate symptoms as a temporary measure (Fig. 6). Occasional use of an intra-articular steroid injection may provide temporary relief; however, repeated injections may accelerate the degenerative process. When continued symptoms restrict activity, surgical intervention may be considered.

Surgical Treatment. Surgical treatment of hallux rigidus is dependent on the degree of arthrosis. For stages marked by synovial proliferation, synovectomy may

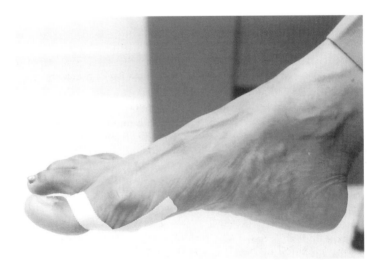

FIGURE 6.   Taping of hallux to minimize dorsiflexion.

be preferred. When an osteochondral defect is present, removal of the loose body along with drilling of the exposed bony surface to promote fibrocartilaginous ingrowth can be performed. For those with limited dorsiflexion without osteophyte formation, a closing-wedge, dorsiflexion osteotomy of the 1st metatarsal may be performed. In the presence of proliferative bone, cheilectomy with debridement of the medial and lateral osteophytes is preferred. When Grade III changes are present, surgical options include fusion, soft tissue interpositional arthroplasty, and prosthetic replacement.[1] At the current time, results of prosthetic replacement have been suboptimal. Therefore, it is not used very often.

Disorders of the Lesser Metatarsals

Metatarsalgia or pain in the region of the lesser MTP joints is a common complaint and can be due to a myriad of causes. It is a non-specific term that serves only to denote the location of pain without describing the pathophysiologic basis, natural history, or treatment plan.[16] Although the differential is broad, pain may be referred from the plantar skin, metatarsal stress reactions or fractures, localized or diffuse synovitis of the MTP joints, interdigital neuroma, osteochondrosis (Freiberg's disease) or arthritis.

PHYSICAL EXAMINATION

As with any musculoskeletal complaint, a thorough examination is essential. The examination begins with inspection, noting the position of each of the joints of the lesser toes as well as that of the big toe. Observation should be made for deformity, swelling, bony prominences, and the condition of the skin. Palpation of the affected areas is then performed. The dorsal and plantar surfaces are examined. Dorsally, attention should be paid to the presence of callosities on the toes and tenderness at the level of the MTP joints. One may detect the presence of ganglion cysts, bony projections, and thickened synovium. Plantarly, examination should be sought for keratotic lesions, bony prominences, fat pad atrophy, and ulceration. The presence of fixed or flexible deformities should also be determined. The interdigital spaces are individually palpated for the presence of interdigital neuritis.[16]

PLANTAR SKIN PAIN

Common lesions of the plantar skin include diffuse calluses, seed corns (deep-seated circumscribed nucleated calluses), plantar keratoses, circumscribed ulcerations, and solitary or multiple warts.[23]

Diffuse calluses, seed corns, plantar keratoses, and ulcerations result from pressure over bony prominences, usually as a result of poorly fitting shoes. These lesions often respond to shaving of the keratotic tissues and/or modification of shoe wear to transfer pressure away from involved areas. If such conservative treatment fails, definitive surgical intervention may be indicated.

A well-localized, discrete hyperkeratotic proliferation under a metatarsal head can cause significant pain and disability. These deep-seated nucleated calluses or "seed corns" must be differentiated from plantar warts, which are viral in etiology. Plantar warts tend to be raised, painful, and discrete lesions that can occur anywhere on the plantar aspect of the foot including non–weight bearing areas. They are highly vascular, exhibiting punctate bleeding when shaved. The intractable plantar keratosis, on the other hand, has a hard core composed of avascular keratotic tissue that is painful to pressure. These lesions are generally found underneath a metatarsal

FIGURE 7. Placement of metatarsal pads within shoe, proximal to lesion.

head or at any site of abnormal pressure, such as a prominent fibular condyle of the metatarsal head.[13]

Initial management should focus on relieving the pressure through the use of metatarsal pads and soft, flat shoes with additional padding if needed. Pads should be placed proximal to the metatarsal head to reduce weight bearing on the lesion (Fig. 7). Shaving the callus at regular intervals in the office (Fig. 8) combined with the use of a pumice stone by the patient after bathing also may control the painful prominence and provide significant symptomatic relief. If symptoms persist, surgical treatment can give satisfactory results. Surgery is aimed at removing the bony prominence formed by the plantar condyles under the metatarsal head, which will relieve the localized pressure. This can be accomplished by plantar condylectomy.[13]

Diffuse plantar painful thickening under the lesser metatarsal heads is the result of abnormal pressure. This is due to an alteration of the normal weight bearing mechanics of the foot. This can be created by a congenital condition such as a short or unstable first metatarsal or cavus foot, or as a secondary phenomenon related to a traumatic event or surgical procedure that elevates the first metatarsal head.

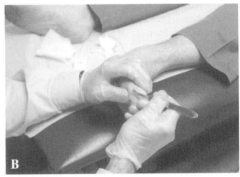

FIGURE 8. *A*, No. 17 blade. *B*, Debridement of callus.

Shortening of the 1st metatarsal, regardless of the cause, may result in transfer lesion under the lesser metatarsal heads as they are forced to bear more of the load. Surgical alteration of any of the lesser metatarsals may create problems in the remaining metatarsals. A fracture of one of the lesser metatarsals can lead to healing in a plantar flexed position, which could cause the bone to bear a greater proportion of the weight. Likewise, subluxation or dislocation of a lesser MTP joint can also lead to formation of a painful keratosis.[16]

Initial management is similar to those for discrete lesions with relieving pressure and redistributing the abnormal forces. The callus is trimmed with a sharp knife to reduce the hyperkeratotic tissue. For deep-seated lesions, several trimmings may be necessary. After debridement, a soft metatarsal support is used to relieve the pressure on the involved area. The soft support can be used initially provided that the patient's shoe is of adequate size. Individuals with significant keratotic lesions must be encouraged to wear broad, soft, and preferably low-heeled shoes to provide more cushioning for the plantar aspect of the foot. The metatarsal support (pad) is placed into the shoe just proximal to the area of the lesion. It is important to instruct the patient that a breaking-in period of 7–10 days is necessary to get adjusted to the feel of the metatarsal support. The patient is then seen periodically for trimming of the lesion, adjustment of the metatarsal support, and possible replacement with a larger and higher one.[13]

A well-molded soft orthotic may be necessary if the patient has postural abnormality of the foot. The custom-molded orthotic device should not be utilized until one has experimented with removable soft inserts first to see whether the patient responds to an orthosis.

Surgery is reserved for those with persistent symptoms despite nonoperative treatment. For an abnormally long metatarsal, a shortening osteotomy may be necessary. A metatarsal with a plantar flexion deformity may be addressed surgically with a dorsally based, closing-wedge osteotomy. In some instances, a 1st MTP fusion may be indicated to minimize forefoot stresses during the heel rise segment of gait. Single metatarsal head resection is ill advised, as it may lead to further deformity or occurrence of new transfer lesions.[16]

Stress Fracture

Stress fractures are defined as spontaneous fractures of normal bone that results from a summation of stresses of which any one by itself is harmless. They occur in the normal bones of healthy people. Patients rarely report a specific injury.[19]

The metatarsals are among the most common sites for these injuries. The 2nd metatarsal is most frequently involved, followed by the 3rd metatarsal. In ballet dancers, fracture at the base of the 2nd metatarsal has been reported.[5]

Stress fractures are often noted in new military recruits who undergo intensive training to which the bones of the foot are not adapted. In addition, metatarsal stress fractures have also been described in young patients engaged in recreational sporting activities.

Clinical and Radiographic Evaluation

The most common presenting complaint is pain. It may occur in the setting of a long march or with increased running on hard pavement. One usually describes this pain as an ache or soreness in the foot. As the pain becomes more intense, a limp develops. Although swelling is absent initially, after approximately 2 weeks, clinical findings begin to appear. They include tenderness, swelling, and ecchymosis over

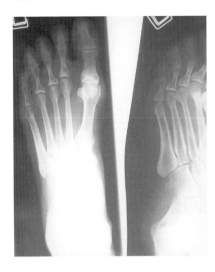

FIGURE 9.   Radiograph in patient suspected of having a stress fracture.

the shaft of the metatarsal. Point tenderness over site of injury on the metatarsal is diagnostic.

Stress fractures are often diagnosed clinically because radiographic findings may lag behind the clinical examination. Radiographs taken within 2 weeks of the onset of symptoms may not demonstrate a metatarsal fracture (Fig. 9). AP and oblique radiographs are most useful in determining fracture (Fig. 10). A technetium bone scan or MRI can be performed when radiographs are negative but a stress fracture is clinically suspected.

Fractures of the 1st metatarsal are typically found in the proximal portion of the bone. Fractures of the 2nd and 3rd metatarsals usually occur in the middle of the

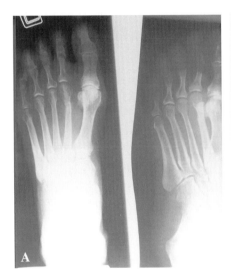
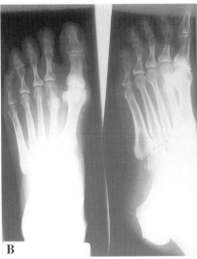

FIGURE 10.   Same patient in Figure 9. Radiograph taken 16 days later, demonstrating fracture of 2nd metatarsal neck (A), callus formation (B).

shaft or in the neck of the bone. In the 4th metatarsal, they tend to occur distally. Fifth metatarsal fractures are often seen near the proximal diaphysis. Displacement of metatarsal stress fractures is rare.[19]

TREATMENT

The treatment options are determined by the pain and disability of the patient. In the most painful situations, a walking cast would be indicated. For others, a wooden-soled or stiff-soled shoe along with restriction of activities until fracture healing has taken place is necessary. Treatment for all patients includes decreasing activity and walking in a wooden shoe until the pain subsides. This usually occurs within 4–6 weeks. Sports or training may then be advanced progressively, or in the non-athlete, the patient may return to their ADLs.

SUBLUXATION AND DISLOCATION OF THE SECOND METATARSOPHALANGEAL JOINT

Subluxation and dislocation of the 2nd MTP joint is a fairly common event.[3] Acutely, MTP joint dislocation may occur after an injury with disruption of the plantar capsule and MTP collateral ligaments. Capsular distention associated with systemic arthritides, connective tissue disorders, as well as non-specific synovitis can lead to capsular insufficiency. Chronic synovitis may lead to deterioration of the collateral ligaments and joint capsule with subsequent instability of the MTP joint.[16]

ETIOLOGY

The typical forces that lead to subluxation and dislocation of the MTP joint are hyperextension and axial loading. Extrinsically, pressure applied to the distal aspect of the longest toe, usually the 2nd toe, by footwear will cause hyper–plantar flexion at the PIP joint and dorsiflexion at the MTP joint. This can lead to dorsal displacement of the proximal phalanx on the metatarsal head. With continued pressure, the plantar soft tissues (capsule, plantar plate, plantar aponeurosis) may stretch and lose their function as stabilizers of the joint. Subluxation may occur, and if left untreated, may progress to dislocation. In long-standing cases, soft tissue contracture may occur involving the extensor tendons as well as the dorsal, medial, and lateral joint capsule. During walking, all of the forces across the MTP joint tend to hyperextend the joint.

Synovitis of the 2nd MTP joint is more commonly associated with attritional changes in the plantar plate due to a long 2nd metatarsal. Capsular and collateral ligament structures may also be involved, leading to a cross-over toe deformity.[4]

Subluxation of the 2nd MTP joint caused by synovitis may also occur in the setting of an inflammatory disorder. Using rheumatoid arthritis as an example, synovial proliferation causing capsular distention and attenuation leads to loss of the stabilizing functions of the capsule and adjacent ligaments. Furthermore, this may also lead to osseous erosion complicating the instability further. Edema and distention of the joint capsule elicit pain that worsens with increasing instability. This thickening of the peri-articular soft tissue may also exert pressure against adjacent interdigital nerves leading to inflammation of those structures as well.[16]

PHYSICAL EXAMINATION

Patients will present with pain localized to the region of the 2nd MTP joint. The development of MTP joint subluxation is insidious. Pain is aggravated by activity and is usually relieved by rest. In the presence of hammer toe deformity, either creating the MTP subluxation/dislocation or as a cause of the subluxation/dislocation,

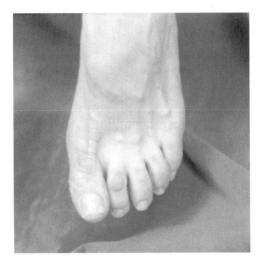

FIGURE 11. Clinical photograph of hammertoe deformity with callus on dorsal aspect of PIP joint.

pain also may be localized to the PIP joint. This is due to its dorsal position relative to the metatarsal head causing the toe to rub against the top of the toe box, creating a painful callus (Fig. 11). The shoe then pushes down on the dorsally subluxated/dislocated proximal phalanx against the metatarsal head, which may lead to a plantar keratotic lesion.

Palpation of the foot may demonstrate warmth, tenderness, and a sense of fullness in the region of the MTP joint. Tenderness may be localized either dorsally or plantarly, medially or laterally, depending on the stage and extent of the disorder. Plantar flexion may be limited. MTP stability may be assessed by the drawer test, described by Thompson and Hamilton.[20] The involved toe should be dorsiflexed approximately 25 degrees at the MTP joint while a vertical stress is applied (Fig. 12).

FIGURE 12. Clinical photo demonstrating drawer test. Forefoot stabilized with one hand, toe grabbed with other performing dorsal translation.

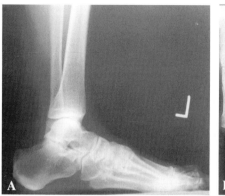
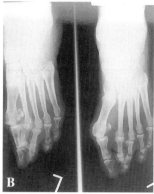

FIGURE 13.   Radiograph demonstrating dislocation of the 2nd MTP joint. *A*, Lateral view. *B*, AP view.

When the toe is vertically translated, pressure is created on the plantar capsule and elicits the characteristic pain.[3,16]

RADIOGRAPHS

Radiographic examination of the MTP joint is less useful than the clinical examination. In early stages of synovitis, AP radiographs may demonstrate widening of the MTP joint space. With subluxation, the base of the proximal phalanx may overlap the metatarsal head as it overrides dorsally, which is seen radiographically as narrowing or disappearance of the joint space. With complete dislocation, the base of the proximal phalanx may lie dorsally over the metatarsal head and is seen as overlapping on the radiograph.

Lateral radiographs may demonstrate dislocation or hyperextension of the MTP joint. Long-standing deformities lead to soft tissue contractures with fixed dorsal dislocation of the MTP joint[3] (Fig. 13).

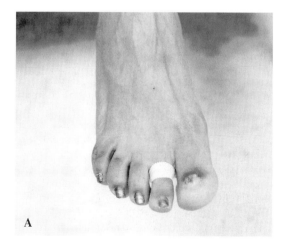
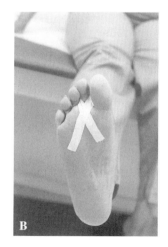

FIGURE 14.   Technique for taping of 2nd toe. *A*, Dorsal view. *B*, Plantar view.

TREATMENT

Conservative management is aimed at controlling symptoms and preventing progression of deformity. This in turn is dependent on the stage of the deformity. A well-fitted shoe with sufficient room in the toe box may suffice. Taping of the toe in a neutral position may offer stability, but it may require several months (Fig. 14). It will not correct deformity but may add stability through scarring of the MTP joint. Taping is not helpful once the MTP joint is dislocated.

The use of a metatarsal pad placed proximal to the metatarsal heads may alleviate plantar discomfort by redistribution of the weight proximally. The use of NSAIDs may also alleviate symptoms; however, they should be used cautiously in an older population.

The use of intra-articular steroid injection has been described for MTP synovitis.[15,21] Intra-articular steroid injection in conjunction with either a rocker sole or shoe with an extended steel shank may provide relief. Injection often yields only temporary relief. Cautious use of intra-articular steroids is advocated because their use may also predispose to capsular degeneration and thus instability.

Mann[14] and Coughlin[2] report on the relatively poor results with nonsurgical treatment of 2nd MTP synovitis and instability and that surgical intervention may be indicated to prevent long-term disability from this condition.

Surgical Treatment. When chronic pain is unrelieved by conservative measures or if subluxation or dislocation has occurred, surgical correction is indicated. Surgical treatment is dependent on several factors. Assessment of the etiology and flexibility of the toe must be made. In addition, co-existing conditions such as hallux valgus also need to be addressed when planning surgical correction of a 2nd MTP joint disorder.

In early stages of synovitis, synovectomy may be performed through a dorsal approach. This allows decompression of the joint with removal of inflammatory tissue. With progressive subluxation, a more complete release of the surrounding soft tissue structures is needed to bring about reduction. This would include capsular release, extensor tendon release, or lengthening and/or flexor to extensor transfer. Further decompression through partial metatarsal head resection or shortening metatarsal osteotomy would be indicated in cases of dislocation. In the presence of a hammer toe deformity, correction of the hammer toe with PIP arthroplasty can also be performed.

INTERDIGITAL NEURITIS/NEUROMA

This condition has been extensively written about over the years. The term *neuroma* is inaccurate, as this condition is a painful clinical entity affecting the common digital nerve.

Interdigital neuritis represents a pathologic condition of the common digital nerve arising from various factors. Most patients with symptoms consistent with IDN are middle-aged individuals, occurring predominantly in women. An interdigital neuroma is usually unilateral, although bilateral neuromas have been observed. The simultaneous occurrence of two neuromas in the same foot is considered rare. The majority of them occur in the third webspace, but an equal number of neuromas in the 2nd and 3rd interspaces have been described. It is believed that IDN does not occur in the 1st or 4th interspaces. The presence of symptoms in either of these regions, suggestive of nerve irritation, should prompt a search for other causes of pain.[11,24]

ETIOLOGY

Anatomic, traumatic, and extrinsic factors have been identified. The medial plantar nerve has four digital branches. The most medial branch is the proper digital nerve to the medial aspect of the hallux. The next three branches are the 1st, 2nd, and 3rd common digital nerves and are distributed to both the medial and lateral aspects of the 1st, 2nd, and 3rd interspaces. The lateral plantar nerve divides into a superficial branch and a common digital nerve to the 4th interspace. The common digital nerve frequently sends a communicating branch to the third digital nerve. It has been speculated that the combined thickness of the nerve makes it more susceptible to injury and neuroma formation. Anatomic studies[8] have disproved this; however, in the same study, the 2nd and 3rd interspace was noted to be narrower than the 1st and 4th, which may predispose the nerve to entrapment.[11]

The mobility between the medial rays and the lateral rays is also thought to be a reason for increased incidence of neuromas in the 3rd webspace. The relative increased mobility of the 4th and 5th metatarsals at their articulation with the cuboid may lead to increased mobility at the 3rd interspace and thus place more tension on the common digital nerve. Nevertheless, the high incidence of neuromas in the 2nd interspace, in part, negates this theory.

Normal gait with dorsiflexion of the MTP joints and plantar flexion of the metatarsal head through the action of the plantar aponeurosis predisposes the nerve to repetitive injury. High-fashion footwear causing the MTP joints to hyperextend has created a greater incidence of neuroma formation in women wearing these shoes. The mechanism for this may be a tethering effect of the nerve as it passes underneath the transverse metatarsal ligament (TML).

Acute trauma from a fall, crush, or from a penetrating object occasionally results in a traumatic neuritis.

A mass located either above or below the TML may exert extrinsic pressure against the nerve. Bursae are usually located above the TML between the metatarsal heads. Although the presence of the bursa itself may not exert pressure against the nerve, inflammation of the bursa may cause a secondary inflammatory process resulting in fibrosis of the nerve. Capsular degeneration leading to instability of the proximal phalanx may cause the toe to drift medially, causing the metatarsal head to move laterally and thus create pressure between the two involved metatarsal heads and create pressure against the underlying nerve. Thickening of the TML, a ganglion, or synovial cyst arising from the MTP joint may likewise cause pressure against the nerve as it passes under the TML. Histologically, perineural fibrosis, neural degeneration with thickening, and hyalinization of the walls of the endoneurial blood vessels are seen.[11]

DIAGNOSIS

The primary complaint of those with IDN is pain localized to the plantar aspect of the foot located between the metatarsal heads. The pain is often characterized as burning in nature and may or may not radiate into the toes of the involved interspace. Typically the pain is aggravated by activities and may also be exacerbated by the use of tight-fitting high-heeled shoes. The pain may be relieved by removing the shoe and massaging the toes. The use of broad, soft walking or jogging shoes may result in a decrease in symptoms. Patients rarely walk with a limp, and malalignment of the foot is often not present.

The diagnosis of IDN is usually made based on history and physical findings. Radiographs and electrodiagnostic testing are rarely helpful.

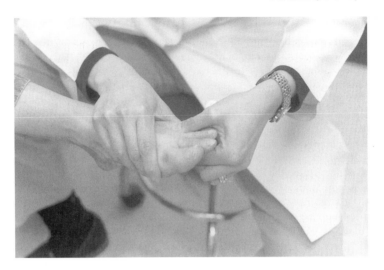

FIGURE 15. Examining for interdigital neuroma. Palpation of webspace proximal to metatarsal head with thumb and forefinger, and compression with opposite hand.

PHYSICAL EXAMINATION

The examination begins with the patient standing. One should look for deviation, subluxation, or clawing of the toes or evidence of fullness in the involved webspace. ROM of the MTP joints is then observed. Palpation is then performed on the MTP joints looking for signs of synovitis, degeneration of the plantar fat pad, and pain around the joint. Typically, patients with IDN do not have tenderness over the metatarsal heads.

Pain in the involved interspace can be reproduced by digital manipulation with pressure applied just proximal to the metatarsal heads by squeezing the forefoot between the index finger and the thumb. Palpation is carried out distally into the webspace. This will usually reproduce the pain with pain radiating out toward the tips of the toes. Pressure is then applied in the mediolateral direction with one hand to increase pressure on the tissue between the metatarsal heads (Fig. 15). This may elicit a painful click, described as Mulder's sign. If it reproduces the patient's symptoms, it may be diagnostically significant. Sensory examination is usually normal, although hypoesthesia may be noted in the involved interdigital space.

Associated conditions of the forefoot include synovitis, bursitis, and metatarsalgia and may present with similar complaints of pain. The pain caused by synovitis may be localized distal to the metatarsal head or dorsal to the MTP joint. Metatarsalgia is associated with pain underneath the metatarsal head and may be accompanied by callosity. The distinction between bursitis and neuritis is difficult. Bursitis may be heralded by swelling in the intermetatarsal space. An diagnostic injection of local anesthetic placed in the involved web space below the TML may provide useful information if diagnosis is in doubt.[11,24]

Radiographic studies are usually not necessary, as the diagnosis is mostly a clinical one. MRI or ultrasound may be useful in cases where diagnosis is unclear or in patients who have had prior surgery.[17]

TREATMENT

The goal of treatment should be to alleviate pressure on the nerve. This is done by decreasing the tension on the intermetatarsal ligament and/or reducing compression of the forefoot. The use of a wide, soft, laced shoe with a low heel may suffice. This type of shoe allows the metatarsals to spread out alleviating some of the pressure on the metatarsal head region and also diminishes hyperextension of the MTP joints.

A metatarsal pad may also be added to the shoe proximal to the metatarsal head region. This diminishes pressure at the involved area and helps to spread the metatarsal heads to relieve pressure on the nerves. On rare occasions, a metatarsal support may be added to a high-heeled shoe provided there is sufficient room in the toe box to accommodate the foot and pad. When using these pads, the patient should be instructed to break these devices in gradually. A protocol starting with 4 hours the first day and then increasing by 1 hour per day is usually successful. In most instances, patients start with a small size and may increase the size of their pad if their symptoms have not been relieved once they are wearing the pad all day.[11,22]

Kilmartin et al. explored the role of orthoses for IDN in those suspected of having flexible deformities contributing to their symptoms. Their study revealed no significant improvement in symptoms in those studied.[7]

Injection of the interspace with local anesthetic alone or in a combination with a steroid may provide pain relief. The effectiveness is often dependent upon using a small quantity that is carefully directed. Long-term use of corticosteroid injections is associated with various complications such as atrophy of subcutaneous fat, skin discoloration, and disruption of the joint capsule.

Most patients respond fairly well to initial conservative treatment, but only approximately 20% of patients will have complete resolution of symptoms. In the majority of patients, symptoms persist and in time, many patients elect to have the affected nerve excised.

Surgical indications include persistent pain and disability despite non-operative measures. Surgical treatment can either be excision, resection of the affected nerve, or release of the TML to decompress the underlying nerve. Surgery carries an approximately 80% success rate.[11]

OSTEOCHONDROSIS OF THE METATARSAL HEAD (FREIBERG'S DISEASE)

Freiberg's disease, or osteochondrosis of the metatarsal, can also be a source of forefoot pain. It is thought to represent an ischemic necrosis of the epiphysis. It is more frequently seen in girls. This entity usually occurs during adolescence and is thought to be caused by avascular necrosis of the underlying subchondral bone. This is believed to be due to repetitive stresses at the metatarsal head creating microfractures and ultimately compromise of the blood supply. Patients typically complain of limitation of motion at the affected joint. Pain is aggravated by activity and relieved by rest.[13]

Physical examination may reveal warmth, swelling, and diminished range of motion secondary to pain. There may also be generalized thickening about the joint secondary to synovitis.

Although this condition may heal with only minimal deformity, some patients have progressive degenerative changes with articular destruction.

Initial radiographs may appear normal. A bone scan can be useful for localizing the process to the metatarsal head. Osteosclerosis in the early stages and osteolysis

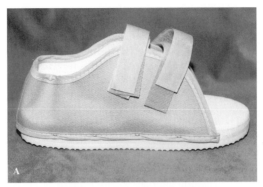

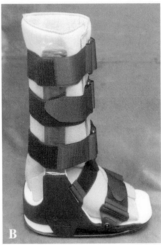

FIGURE 16. *A*, Postoperative shoe. *B*, Short-leg walking boot.

with collapse in later stages may be seen radiographically. MRI often shows changes consistent with AVN. Follow-up radiographs are helpful in demonstrating progressive deformity of the metatarsal head, with irregularity, fragmentation, and flattening.

TREATMENT

A non-operative approach is aimed at protection and alleviating discomfort. This can be accomplished through the use of a wooden-soled post-op shoe; removable boot or short-leg walking cast, which will minimize the stress across the involved joint (Fig. 16).

If pain persists and is associated with limited motion and there is evidence of proliferative bone formation or degenerative changes, surgical intervention is indicated.

Surgical treatment includes exploration of the joint, synovectomy, and debridement of bony fragments and osteophytes. A more extensive deformity requires decompression of the MTP joint.[13]

ARTHRITIS OF THE MIDFOOT

Degenerative arthritis of the tarsometatarsal joints often is a sequela of trauma. It may be the result of a Lisfranc's fracture or dislocation. Arthrosis can also develop

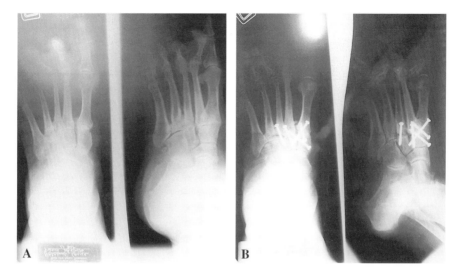

FIGURE 17.   Radiographs demonstrating arthritis of the 1st, 2nd, and 3rd MTC joints (*A*), after fusion (*B*).

spontaneously in the midfoot from primary osteoarthritis, or inflammatory arthritis. A disabling situation develops because of stress placed on the longitudinal arch with weight bearing. Progressive pain with the development of a flatfoot deformity makes walking difficult. Shoe wear likewise may be made more difficult in the presence of proliferative osteophytes on the dorsal aspect of the foot. In patients with peripheral neuropathy, midfoot arthritis can be caused by Charcot arthropathy.

Physical examination involves inspecting the foot for a flat foot deformity and the presence of bony prominences. Hindfoot and forefoot position is also noted. Palpation of the midfoot metatarsocuneiform and metatarsocuboid articulations is then carried out. Passive manipulation of the midfoot, abduction of the forefoot, and pronation stress test can help to determine the location of maximal pain. This is important in the decision making process for either surgical or nonsurgical treatment. Midfoot arthropathy may also be associated with malalignment at the transverse tarsal joint.

Radiographs are obtained in the AP, oblique, and lateral projections. These should be done with the patient bearing weight. Radiographs will demonstrate narrowing of the joint spaces, osteophyte formation, sclerosis and, cyst formation (Fig. 17). Depending on the degree of arthritis, subluxation (abduction/dorsiflexion) of the affected joints may be seen. CT scan can be useful in determining the extent of arthrosis.[1,10]

Treatment

Conservative management of midfoot degenerative arthritis includes the use of a soft or rigid custom molded orthosis that provides support to the longitudinal arch. It also eliminates motion at the affected joints, and in so doing may alleviate pain and may aid in ambulation.[10] Bracing can be effective in the treatment of arthritis of the foot. Braces should be custom molded and padded appropriately over any bony deformity. The patient must understand that bracing treatment does not cure his or her problem but may offer an effective means of controlling symptoms.[22] Shoe modifications include utilization of a stiff insole and a rocker bottom outer sole that may improve ambulation. For more advanced arthritis, an AFO or UCBL orthosis should be utilized. For arthritis restricted to the tarsometatarsal joints, a UCBL is very effective. The application of a SACH and rocker bottom can increase the effectiveness of the brace and afford the patient a more normal gait pattern. Again, these orthoses do not correct the deformity, but they do add support and stability.

With progression of the deformity and/or if bracing treatment fails, surgical intervention is indicated. Arthrodesis of the affected joints is the procedure of choice. Surgical correction is aimed at the affected joints with restoration of the normal alignment of the midfoot articulations.[10]

REFERENCES:

1. Coughlin MJ: Arthritides. In Mann RA, Coughlin MJ (eds): Surgery of the Foot and Ankle, 7th ed. St. Louis, Mosby, 1999, pp 560–650.
2. Coughlin MJ: Second metatarsophalangeal joint instability in the athlete. Foot Ankle 14:309–319, 1993.
3. Coughlin MJ, Mann RA: Lesser toe deformities. In Mann RA, Coughlin MJ (eds): Surgery of the Foot and Ankle, 7th ed. St. Louis, Mosby, 1999, pp 320–391.
4. Fortin PT, Myerson MS: Second metatarsophalangeal joint instability. Foot Ankle Int 16:306–313, 1995.
5. Harrington T, Crichton KJ, Anderson IF: Overuse ballet injury of the base of the second metatarsal: A diagnostic problem. Am J Sports Med 21:591–598, 1993.
6. Karasick D, Wapner KL: Hallux rigidus deformity: A radiologic assessment. AJR 157:1029–1033, 1991.
7. Kilmartin TE, Wallace WA: Effects of pronation and supination orthosis on Morton's neuroma and lower extremity function. Foot Ankle Int 15:256–262, 1994.
8. Levitsky K, Alman BA, Jensevar DS, Morehead J: Digital nerves of the foot: Anatomic variations and implications regarding the pathogenesis of interdigital neuroma. Foot Ankle 14:208–214, 1993.
9. Mann RA: Adult hallux valgus. In Mann RA, Coughlin MJ (eds): Surgery of the Foot and Ankle, 7th ed. St. Louis, Mosby, 1999, pp 150–269.
10. Mann RA: Arthrodesis of the foot and ankle. In Mann RA, Coughlin MJ (eds): Surgery of the Foot and Ankle, 7th ed., St. Louis, Mosby, 1999, pp 651–701.
11. Mann RA: Disease of the nerves. In Mann RA, Coughlin MJ (eds): Surgery of the Foot and Ankle, 7th ed. St. Louis, Mosby, 1999, pp 502–524.
12. Mann RA: Disorders of the first metatarsophalangeal joint. J Am Acad Orthop Surg 3:34–43, 1995.
13. Mann RA, Coughlin MJ: Keratotic disorders of the plantar skin. In Mann RA, Coughlin MJ (eds): Surgery of the Foot and Ankle, 7th ed. St. Louis, Mosby, 1999, pp 392–436.
14. Mann RA, Mizel MS: Monarticular nontraumatic synovitis of the metatarsophalangeal joint: A new diagnosis? Foot Ankle 6:18–21, 1985.
15. Mizel MS, Michelson JD: Nonsurgical treatment of monarticular nontraumatic synovitis of the second metatarsophalangeal joint. Foot Ankle Int 18:424–426, 1997.
16. Mizel MS, Yodlowski ML: Disorders of the lesser metatarsophalangeal joints. J Am Acad Orthop Surg 3:166–173, 1995.
17. Resch S, Stenstrom A, Jonsson A, Jonsson K: The diagnostic efficacy of magnetic resonance imaging and ultrasound in Morton's neuroma: A radiological-surgical correlation. Foot Ankle 15:88–92, 1994.
18. Rodeo SA, O'Brien S, Warren RF, et al: Turf-toe: An analysis of metatarsophalangeal joint sprains in professional football players. Am J Sports Med 18:280–285, 1990.
19. Sanders R: Fractures of the midfoot and forefoot. In Mann RA, Coughlin MJ (eds): Surgery of the Foot and Ankle, 7th ed. St. Louis, Mosby, 1999, pp 1574–1605.
20. Thompson FM, Hamilton WG: Problems of the second metatarsophalangeal joint. Orthopedics 10:83–89, 1987.
21. Trepman E, Yeo S-J: Nonoperative treatment of metatarsophalangeal joint synovitis. Foot Ankle Int 16:771–777, 1995.
22. Wapner KL: Conservative treatment of the foot. In Man RA, Coughlin MJ (eds): Surgery of the Foot and Ankle, 7th ed. St. Louis, Mosby, 1999, pp 115–130.
23. Wapner KL: Foot pain: Where and why? Hosp Med 28:105–121, 1992
24. Weinfeld SB, Myerson MS: Interdigital neuritis: Diagnosis and treatment. J Am Acad Orthop Surg 4:328–335, 1996.

JOHN A. DiPRETA, MD
WEN CHAO, MD
KEITH L. WAPNER, MD

CONSERVATIVE MANAGEMENT OF ACQUIRED FLATFOOT

From Pennsylvania Orthopaedic
   Foot and Ankle Surgeons
Philadelphia, Pennsylvania

Reprint requests to:
Pennsylvania Orthopaedic Foot
   and Ankle Surgeons
230 West Washington Square
Fifth Floor
Philadelphia, PA 19106

Flatfoot encompasses a spectrum of clinical and radiographic presentations. In broad terms, flatfoot can be congenital or acquired. Congenital causes range from asymptomatic and flexible to symptomatic and rigid.[12]

Acquired flatfoot in the adult, in contradistinction to congenital flatfoot, is a deformity that developed secondary to an underlying condition. In long-standing cases, the ankle may be involved as well. This chapter focuses primarily on posterior tibial tendon dysfunction as one of the more common causes of acquired flatfoot in the adult.

ANATOMY AND PATHOPHYSIOLOGY

A review of the normal function of the tibialis posterior muscle is imperative in order to comprehend the pathophysiology of the condition and the rationale behind the non-operative care of this disorder.[11,13,14]

The posterior tibial tendon (PTT) courses behind the medial malleolus, posterior to the axis of the ankle, and medial to the axis of the subtalar joint. It then inserts into the plantar and medial aspect of the navicular, plantar aspect of the three cuneiforms, and the bases of the second, third, and fourth metatarsals. By its insertion on the midfoot, the PTT adducts and supinates the forefoot secondarily inverting the subtalar joint. Because of its position relative to the subtalar joint axis, it has a significant degree of leverage to bring about inversion of the subtalar joint. The mechanism of these joints is such that when the hindfoot is everted the transverse tarsal joint (talonavicular, calcaneocuboid) is unlocked and the axes are parallel. This allows the foot to remain supple. When the hindfoot is inverted, the axes of the transverse tarsal joint become divergent. This locks the transverse tarsal joint, and the foot becomes rigid.[11,22] This relationship is critical during the gait cycle. Immediately after heel strike, initially there is eversion of the subtalar joint and the foot is supple. Then there is progressive inversion (initiated by the PTT adducting the transverse tarsal joint). The divergence at the transverse tarsal joint allows the subtalar complex to become rigid. This enables the gastrocnemius-soleus complex to provide a plantar flexion force against a rigid lever to allow forward progression during the toe-off phase of the gait cycle. Thus, the PTT is critical in inverting the hindfoot and locking the transverse tarsal joint for normal gait and ambulation.[11]

In patients with PTT dysfunction, the ability to invert the hindfoot is diminished. The gastrocnemius-soleus complex subsequently acts upon the talonavicular joint. In addition, loss of PTT function results in the peroneus brevis acting unopposed, with a dynamic abduction-eversion force. Through these continued dynamic forces (the gastrocnemius-soleus complex action on the talonavicular joint and the unopposed pull of the peroneus brevis), a progressive attenuation of the medial static restraints of the longitudinal arch occurs. The integrity of the talonavicular joint is maintained by the spring ligament complex, which is comprised of the stronger medial superior calcaneonavicular ligament and the inferior calcaneonavicular ligament. Portions of the superficial deltoid ligament also help to support the talonavicular joint. In normal individuals, the PTT protects this structure and the spring ligament complex. Loss of normal function leads to attenuation of these important ligamentous structures. During the gait cycle, the center of pressure passes toward the metatarsal heads and if the transverse tarsal joint is not stabilized in adduction, this places stress across the medial aspect of the talonavicular joint complex, worsening the abducted position of the transverse tarsal joint. Loss of the secondary soft tissue constraints (deltoid ligament, talonavicular capsule, spring ligament) allows increasing valgus angulation of the heel. With continuing deformity, medial subluxation/plantar flexion of the talus occurs, along with valgus alignment of the calcaneus and increased abduction of the forefoot. As the heel assumes an increased valgus position, the Achilles becomes lateral to the axis of rotation of the subtalar joint and assumes a role as an evertor of the calcaneus. Over time, this shortened position of the heel results in an Achilles tendon contracture.[11,12,22]

Secondary changes develop over time with chronic valgus angulation of the heel with horizontal orientation of the subtalar joint. Although initially flexible and reducible, the chronic malalignment leads to a fixed deformity with the development of secondary arthritis. Eventually, with an extreme valgus angulation of the heel, subfibular impingement can occur, creating significant pain in the lateral aspect of the ankle and sinus tarsi.

ETIOLOGY

Extrinsic and intrinsic factors have been identified in contributing to PTT dysfunction. Most cases of spontaneous PTT dysfunction are due to intrinsic tendon degeneration. Frey[5] describes a region of hypovascularity within the tendon in a 1.0–1.5 cm region distal to the medial malleolus. It has been shown that this distinct region corresponds to the degenerative changes and ruptures of the PTT. Dysfunction has also been linked to inflammatory arthropathies (Reiter's syndrome, spondylosing arthropathy, psoriasis)[19] and extrinsic causes such as corticosteroid[8] exposure and fracture/dislocations of the ankle.[17]

HISTORY, SYMPTOMS, AND PHYSICAL EXAMINATION

Often the history, symptoms, and physical examination demonstrate typical findings. With increasing awareness of this condition, the correct diagnosis and staging of the disease process can be made and appropriate management initiated.[11]

The patient with PTT dysfunction usually denies any acute, significant traumatic event. Instead, the majority of patients describe a gradual onset of symptoms and deformity. While obtaining a history, it is important to elicit any information regarding a systemic inflammatory process.[19]

Initially, it may be difficult for patients to localize the discomfort. Tenderness may be elicited along the medial aspect of the ankle, especially upon stress with activities. As the tendon dysfunction progresses, patients may localize or describe mild to moderate tenderness in the region of the medial malleolus. Discomfort along the PTT or tendon sheath also may be elicited along the medial malleolus to its attachment on the undersurface of the navicular. When localized, the site of tenderness usually corresponds to the areas of PTT involvement. Upon increasing dysfunction of the PTT, significant discomfort may occur laterally in the sinus tarsi and lateral ankle secondary to extreme valgus angulation of the calcaneus and lateral impingement upon the fibula.

After the initial history has been obtained, a careful physical examination should be performed.[21] Initially the patient is evaluated walking down a hallway. The presence of any limp or antalgic gait on the involved side should be noted. If the patient has pain in the foot or ankle, the affected limb may externally rotate during gait in comparison with the unaffected limb. This external rotation decreases the stresses on the subtalar-ankle joint complex and the painful motion in these joints. Additional areas to evaluate include the initial ground contact of both feet and the timing of the heel rise.

After observation of gait, a thorough physical examination is performed. The mobility of the ankle and subtalar joint should be assessed. With the increased valgus angulation of the heel, the Achilles tendon lies lateral to the axis of rotation of the ankle. This results in a gradual contracture of the gastrocnemius-soleus complex. If the subtalar joint is supple, care should be taken to check the dorsiflexion of the ankle with foot in slight inversion. This reveals the true motion at the ankle joint rather than the breaking phenomenon that may occur through the transverse tarsal joint. Ankle motion should be assessed with the knee extended and flexed at 90 degrees. Normally, approximately 20 degrees of dorsiflexion and 50 degrees of plantar flexion occur at the ankle joint.[21]

Motion at the subtalar joint is evaluated by grasping the calcaneus with one hand and locking the ankle joint with the other. By stressing the calcaneus into varus (inversion) and valgus (eversion), the motion of the subtalar joint can be determined. Normally, there are 30 degrees of varus and approximately 10 degrees of valgus within the subtalar joint. Motion may be restricted if arthrosis is present.[11]

The range of motion of the transverse tarsal joint is evaluated next. The motion of this joint consists of abduction and adduction, with some extent of dorsiflexion and plantar flexion. The mechanics of the transverse tarsal joint are such that when the heel is in valgus alignment, there is relative freedom within the joints. When the heel is placed into an inverted position, there is a moderate degree of rigidity to the transverse tarsal joints. As in the subtalar joint, degenerative processes in these joints may restrict motion.

It is important to evaluate the relationship of the hindfoot to the forefoot. By grasping the calcaneus and aligning it into a neutral position, the forefoot-hindfoot relationship can be determined. Normally the forefoot alignment remains neutral and plantigrade when the subtalar joint is reduced into a neutral position. The presence of a minor malalignment is of minimal clinical significance unless the foot is rigid. However as the PTT dysfunction progresses, a fixed supination deformity of the forefoot occurs. Rigid forefoot malalignment may result in secondary callus formation or pain beneath the border the foot as a result of increased weight bearing in these areas.

After documenting the range of motion, a careful examination of the affected PTT region should be performed. Swelling may be present early in the clinical course. Gradually, the inflammation and tenosynovitis of the PTT result in a fullness of the tendon sheath. To best appreciate these findings, it is necessary to view the standing patient from behind to compare the affected and unaffected sides. Fullness of the tendon sheath, just retromalleolar, often is evident only when comparing the involved to the uninvolved side.

In regard to the subtalar joint, significant tenderness upon palpation often exists within the sinus tarsi. When secondary deformities occur, tenderness over the lateral sinus tarsi exists as the anterior portion of the talar posterior facet impinges on the dorsal aspect of the calcaneus. Gradually, significant limitations in motion of the subtalar joint occur, especially with restriction of eversion-inversion range of motion. With progressive heel valgus, tenderness may be present in the lateral aspect of the ankle secondary to subfibular impingement.

It is critical to evaluate the strength and integrity of the posterior tibial tendon. This involves an assessment in the standing and sitting position. While standing, viewing the posterior aspect of the weight bearing foot, the hindfoot is in valgus; a marked prominence is noted medially secondary to medial and plantar subluxation of the talar head; the longitudinal arch is flattened, and the forefoot exhibits abduction.[13] Abduction of the forefoot creates the characteristic finding of "too many toes" laterally (Fig. 1). Heel rise tests are performed with the patient standing approximately 2 feet way from a wall with the palms placed flat against the wall. The patient is then asked to rise up on the balls of the foot with the knees extended. As the

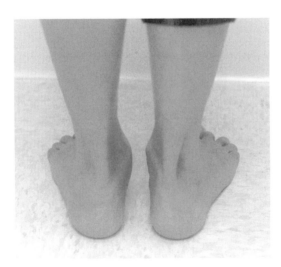

FIGURE 1.   Flatfoot deformity with "too many toes" noted in the left foot.

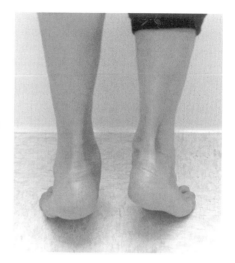

FIGURE 2. Absence of hindfoot inversion with heel rise on left.

heels rise, calcaneal motion is observed. Those with a functioning PTT will demonstrate brisk inversion of the heel. Failure of inversion suggests PTT dysfunction (Fig. 2). A single heel rise test is then performed, with weight bearing on the limb being examined. Inability to raise the heel rapidly and to maintain heel elevation suggests dysfunction. The knee must remain extended, as knee flexion may allow the patient to roll the heel off the floor.[2,13]

It is critical to next evaluate the strength and integrity of the PTT. This is accomplished further with the patient in the seated position. The patient is asked to plantar flex and invert the foot against resistance. Care should be taken to eliminate action of the tibialis anterior muscle to allow a more accurate assessment of the tibialis posterior strength. This is accomplished by fully everting and abducting the foot and asking the patient to invert and adduct the foot against resistance.[2] During testing, the tendon should be palpated as well. This is done along the posterior margin of the tibia as well as in the interval between the medial malleolus and the navicular. Complete absence or thickening of the PTT implies dysfunction. Side-to-side comparison is essential.

Although PTT dysfunction may be identified in its advanced stages, early clinical presentation may be difficult to detect. Hinterman and Gachter[7] describe the first metatarsal rise sign. With external rotation of the leg or moving the heel into varus manually, elevation of the first metatarsal head may be seen with PTT dysfunction. In those with normal PTT function, the first metatarsal head will remain on the floor. This may be an indication of early PTT dysfunction.

In addition to PTT dysfunction, care should be taken to exclude the other causes of acquired flatfoot deformity. The differential diagnoses, as mentioned earlier, include neuropathic arthropathy and post-traumatic deformation. Arthritis of the ankle, talonavicular, or tarsometatarsal joints can also cause acquired flatfoot deformity.[13]

CLASSIFICATION AND STAGING

Johnson and Strom[10] were the first to describe a classification system for dysfunction of the posterior tibial tendon. They classified the abnormalities of the dysfunctional tendon into three distinct stages, based on the presence or absence of hindfoot or transverse tarsal deformities and the ability to achieve flexible reduction of the involved articulations. Stage I consists of a normal-length PTT, afflicted by inflammation with associated peritendinitis or tendinosis. Mild weakness and minimal, if any, deformity are present in Stage I. The subtalar joint is flexible. Since the length of the tendon is normal, the patient is able to perform single heel rise. Stage II is a progression of the inflammatory/degenerative process that results in an elongated PTT. Secondary deformities exist as the midfoot pronates and the forefoot abducts. Although the arch of the foot may be flattened, the hindfoot and transverse tarsal articulations remain supple, allowing easy reduction of the deformity. Motion about the transverse tarsal and hindfoot articulations remain normal in the non–weight bearing state. The patient is unable to perform a single heel rise. Stage III is characterized by the development of a rigid hindfoot and forefoot. The hindfoot is fixed in eversion, while the forefoot is in abduction. When the heel is held in neutral, and the foot is viewed from the front, there is a fixed forefoot varus deformity. The patient is unable to perform single heel rise with Stage III changes. Myerson[18] modified Johnson's classification with the addition of a fourth stage. Stage IV proposes that the increasing progression of the valgus talus leads to degenerative changes in the tibiotalar joint.

RATIONALE FOR NONOPERATIVE TREATMENT OF POSTERIOR TIBIAL TENDON DYSFUNCTION

The goals of aggressive nonoperative management of PTT dysfunction include the elimination of clinical symptoms, stress reduction of compromised tendon, support of the flattened arch, improvement of the hindfoot alignment, and prevention of progression of foot deformity. Appropriate conservative nonoperative measures are extremely useful as a part of the initial treatment, especially in the presence of various factors, such as advanced age, existence of medical problems that preclude surgery, low activity levels, or the presence of minimal discomfort.[11]

Prior to discussion of the authors' method of treatment, a review of previous protocols shall be presented. In 1963, Williams[23] reported on a series of 52 patients with "chronic nonspecific tendovaginitis of the tibialis posterior." Measures included restriction of activities, arch supports, foot baths, casting, strapping, and injection with hydrocortisone. Although most patients improved, 12 patients failed to improve despite several months of treatment. Few details of the protocol were discussed, and an analysis of these patients using an outcome or functional scoring system was not available.

In 1982, Jahss[9] reported on a series of 10 sedentary patients older than 52 years with the diagnosis of spontaneous rupture of the PTT. The first five were treated nonoperatively, as it was thought that surgical procedures at the time were less than optimal. The treatment consisted of orthopaedic oxfords, with long medial counters, low rubber scaphoids, and medial heel wedge, and administration of NSAIDs. No relief was noted, and Jahss thought it necessary to surgically explore the tendon in all except those who lived sedentary lives.

Frey and Shereff[6] recommended a conservative course of rest, ice, NSAIDs, and a medial posted orthotic to limit the extent of pronation during ambulation. For acute tenosynovitis in young adults, immobilization in non–weight bearing casts with the foot in inversion was employed. In a chronic setting, treatment was augmented with the use of shoe modifications with medial sole and heel wedge with longitudinal arch support. These were thought to limit the tendon's extent of excursion.

Mann[15] believed that the goal of nonoperative care was to support the medial longitudinal arch and valgus deformity of the calcaneus. He recommended the use

 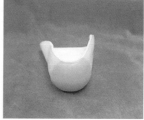 

FIGURE 3. University of California Biomechanics Laboratory (UCBL) braces (three views).

of an orthosis with a small correction and progressive build-up as the patient becomes more tolerant of the pressure beneath the longitudinal arch. The use of a University of California Biomechanics Laboratory (UCBL) orthosis was proposed for its ability to decrease eversion of the calcaneus while establishing some support beneath the arch (Fig. 3).

In 1996, Myerson[18] presented his protocol for the treatment of PTT dysfunction. For those with acute tenosynovitis of the PTT, an initial regimen consisting of rest, NSAIDs, and immobilization was recommended. Corticosteroid use was discouraged, with its risks of rupture. Immobilization in a weight bearing rigid below-knee cast or removable boot was recommended for 6–8 weeks. For those who demonstrated significant improvement with immobilization, a molded heel and sole wedge, hinged ankle-foot orthosis, or orthotic arch support is used to invert the hindfoot. If only mild or moderate improvement is noted, further immobilization may be warranted. Otherwise, consideration is given to a surgical approach to the problem.

Recommended initial treatment for those presenting with acute tenosynovitis of the PTT include a period of rest, NSAIDs, and casting of the involved foot. Use of corticosteroids is contraindicated because of their associated morbidity. After a period of 4–6 weeks of immobilization, a permanent foot orthosis should be used.[11]

Using the staging system of Johnson and Strom,[10] treatment of the patient can be based on the clinical stage. We advocate the use of either a UCBL shoe insert with medial posting or a custom molded ankle-foot orthosis (MAFO) for the treatment of PTT dysfunction prior to consideration of any surgical intervention. For those with Stage I dysfunction (functioning tendon) or Stage II (non-functioning tendon, but deformity is correctable), the use of a UCBL shoe insert with medial posting is recommended. The goal is to correct the flatfoot deformity and to prevent progression of the deformity by decreasing stress across the PTT. Other bracing choices include a MAFO, articulated MAFO, and Marzano brace (Fig. 4). Care should be taken to evaluate the suppleness of the foot to determine adequate correction of the hindfoot as well as the forefoot alignment with the heel in neutral position. Pronation of the first metatarsal with a fixed forefoot varus deformity greater than 10 degrees is not optimally treated with a UCBL shoe insert with medial posting. For individuals with Stage III or Stage IV dysfunction, the goal of nonoperative treatment is to use the custom orthosis to prevent further progression of the deformity by bracing the foot in an in situ position. Bracing choices include a MAFO or Marzano brace.

Successful use of an UCBL brace is dependent on controlling the position of the calcaneus and preventing the heel from going into valgus. If the heel is not held in neutral, the UCBL brace will not, in of itself, be able to support the medial longitudinal

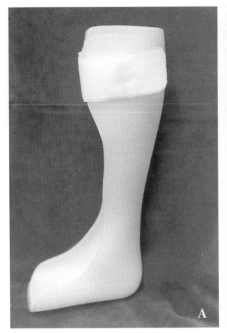 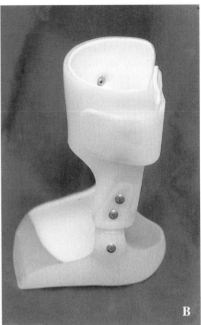

FIGURE 4. *A*, Molded ankle foot orthosis. *B*, Short articulated ankle-foot orthosis (Marzano brace).

arch. The orthotist must mold the brace with the heel held in a neutral position. The brace must be fitted to adequately grip the posterior body of the calcaneus. It is often necessary to add medial posting to the brace in order to maintain the heel in a neutral position and maintain the transverse tarsal joints in a more rigid position.[22]

If the patient is unable to tolerate the use of the UCBL brace, a Marzano or MAFO type brace may be employed. They can also be used in a patient with a flexible deformity. It has been our experience that lining the brace with Plastizote and accommodating any bony deformities by creating a relief in the polypropylene and placing polyurethane foam (PPT) below the Plastizote in these areas increase the success of bracing. Patients with clinical obesity have a lower rate of success with the UCBL brace and often require a more rigid support with the brace that comes above the axis of the subtalar joint.

When manufacturing a MAFO brace, it is important to accommodate the bony prominences of the patient's foot. This is best accomplished by creating a relief within the polypropylene, placing a bed of PPT within that relief, and then covering the entire brace with Plastizote. By keeping the pressure off the bony prominences such as the prominent talar head, patients are able to obtain comfort with the use of the brace without developing pressure points.[22]

Chao et al.[3] have reported on the success rate of bracing in a study of 52 patients with the diagnosis of PTT dysfunction treated over a 4-year period with either a MAFO or UCBL insert with medial posting. Forty-nine patients were included in the study because three patients were lost to follow-up and one patient died of unrelated causes. The diagnosis of posterior tibial tendon dysfunction was made on the basis of history and physical examination.

In patients with flexible deformities, less than 10 degrees of residual forefoot varus with the heel in neutral, and no clinical obesity, a UCBL insert with medial posting was utilized. All other patients were treated with a molded ankle foot orthosis. A functional scoring system was devised based on pain, limp, use of assistive devices, distance of ambulation, and patient satisfaction.[4] All patients were interviewed by an independent investigator. There were 40 feet treated with a molded ankle-foot orthosis and 13 treated with a University of California Biomechanics Laboratory insert with medial posting. The mean age of patients was 66 years, ranging from 42 to 89 years. The average follow-up was 20.3 months (range, 8–16 months). Patients were divided into three groups for assessment of treatment of results: Group I, patients with good to excellent results; Group II, patients with fair to poor results who elected not to undergo operative treatment; and Group III, patients who did not respond to nonoperative treatment and elected to undergo surgery.

In group I, 33 patients (67%; 27 women and 6 men) had excellent to good results. Three patients had bilateral involvement Twenty-six feet were treated with a molded ankle-foot orthosis and 10 were treated with a UCBL insert with medial posting. At the time of the study, six patients had stopped using the orthosis because of complete resolution of their symptoms and return of posterior tibial tendon function. Twenty-six patients continued to use their orthotics. One patient elected to undergo surgical reconstruction to eliminate the need for long term orthotic treatment despite excellent functional results.

In group II, 12 patients (24%; nine women and three men) had fair to poor results. One patient had bilateral involvement. Ten feet were treated with a MAFO, and three were treated with a UCBL brace with medial posting. The mean functional score was 10.7 with the average length of orthotic wear being 3.9 months (range, 1–15.5 months). At the time of the study, all of the patients in this group discontinued using the orthoses, and despite continued symptoms, refused to undergo surgical intervention.

Group III consisted of four patients (9%) who did not respond to treatment with a brace and who subsequently underwent surgical intervention. All four patients had been treated with a MAFO brace and had continued the use of the brace for an average of 6.4 months (range, 2–12 months). The patients elected to undergo surgical correction of their deformity.

Marzano and Alexander[16] have reported on the results of the Marzano brace, which has a theoretic advantage of being shorter than a molded ankle-foot orthosis and being articulated at the ankle. The brace combines a UCBL brace with a custom molded total contact anterior shell on the distal tibial crest secured with a posterior strap connected with a thermoplastic hinge. The UCBL is molded with the heel corrected to neutral for flexible deformities and in situ for fixed deformities.

Marzano and Alexander reported 79% overall satisfaction rate; 16% of the patients in their study group were satisfied with some reservations. Fourteen percent of the patients in their study had posterior tibial tendon dysfunction. The remaining diagnoses included subtalar osteoarthritis, calcaneal fractures, tarsal coalitions, inversion and eversion instabilities, and peroneal tendon dysfunction. The study emphasized the ability of the device to control hindfoot motion and alleviate symptoms while being easy to apply and acceptable to the majority of patients.

In patients who do not respond to treatment with the UCBL brace or the Marzano brace because of discomfort with brace wear or continued pain, a molded ankle-foot orthosis usually will prove satisfactory. Some patients, however, find the loss of ankle motion too cumbersome. In these patients, an articulated AFO using the same thermoplastic ankle hinge used in the Marzano brace can be incorporated.

Nonoperative treatment of the acquired flatfoot deformity caused by posterior tibial tendon dysfunction can be successful, especially for elderly patients with relatively sedentary lifestyles or patients who have high surgical risks because of concurrent medical problems. The goal of brace treatment is to maintain and immobilize the initial deformity and prevent additional progression of the flatfoot deformity. Depending on the flexibility of the deformity, various bracing choices currently are available in the armamentarium of nonoperative treatment of posterior tibial tendon dysfunction.

SURGICAL INDICATIONS

Nonoperative care is successful in a majority of patients. However, despite appropriate management, symptoms and deformity can progress. It is in these patients that a surgical approach to the problem is considered. Operative intervention should be considered after failing a 3–6 month period of nonoperative treatment.[20]

Surgical treatment of PTTD is dependent on the clinical stage and radiographic changes of the foot. For those with early Stage I disease, the PTT should be explored, tenosynovial tissue resected, and any tears debrided and repaired. If degenerative changes are noted within the substance of the tendon, a flexor digitorum longus transfer to the navicular or medial cuneiform should be considered to supplement the function of the PTT.

For those with Stage II dysfunction, deformity has occurred as a result of the elongation of the PTT. Therefore, a reconstructive procedure is indicated. Transfer of the flexor digitorum longus is done, often in combination with a bony procedure to correct the flatfoot and to protect the reconstruction. Combination procedures including FDL transfer with a lateral column lengthening (through the anterior calcaneus or through the calcaneocuboid articulation) or medial displacement calcaneal osteotomy have been described. Furthermore, reconstruction of the spring ligament has also been advocated.

For those with Stage III changes (rigid valgus deformity of hindfoot with or without associated degenerative changes), arthrodesis is the preferred procedure. Limited arthrodesis in combination with tendon transfer have been described. However definitive correction of the foot and alleviation of pain are best accomplished with a triple arthrodesis (fusion of the subtalar, talonavicular, and calcaneocuboid joints).

In Stage IV, where tibiotalar changes are also seen, the site causing most of the symptoms needs to be determined. Surgical correction is directed at the most symptomatic site. In severe cases, a pantalar fusion (fusion of the tibiotalar, subtalar, talonavicular, and calcaneocuboid joints) may be necessary.

Postoperative recovery for tendon transfer requires a period of non–weight bearing immobilization with the foot plantar flexed and inverted. At approximately 4 weeks after surgery, the foot may be placed in a plantigrade position and ambulation begun with a removable cast-walker. At this time, ROM exercises can begin. After 8 weeks, strengthening can begin. Optimal recovery can be expected approximately 6–8 months after surgery. For those undergoing arthrodesis, a period of non–weight bearing immobilization with the use of a cast for approximately 4–6 weeks is employed. If the fusion appears satisfactory on radiographs, the patient may bear weight as tolerated with protection with a cast or removable brace. Twelve weeks after surgery, radiographs are repeated. If the fusion has consolidated, the patient may bear weight as tolerated with an elastic stocking to control residual swelling. Range of motion exercises and strengthening may also be incorporated at this time.[12]

REFERENCES

1. Alexander I: Basic foot kinematics. In Alexander I (ed): The Foot Examination and Diagnosis, 2nd ed. New York, Churchill Livingstone, 1997, pp 41–53.
2. Alexander I: Tendon disorders of the ankle and hindfoot. In Alexander I (ed): The Foot Examination and Diagnosis, 2nd ed. New York, Churchill Livingstone, 1997, pp 123–143.
3. Chao W, Wapner KL, Lee TH, et al: Nonoperative management of posterior tibial tendon dysfunction. Foot Ankle Int 17:736–741, 1996.
4. Chao W, Lee TH, Hecht, PJ, et al: Conservative management of posterior tibial tendon rupture. Orthop Trans 18:1030, 1994–1995.
5. Frey CC, Shereff M, Greenridge N: Vascularity of the posterior tibial tendon. J Bone Joint Surg 72A:884–888, 1990.
6. Frey CC, Shereff MJ: Tendon injuries about the ankle in athletes. Clin Sports Med 7:103–118, 1988.
7. Hinterman B, Gachter A: The first metatarsal rise sign: A sensitive sign of tibialis posterior tendon dysfunction. Foot Ankle Int 17:236–241, 1996.
8. Holmes GB Jr, Mann RA: Possible epidemiologic factors associated with rupture of the posterior tibial tendon. Foot Ankle 13:70–79, 1992.
9. Jahss MH: Spontaneous rupture of the tibialis posterior tendon: Clinical findings, tenographic studies, and a new technique of repair. Foot Ankle 3:158–166, 1982.
10. Johnson KA, Strom DE: Tibialis posterior tibial tendon dysfunction. Clin Orthop 239:196–206, 1989.
11. Lin SS, Lee TH, Chao W, Wapner KL: Non-operative treatment of patients with posterior tibial tendinitis. In Wapner KL (ed): Foot and Ankle Clinics Tendon Injury and Reconstruction, Vol 1, No. 2. Philadelphia, WB Saunders, 1996, pp 26–277.
12. Mann RA: Flatfoot in adults. In Mann RA, Coughlin, MJ (eds): Surgery of the Foot and Ankle. St. Louis, Mosby, 1999, pp 733–767.
13. Mann RA: Biomechanical approach to the treatment of foot problems. Foot Ankle 2:205–212, 1982.
14. Mann RA: Biomechanics of the foot. Inst Course Lect 31:167–180, 1982.
15. Mann RA: Rupture of the tibialis posterior tendon. Inst Course Lect 33:302–309. 1984.
16. Marzano R, Alexander I: Short articulated ankle foot orthosis for hindfoot disorders. Proceedings of the American Foot and Ankle Society Eighth Annual Meeting, Napa, CA, 1992.
17. Monto RR, Moorman CT III, Mallon WJ, et al: Rupture of the posterior tibial tendon associated with closed ankle fracture. Foot Ankle 11:400–403, 1991.
18. Myerson MS: Adult acquired flatfoot deformity: Treatment of dysfunction of the posterior tibial tendon. J Bone Joint Surg 78A:780–792, 1996.
19. Myerson M, Solomon G, Shereff M: Posterior tibial tendon dysfunction: Its association with seronegative inflammatory disease. Foot Ankle 9:219–225, 1989.
20. Pomeroy GC, Pike RA, Beals TC, Manoli A: Acquired flatfoot in adults due to dysfunction of the posterior tibial tendon. J Bone Joint Surg 81A:1173–1182, 1999.
21. Shereff MJ, Cohen BE: Clinical evaluation of the foot and ankle. In Sammarco GJ, Cooper PS (eds): Foot and Ankle Manual. Baltimore, Williams & Wilkins, 1998, pp 45–55.
22. Wapner KL, Chao W: Nonoperative treatment of posterior tibial tendon dysfunction. Clin Orthop 365:39–45, 1999.
23. Williams R: Chronic non-specific tendovaginitis of the tibialis posterior. J Bone Joint Surg 45B:542–545, 1963.

INDEX

Entries in **boldface type** indicate complete chapters.